FLYING FROM MY MIND

ETERNITY

He who binds to himself a joy
Does the winged life destroy;
But he who kisses the joy as it flies
Lives in eternity's sunrise.

W. Blake

FLYING FROM MY MIND

MY MIND

Innovative and Record-breaking Microlight and Aircraft Designs

David Cook

Pen & Sword
AVIATION

First published in Great Britain in 2007 by
Pen & Sword Aviation
an imprint of
Pen & Sword Books Ltd
47 Church Street
Barnsley
South Yorkshire
S70 2AS

ISBN 978 1 84415 588 0

Typeset in Palatino by
Phoenix Typesetting, Auldgirth, Dumfriesshire

Printed and bound in England by
CPI UK

Pen & Sword Books Ltd incorporates the imprints of Pen & Sword Aviation,
Pen & Sword Maritime, Pen & Sword Military, Wharncliffe Local History,
Pen & Sword Select, Pen & Sword Military Classics and Leo Cooper.

For a complete list of Pen & Sword titles please contact
PEN & SWORD BOOKS LIMITED
47 Church Street, Barnsley, South Yorkshire, S70 2AS, England
E-mail: enquiries@pen-and-sword.co.uk
Website: www.pen-and-sword.co.uk

To my wife Catherine

Acknowledgements

May I acknowledge the people who have assisted me without wanting anthing in return:

Terry Aspinall, Tony Batten, Dennis Brett, Colin Buck, Peter Clack, Robert Cassidy, David Clarke, Catherine Cook, Jacob Cook, Gary Cook, Chloe Cook, Steven Emmersen, Dr David Foreman, Joan Galway, Rex Garrod, John Gill, Bob Hammond, Tim Hardwick-Smith, Brian Harrison, Mary Higgs, Mike Hilling, George Ireland, Joseph Iszard, Robert Jelliff, Frank Johns, Brian Johnson, Dick Kimmerling, Fiona Luckhurst, Christopher Meynell, Neil Moran, Tim Moy, Dr Martin Pickford, Mike Plewman, Harry Potter, David Raeburn, Chris Reilley, David Robb, Chris Sinclair, Wendy Sinclair, David Southwell, Dr Ian Tait, Chris Tansley, Gerald Townsend, Nigel Townsend, Peter Try-Davies, John Wells, Patrick White, John Wibberley.

In memory of my two good friends:-

Zaka Ullah Bhangoo and Mick Newman tragically killed in a Sky Arrow, 2007.

Foreword

by Wing Commander K. H. Wallis

I had first met David Cook when we were flying at the finale of 'It's a Knock-out' at a small field at Arundel in Sussex. I witnessed his 'running take-off' in one of his early experiments in 'real flying'. We had several laughs together on that occasion. It was only when I read his 'Flying from My Mind' that I learned that we had something else in common besides a desire to fly.

David had been rejected as an RAF pilot on the grounds of migraine affecting his eyesight. I had been rejected by the RAF before World War Two because I had a defective right eye from birth, although I had qualified for a Pilot's 'A' licence in 1937. I was in the Civil Air Guard when war came and by a series of lucky chances I was able to fly in the RAF and to continue even after being 'discovered'!

I was interested to learn that David was also a competent marksman. I used to represent the RAF at Bisley and elsewhere. After our first memorable meeting at Arundel I was later to witness the steady progress of David's designs to the standard of the practical and proven 'CFM Shadow'. I admired the way in which he enlisted help and started production. Safe flying at low cost became available to many desiring the special pleasure of flight. I had been aware of David's best use of modern technology and the use of Fibrelam and the bonding produced by Aero Research at Duxford. However, it was only when reading 'Flying from My Mind' that I realised the full extent of David's work and the very interesting aspects so well described in detail.

The overseas production of his designs, in widely differing situations and the very many problems encountered and overcome could well be the sole subject of an interesting book. His innovation and common-sense approach to a practical aircraft design is an example to all. The fact that he constructed, flew them and experienced the problems and emergencies and learned from them, led to the refinement and subsequent safe operation by so many. His acceptance of the challenge to adapt a 'CFM Shadow' so that it could safely be flown by a tetraplegic ex-military pilot, coupled with the testing and ultimate acceptance by the CAA is another interesting facet so well described. David certainly tells the whole story of his practical approach, 'warts and all'. Some of the views he expresses may well be regarded as controversial but they make for interesting reading and I can certainly see the sense in his arguments.

The World Record flights, their background and the difficulties of compliance with the rigorous FAI requirements are well described. It gives the reader some feel of the effort involved in addition to just getting in the aircraft and the flying performance. As one who has been involved in Police searches and military trials and exercises, carrying remote-sensing equipment such as infra-red line-scan and special camera packs, I found the description of the use of David's economical aircraft in such roles a further proof of his contribution in a special aspect of aviation. I was particularly pleased to read of the problems and hazards of film-making, after flying at Pinewood Studios, which I too know, is hardly a suitable place. I had flown for films in Brazil, Japan, Italy, Spain, Malta and Lanzarote. Most people think film-making must be 'fun flying'. David gives the reader a true account of the actual flying involved, the number of flights and time in the air for a few minutes on the screen, together with the hazards encountered. It is just like the repetitive filming on the ground, with the word 'Action', soon to be followed by 'cut, do it again' time after time before the desired recording is achieved.

The same seems to occur in aerial filming, but when this entails a take-off and landing from a marginal site, climbs over rugged terrain for a brief shot in a canyon or over a mountain and return for a difficult landing it can be very different. To then be told such as ' Number Two camera had a "hair in the gate", do it again!' is not good news to the pilot who is aware of the potential hazards. David's account of his experiences in this special field of aviation should certainly dispel the illusion that flying for a film is fun.

The presentation of the Segrave Trophy to Eve Jackson for her flight from England to Australia in 1986 was well deserved, as was the award of the Segrave Medal to David for his significant part in the design and construction of the aircraft and some support work in India. Brian Milton also received the Segrave Trophy, thanks to David's fine support.

His final description of the ultimate liquidation of his fine project makes for sad reading, but it bears out the old saying, 'If you want to make a small fortune out of aviation you must start with a large one!' However, over all David's project was a great success, bringing the affordable pleasure of flight in safety to very many who would not otherwise have enjoyed the experience. 'Flying from My Mind' is a true and detailed description, combined with many illustrations. It is necessary reading for all those who have an interest in the pleasure of flying and its many aspects.

Wing Commander K. H. Wallis
MBE DEng(hc) PhD(hc) CEng FRAeS FSETP FlinstTA(hc) RAF(ret'd)

Contents

Introduction   1

Chapter One   **VJ-23**   3
    Birdman at Selsey and Ridge Soaring   3
    Powered Hang Gliding   8
    The English Channel   10
    Volmer Jensen and California   17
    SBAC Farnborough and Air Displays   22
    VJ-24   28

Chapter Two   **Designs**   30
    MUSFLY   30
    The Shadow   32
      Design Concepts   38
      Materials   39
    Streak Shadow   61
    Image   66
    Tetraplegic   73
    'D' Series and Korean side-by-side   78
    CDG glider, microlight regulations and
      airworthiness   81
    Glint   86
    Design Proposals   90

Chapter Three   **Shadow Achievements, Records
      and Awards**   92
    Distance, Norfolk Air Race, England to Australia,
      Eve Jackson, India, Segrave Trophy   92
    Dawn to Dusk   98
    Design Awards   101
    The Long Distance Traveller   103
    Altitude Record   105
    Time to Climb   114

Chapter Four   **Overseas**   116
    Zimbabwe, World Wide Fund for Nature   116
    Europe   121
    Antipodes   125
    Yemen   130
    Shadow Meets   133
    Denmark and Paris Airshow   135
    Guernsey and Starstreak   142
    Botswana   144
    Arlington Airshow, Back to Texas   148
    Thailand   157
    Isle of Man   160

Chapter Five   **Production Overseas**   162
    United States of America   162
    Production – South Africa   169

Chapter Six   **Military**   180
    Turkish Air Force, Iraqi Air Force and RAF   180
    Surveillance, Linescan, SAS, Indian Air Force,
        DEA and RAF   181
    Lt-Col Thompson   186
    Working with the Law   188

Chapter Seven   **Films**   191
    Slipstream   191
    Shell Advertisement   201
    Superwings   203
    Dragonheart   204

Chapter Eight   **Shadow D Series and CFM Liquidation**   216

Epilogue   217

David Cook-Aviator-Achievements   223
Final Note   228

Introduction

The P51D Mustang fighters roared aggressively as they swept low, skimming the roof of our cottage in the tiny village of Thorpeness on the Suffolk coast. It was the summer of 1944 and I was four years old. Rigid with excitement, I stood with my mother at our gate and breathlessly watched as these gleaming, silver aircraft flew out over the sea.

The North American P51 planes came from Leiston airfield, a mere 3 miles away. This was the nearest fighter base to Germany from England. Their role was to escort the B17 bombers on their missions across Europe. As I was later to learn, this base had produced forty-two aces amongst its pilots. These were special men indeed, for to be an 'ace' one had to have made five or more kills in battle. Chuck Yeager was one of these very pilots and he later became the first man to succeed in breaking the sound barrier.

These vivid scenes from my childhood formed indelible images in my mind and became the seeds of my lasting desire to be an aviator.

Nearby RAF Bentwaters was activated in the early 1950s as an American base. It became the home of hundreds of jets, including the F84 Thunderjet and the best fighter plane in the world at that time – the F86 Sabrejet.

Some of the American pilots and their families were billeted in Thorpeness. This was a heaven-sent opportunity for a group of village lads, who were desperate to be associated with anyone who was remotely connected to the ultimate machines in our lives – jet aircraft. We were encouraged and helped by the American aircrew to build model aircraft and to fly them from our local cricket field. I bet we were the first English boys to experience the delights of

Coca-Cola and hot dogs and to wear the coveted Levi jeans. The Americans were so generous. They were a constant source of wonder to us children raised in a war-impoverished England. Once I was taken to Bentwaters and sat in a Sabre F86 that had only recently returned from the war in Korea and sometimes at my request, I was given a 'beat up' by an F86, just for me, above the village.

As I entered my late teens, I joined the RAF initially as an airframe fitter, then later applied to aircrew. This approach would skill me in systems, engineering and flying, an invaluable asset for the future. Unfortunately, however, my career in the RAF was not to be. My progress from TII Vampires, jet Provosts and other fast jets was brought to an abrupt halt, whilst with the Victor V bomber. I suffered a migraine with fifteen minutes' impaired vision and I was immediately grounded from any career flying in the Air Force.

There was no alternative but to leave the RAF, as it was no use to me unless I could fly. In fact, this part of my life ruined much of my desire to have anything else to do with aviation. It was not till ten years later that my deep, smouldering love of the aerial was reignited.

To view colour photographs relating to this book visit
www.davidcookaviator.com

CHAPTER 1

VJ-23

BIRDMAN AT SELSEY AND RIDGE SOARING

I first saw it in 1972. There, in *Pilot* magazine, was a man in America bearing the typically transatlantic name Volmer Jensen. The magazine pictured Jensen flying a foot-launched glider named the VJ-23 Swingwing. It was a rigid wing hang glider with aerodynamic controls. This glider, which had a conventionally styled wing and tailplane and with a control stick was totally unknown to me; the hang gliders at that time were foot-launched, flexwing, weight-shift kites. It claimed to have a 9:1 glide ratio (9 feet distance for every 1 foot descent). Immediately my interest was aroused. This was a machine that with my traditional training, I could build and fly.

The Birdman Rally at Selsey Bill, Sussex, was an annual event, which offered £3000 to the first person who succeeded in flying the distance of 50 yards when leaping from their pier. The 'take-off' platform on the pier was said to be 30 feet above the sea, so I calculated that this could be achieved in a machine with a 1:5 glide ratio. 'Piece of cake,' I thought. I could win this money, which was equivalent to the purchase price of a house in those days.

My income in 1973 was approximately £25 a week. I had married two years previously and Catherine and I were expecting our second child shortly. All our funds had gone into purchasing our home. This is an extraordinary house built over, under and around a Great Eastern Railway carriage – 3rd class – dating 1840. With our mortgage reducing my income by 45 per cent, not much cash could be apportioned to building a glider. But the £3000 seemed attainable and our home had the overwhelming benefit of possessing a basement beneath the propped up railway carriage, which would enable me to build the glider 'in house'.

I sent for the $80 plans from Mr Jensen. They showed a wooden airframe with fabric flying surfaces weighing about 100 lb. At the time I was a draughtsman at the local engineering company, Richard Garrett, in Leiston. My colleagues in the pattern shop sorted me out two beautiful planks of yellow pine – straight grain, no knots and very well seasoned. There was no inventory with the VJ-23 plans, thus I had to compile a list of all the various sizes of wood required. For example, 150 feet of ¼-inch x ¼-inch, 90 feet of ¾-inch x ½-inch, etc. With careful planning and great skill, a local carpenter, Brian Staff, then cut all the sizes needed from the two planks. My engineering friends at Richard Garrett helped me make the metal parts and control system. We all thought it a wonderful project. Finally I named the glider *AINITA TYB* (All I Need is the Air that You Breath) after the hit song recently performed by the Liverpool group called The Hollies), which was displayed on each side of the boom tube in large letters.

After a year of my spare time and a final cost of £128, the glider was complete and ready to fulfil its intended duty, which was to win the Selsey Birdman Rally. It was a sound investment, I considered, for an eventual gain of £3000.

It was July 1974 and the day of the Rally dawned. Eighteen of us set off from Suffolk to take the glider on its hastily constructed trailer to Selsey for the big day and, in our minds, the prize. We were programmed to fly after ten or so other competitors. Some entrants had come for a laugh and merely jumped off the launch platform wearing only a duck-suit with fairy wings, but others were as serious as us. One was a beautifully made canard-wing aircraft, entered by a university. It looked as if many hundreds of hours had been spent on its construction. The transparent Mylar covering showed numerous intricate wooden ribs. Its presentation and appearance was that of a potential winner. However, the lovely machine flew only a few feet in distance before plunging into the water. It seemed to me that the university that had built it had done everything right mechanically but failed in its choice of pilot.

The moment of truth had arrived. The culmination of a year's work and theoretical calculations would be proved either to work or fail within the next few minutes. There I stood, like an ungainly bird awaiting its first flight, precariously perched between sea and sky with 20,000 eager spectators watching my every move from the shore. The platform was 10 feet long and 4 feet wide. Helping me lift the 100-lb glider were Chris Reilley and Neil Moran. We could see that as the tide was high, the water was only 20 feet below – not 30 feet as proclaimed by the organisers. The buoys marking the finish line looked more like 75 yards in distance rather than the stipulated 50 yards because the lateral flow of the tide had swept them further from their anchors. My 1:5 glide ratio calculation was no longer valid. I ran the 6 or 7 feet to the end of the platform and leapt.

Diving or falling towards the water, the VJ-23 picked up sufficient airspeed to fly within 6 feet of the finish line. After struggling to free myself from beneath the floating glider, I was hauled out of the sea by the men in the RNLI rescue boat. There was a massive cheering ovation from the enthusiastic crowd. No one had ever flown this far before. My calculations had proved correct. However, there was no £3000, just a cheque for £30 presented by the astronomer Patrick Moore and a pretty lady to shake my hand, but my mind was already planning for the 1975 event!

I had been very concerned about the launching of the glider. It was crucial to obtain 15–20 mph over the wings for flight. For safety reasons, I needed assistance to help me acquire sufficient launch speed and to prevent the ventral rudder from striking the end of the platform, as it so nearly had on my first attempt.

I practised with three able launchers sprinting from a standing start, carrying the 100-lb glider. With 10 mph over the wings the plane is almost weightless, so this task was not as strenuous as it sounds, but 10 feet was a very short distance. The solution would be for the helpers to launch themselves as well, which would inadvertently also provide extra entertainment for the onlookers!

A year later at the 1975 Selsey Birdman Rally, the plan of campaign was put into practice. My three fellow launchers, Chris

Tansley, Robert Jelliff, Bob Kent and I sprinted with the VJ-23 to the end of the platform and hurtled towards the sea. The entertainment level of the crowd would have been increased even more had they known that one of the launchers, Chris Tansley, could not swim! He had to be rescued 100 yards from the shore by Robert Jelliff and Bob Kent. His action was one of pure self-sacrifice and could truly be described as the meaning of 'having a mate'.

My launching strategy was a success. I achieved a distance of 66 metres (the standard of measurement having been changed from imperial to metric from the previous year), but once again no prize money was offered. The organisers argued that the spirit of the competition had been flaunted and the flight was not 'by the sole means of the pilot'.

Later, when we discussed the day, my helpers told me that when they surfaced from their plunge into the sea, they could still see me in the air, gliding using ground effect, to the accompaniment of stupendous roars of encouragement from the people lining the beach.

My knowledge of 'ground effect' emanated from my RAF days when flying the Victor V bomber at low levels. Flying at close to 500 knots, 50 feet above the sea, one had to apply positive forward control, otherwise the aircraft would climb because it was riding on its own created bubble of air.

My technique at Selsey was to obtain maximum acceleration, dive to the sea, level out and float in ground effect. This I accomplished and then, just before the energy gave out, I pulled up, gained a little height and nosed down into the water. The VJ-23 floated well and survived its two sea-water immersions, but what was now to be its purpose? I had failed to attain the £3000, which was to justify its existence. Further achievement targets had to be found. The competitive world of hang gliding provided the answer.

For competition purposes, hang gliders were categorised in three classes. The VJ-23, possessing aerodynamic controls and being foot-launched, was categorised as Class 3. Class 1 comprised original-generation flexwing hang gliders and Class 2 the state of the art – at the time – manufacturers' types. The outstanding VJ-23

L/D ratio (lift over drag) of 9:1 prohibited the hang gliding manu-facturers of the period from claiming outrageous performance figures for their machines, as the VJ-23 and I won every Class 3 event, whether national or international, in which it was entered.

There were, though, distinct disadvantages with this type of machine. The most memorable disadvantage was the difficulty of retrieving it and returning to the top of a 500-foot hill following a spot landing at the bottom! Pilots who owned a flexwing could disassemble their hang glider at the base of the hill, put all the components in a bag and march back with the minimum of time loss, stress and discomfort. My solution in the future was to develop a clip-on engine and fly the return journey to the summit.

The cliffs in Suffolk are only 30–50 feet in height, so the lift band of generated air when the wind is blowing on-shore is very narrow. I therefore became very proficient at keeping in this wave lift when gliding along our coastline. This knowledge of handling minimal air-wave lifts stood me in great stead and was one of the main reasons why I appeared to win so easily in competition flying, competitions always being held in the vicinity of large hills! But in reality I was only able to fly when the winds were from an easterly or north-easterly direction in Suffolk and these did not occur nearly enough to satisfy my desire to be airborne.

I made a study of the soaring capabilities of the different species of gull. In light winds, only large gulls could soar on the lift band. The VJ-23 was roughly the equivalent to a herring gull's per-formance, so we were better than some of the gull family but nothing could touch the ability of the fulmars. Watching the effort-less skill of a fulmar skimming a cliff top in minimal lift, must surely be one of the world's wonders to a flyer like myself.

The reward for making these observations was that I was able to assess whether or not the VJ-23 could glide that day by merely watching which gulls were soaring the cliff top.

The minimum wind speed needed was 12–15 mph in order to maintain launch height or rise. I have soared in 30+ mph and reached over 200 feet above the cliff tops in the 'ridge lift' but once out of this lift a glide to the beach was inevitable.

Powered Hang Gliding

Our local weather only occasionally provided the right conditions for gliding, so I had decided, by 1977, that the best answer would be a small engine to assist flight. I would then be able to fly whatever the wind direction.

The McCulloch 101 Go-Cart engine seemed the best choice. It weighed only 12 lb and a 5-litre fuel can inside the wing would provide thirty minutes of running time. I quickly designed an engine mount, attaching it to the machine using only three bolts (one already existing) and set about making a propeller. This first attempt to carve a propeller took about twenty hours and produced 45 lb thrust. This proved insufficient to fly, though it only just failed in its task. I used to run along our beach for nearly a mile, making an ungodly racket caused by the engine's open exhaust. It was unsilenced and revving at 8000 rpm with my 28-inch diameter propeller. Reaching 15 mph at full sprint, I could bound into the air and fly about 50 yards before having to repeat the running procedure.

It was exhausting work. On one such occasion of running for what seemed at the very least a mile, with the McCulloch engine screaming like a demonic creature trapped on the wing above my head, I had to admit defeat and stop to rest. As I tried to recover what physical powers I might still possess, I was approached by a sweet old lady from one of the beachside cottages, offering me a cup of tea. She was under the illusion that I had just come in to land in my extraordinary machine and accomplished some lengthy flight. Not wishing actually to lie about my complete and utter failure to fly and to retrieve some dignity from the situation, I pointed vaguely behind me as I thanked her and said that I'd come from that direction!

Numerous amusing incidents took place during my testing of the VJ-23 plus engine in that period of 1977–8. One of these was when, yet again, I was attempting flight on the beach path between Thorpeness and Aldeburgh with Mike Hilling assisting me as ground crew. I was halted by a local policeman who tried to arrest me. He was unable to specify the offence I was committing but presumably my bizarre behaviour and general disturbance with the aircraft was sufficient to provide an adequate reason for my arrest. I went through the procedure of proving my aerial experience by showing the policeman my hang gliding proficiency papers. Mike, meanwhile, was busy making his body as small as possible behind the tailplane! The policeman, unaware of Mike's presence, and I confronted each other nose to nose, neither willing to budge from our predetermined stance, when suddenly a disembodied voice struck up from the back of the aircraft . . . 'Whilst facing in a south-westerly direction, I apprehended this 'ere birdman who was stark naked but wearing boots with no laces. He was seen on seventeen separate occasions, running to take off from this 'ere public footpath which 'e was usin' as a runway at the time.'

The police constable's face darkened with rage at this monologue of mimicry and without another word, he strode furiously back to his Panda car to report our misdoings to his superiors.

I awaited the inevitable summons that to my mind would be forthcoming in the near future, which would curtail any more adventures into experimental flight. However, weeks passed and nothing transpired. I later heard that the Sergeant's reaction to the report had been 'Oh that's just David Cook – forget it'!

Another take-off with the powered VJ-23E (E for engine) was in the presence of my SAS cousin, Major David Gibley. I really wanted to impress him with my achievements, as he had succeeded in the Army whereas I had not in the RAF.

The demonstration of flying brilliance, however, was not to be. A normal take-off and launch was followed by a violent pitch up and wing over. Whilst totally out of control, I switched off the engine and prepared to crash. I smashed into the ground with a resounding thud to the accompaniment of tearing, splintering wood as the aircraft broke apart. As I lay beneath the VJ-23E, pinned to the ground, the horrifying realisation dawned on me that I could not see. Overwhelmed with panic, I deduced that the force of the impact had made me blind. My ground crew rapidly lifted off the wrecked aircraft and hoisted me to my feet, whilst I frantically tried to inform everyone present of my lack of vision.

Suddenly I felt my head being forcibly wrenched and, to my joy and disbelief, light flooded my world once more – I was not blind! It had merely been my helmet rammed down over my face.

We never did discover the cause of the crash and the powered glider was soon repaired. Major David Gibley was no doubt very impressed with my achievements!

And so continued the process of testing my prototype propellers. By my fourth attempt I had produced a propeller that gave 62 lb thrust and, with this, I was capable of flight and even launching in zero wind conditions with assistance from friends such as Harry Potter, Chris Tansley, Mike Hilling and Martin Pickford. They had all become used to the idiosyncrasies of the VJ-23 from its conception and knew what was required to boost take-off, i.e. a javelin-type throw!

The powered foot-launched glider weighed about 150 lb, but this weight was quickly reduced when the airflow began to pass over its wings. With the addition of the engine revving on full power, it was imperative that one kept pace with the increasing speed whilst running with the machine, or the aircraft would be flying itself and out of one's control. The most difficult manoeuvre of this take-off run was the leap for the suspended seat at the precise moment of lift-off (a seat that was slung beneath the wing and supporting frame construction). Once this technique had been mastered, it was an absolute thrill to run, be lifted up and become airborne.

THE ENGLISH CHANNEL

In the winter of 1977/8, it came to my notice that an American had flown from the west coast of California to the island of Catalina in a foot-launched hang glider, a distance of 25–30 miles, and that his next target was to come to England and fly to France across the English Channel to achieve another aviation first. I was outraged, patriotic fervour and a British sense of justice immediately rushed to my head. I felt instinctively that this first had to be made by an English person – after all, it is our Channel and I was absolutely determined that come what may, I would be the Englishman to make that flight.

Actually, I have a fundamental fear of water and do not swim well. For although I was brought up in Thorpeness, a seaside village, it was wartime and the beach was heavily mined and out of bounds until 1946/7. Thus, swimming and the sea were unknown experiences in my childhood. Consequently, I did not relish the idea of a flight over such an extensive span of water. However, I set about planning in my mind what would be required for such an undertaking. Financial help was going to be paramount for such a venture.

Duckhams Oils became my main sponsor, kindly donating £100, which in 1978 was worth considerably more than today, the other contributor being Revell Models. Duckhams Oils head of marketing was Frank Johns. He was very enthusiastic about the project as it was their founder, Alexander Duckham, who had funded the very first Channel crossing by air in 1909 by Louis Blériot. The strange coincidence was that he was the same age as myself, thirty-seven, and accomplished the flight on my birthday, 25 July! The difference between Blériot and myself, though, was that he had an aircraft with 25 hp and mine would be 9 hp.

My powered VJ-23E was still in the development stage and the problem of carrying enough fuel for a flight of 25–30 miles had to be resolved. Testing became a matter of urgency!

With two 5-litre cans in the wing 'D' box, the engine should be able to run for up to an hour – just about sufficient in my estimations to fly to France. Fuel testing took place in our bathroom, using water to fill the two 5-litre cans. The cans were connected to a common outlet tee piece, the result being that even if one can was only 25 per cent full and the other can 100 per cent, they would still both empty at the same time. The law of gravity and physics assured me that no air could enter the system by one tank draining before the other. Basic stuff, but good to see it in action!

The next stage was to prove my theory with a long-range flight, so I embarked on a journey following our Suffolk coast. I had flown only approximately 8 miles when the engine suddenly stopped. The VJ-23E, consisting as it did of a set of wings above a suspended plank seat, did not allow any storage room for an emergency tool kit, so it was with great relief when I discovered that the problem was due to a blockage of the air vent on the fuel tank. This was resolved by the judicious use of my penknife and I thankfully achieved the return flight. I reckoned I was now ready for the challenge.

It was now April 1978. I gathered together a team of friends and supporters who were willing to help in any way. I took my two weeks' yearly holiday due from work. Contact was made with the Kent Hang Gliding Club. They gave me every possible assistance as regards planning a likely take-off site, obtaining a chase boat and many other things. Especially helpful were Police Inspector Ted Battersea and Paula Lewis, who gave my friends and me shelter for several nights whilst making the attempt. An endless array of authorities such as the police, customs, coastguards, Duckhams Oils and other people would have to be informed when the day of the flight was decided; the only exception would be the French authorities, for if they refused permission, the whole project would have to be cancelled. It all entailed so much more organising than I could possibly have envisaged at the start. Most importantly, meticulous studies of meteorological charts and fore-casts were made. It was critical that I flew in the right conditions, for the success of the crossing would depend on having made the correct assessment of the winds and weather.

The weather that April was awful. Feeling totally depressed and frustrated and with my holiday time slipping away, I made the decision to go. A fated decision from the start. With a far from ideal weather forecast for the following day, Chris Tansley and I left for Kent, towing the VJ-23E in a trailer behind my VW camper van. In the rain and dark, whilst travelling on the M2 in Kent, the engine blew. Stranded by the side of the motorway, we spent an un-comfortable night in the van. The next morning the police appeared. They had been keeping a watchful eye over us during the night, aware of our predicament. With their help, we found a scrap yard. It was a far from idyllic scene, made worse by what was now appalling weather. We scrabbled amongst the dripping heaps of rusted vehicles and finally, to our relief, unearthed a VW Beetle car. The engine was of a smaller capacity, but at least it would fit. Tearing at the wrecked car with a minimum of tools, we succeeded in freeing the engine from its mount. The owner of the establish-ment looked as pleasant as his property and also possessed a large dog of an obviously vicious temperament, so negotiating the requested price of £25 for the engine was not even considered. All we now had to achieve was its transportation back to the camper van. The discovery of an ancient wheelbarrow solved this problem, even though it had only one handle and a cast iron wheel. The engine was secured in place and whilst Chris gripped the one handle, I grimly held onto the rope that was tying the whole precarious enterprise. And so we trudged. The 3-mile return journey was not easy.

'For goodness sake, we're only trying to fly the Channel,' I recall muttering to Chris in desperation as we wearily pushed our way back to the camper van.

The replacement engine was eventually in position and we were once more on our way through Kent. The conditions were in-describably awful. A raw, bleak wind blew bitter cold and the rain fell without ceasing. The window of flyable weather that I had fore-seen when I made my decision, did not arrive. The rain was unrelenting. We stayed with Paula Lewis, who had so generously offered her house as a base for the crossing attempt, but after several days of frustration with no break to the weather in the fore-seeable future, I made the decision to abort the attempt and we dejectedly drove back to Suffolk.

My paid holiday period was now over and I had achieved nothing. I felt very dispirited; the weather had to change. I requested a further unpaid extension of leave from the drawing office at Richard Garrett.

At long last, my patience was rewarded. On the evening of Wednesday 7 May, the weather forecast for the next few days showed promise. The flight to France became feasible. Later that night my ground crew and I were installed once more with Paula Lewis in Kent. By Friday 9 May, the weather had improved. The wind was an unhelpful 12 mph from the north-west and there was only horizontal visibility of one mile, but the sun was shining! With all my necessary helpers standing by, I could not delay any longer. The decision to fly was made.

Just prior to the launch, an ace hang glider pilot, Gerry Breen, arrived on Walmer Beach with his American design and built flexwing powered hang glider, with the sole purpose of also flying the Channel for an aviation first. It did seem unbelievable to me that two of us should be at the same place, at the same time, on the same day to attempt this record-making flight. I certainly had no knowledge of his intentions; whether he had knowledge of mine, I'll never know. I was not unduly perturbed concerning his presence for the flight, as we would both claim firsts for our different types of powered hang glider. What was far more worrying was the question of the chase boat. If my chase boat had to stop to help him in difficulties, what would happen to me if an emergency developed later in my flight? I could drown.

I was not happy about the situation that now confronted me at a time when I was meant to be focusing on carrying out my final checks. I asked Gerry Breen if he had organised a chase boat and he assured me that his boat would be appearing in due course. I postponed my take-off for over an hour. His chase boat never materialised. I must admit I was suspicious. Did he even have one? Frank Johns, Duckhams' Chief of Marketing, was understandably not amused by Gerry Breen's intrusion and finally told him in no uncertain terms, 'This is "our" beach so piss off!'

I took off for France without him.

Les Wallen from Ramsgate provided my excellent chase craft, which was named the *African Queen* (can you believe it?). An over-powered tub using two 150-hp outboard engines, the boat was to be crewed by Les Wallen, Martin Lanham, Chris Tansley (the non swimmer!) and Harry Potter who had volunteered to rescue me if necessary. Les Wallen, being a local, had stated it was too dangerous to cross the Goodwin Sands in his craft so we both turned south from the beach at Walmer Castle and headed towards Dover. At 25 mph the VJ-23E was slow in flight, but for the *African Queen* trying to keep pace, it meant a rough ride. Hitting the wave chop hard in the grey waters of the Channel resulted in her being airborne much of the time.

At full climb, I was gaining height at about 3 feet a minute – not very impressive, but enough. It required very delicate handling for if one applied too much up elevator movement, overload of the climb could occur, resulting in a rapid loss of altitude.

Thirty minutes into the flight I was horrified to see, emerging from the mist to my right, a supertanker of gigantic proportions. It was on a course that would directly cut across the path of the *African Queen* and me. A collision seemed unavoidable, as her speed of progress appeared to exactly match ours. Les Wallen was already having to contend with extremely difficult conditions for his boat and there was no way he wished to be caught in the turbulent waters of the supertanker's wake, so he passed across her towering, fast-approaching bows as I skimmed over the main deck of her hull, the fo'c's'le looming above me to my right! It was all rather an unnerving experience.

It was not long after the negotiation of the supertanker that the *African Queen*'s engines stopped dead. Anxiously, I circled the boat. I did not dare to venture on alone, as France was still not in sight, due to the foggy horizons. I watched Chris Tansley below – a real 'do anything' man – frantically sort wires of all colours in the engine bay. His intensity was such that I could see his face was bright red with exertion and effort. He was only too aware that the aircraft had a very limited fuel capacity for this flight. Eventually, to my overwhelming relief, the engine returned to life and we once more set course for France, only for the same fault to reoccur a few miles further on. Fortunately, the coast was now visible to my right and I flew the remaining 4 miles or so unaccompanied, knowing that my fuel must be getting low. To cheers from watching passengers, I overflew a Channel ferry and reached France at Blériot-Plage – my intended destination, just south of Calais. The record-making flight had lasted one hour and fifteen minutes, during which I had reached a height of approximately 250 feet above the waves. On landing, there was three minutes of fuel remaining in my two tanks, sufficient only to fill an egg cup!

It was 11:55 a.m. when I touched down on the windswept sand, the sea now thankfully behind me. As I secured the VJ-23E to a nearby sea defence, an elderly German strolled past. 'Where have you flown from?' he asked. 'England,' I replied. He gave me a look of total disbelief and astonishment.

'All zer English are crazy!' he muttered, as he walked on surveying the wild waves and rough sea.

Meanwhile, I could now see the *African Queen* just beyond the breaking waters, but the waves were far too ferocious for the boat to attempt a shore landing, so the crew turned her and aimed for Calais.

My next job was somehow to inform the French authorities of my presence. I walked to the nearest beachside house, where the owner, an old lady, was conveniently working in her garden. I must have made a strange sight, standing before her in my life jacket, wetsuit and overalls. With a lot of arm movements and gesticulations, I tried to explain that I was English and that I spoke no French. I followed this by handing her a note, which I had carefully carried from England. It had been written by a friend of mine in the drawing office who could converse in French and it requested help in contacting the Calais Customs Officer. She read the note and, smilingly, went indoors to make the necessary 'phone call.

All I could now do was to await the arrival of my ground crew with the car and trailer. The launch crew had been John Wells, Brian Pattenden and Catherine. Once I had successfully taken off and the flight was obviously underway, they had driven straight to Dover to board the next available ferry to France. At Calais, they were delayed by the French officials who were very suspicious about the empty trailer and a careful explanation of the purpose of the visit had to be made. It must have been the middle of the afternoon before they eventually found me, hovering beside the coast road, my VJ-23E still tethered on the sands behind me. Word had by now begun to spread of my flight. Press photographers and journalists were congregating on the beach and the Customs Officials arrived. Problems now ensued.

I had undoubtedly done wrong. I had landed illegally in a foreign country without any prior notification to the authorities. As I have previously stated, this was to prevent the likelihood of the flight being banned by the French. The Customs Officer was not amused by my reckless act and made a detailed study of my passport and licence. He wanted to have me detained for having none of the necessary permits. It was a tricky situation. Was I about to be arrested? It was during this difficult conversation that I suddenly realised that my main offence was that I had insulted the Provost of Calais by not informing him of my intentions. With that knowledge, I apologised profusely and the atmosphere immediately became less tense and the confrontation was resolved. Due to the aviation record that I had achieved, the offence I had committed was waivered and we were free to return to England.

My sponsors Duckhams Oils, much to their credit, pulled out all the stops and were delighted at this success and gave a huge party that evening back in Kent. I had achieved the lowest powered flight across the English Channel in the history of aviation. It was 9 May 1978.

The very next day, Suffolk's football team, Ipswich Town, won the FA Cup at Wembley. It was a double achievement for us 'tractor boys'. As we drove back, the main road in Suffolk was lined with Ipswich Town supporters awaiting the triumphal return of their team. They all enthusiastically waved and cheered when we passed. It was an appreciative homecoming.

As a result of this record-making flight, I was signed up as a flying advertisement for Duckhams Oils, presenting the VJ-23E at major air shows and events throughout the country.

I was later awarded the Royal Aero Club bronze medal for aviation achievement at the Royal Aero Club in London. The presentation was made by His Royal Highness Prince Charles, who confidentially told me that because the VJ-23E only possessed one engine, he would be forbidden to fly the machine and that he even had to be accompanied to the 'bog'. I felt real sympathy for him, for his restricted life and his loss of personal freedom.

VOLMER JENSEN AND CALIFORNIA

Volmer Jensen, the glider's designer, was so delighted at the Channel crossing success, that he invited me to visit him in Glendale, California, and purchased the engine installation rights. He fitted the system to his original VJ-23. I had the privilege of flying this machine and several of his other designs during my stay. V.J. were his initials and 23 stood for his twenty-third aircraft design. Whilst with him, Volmer showed me an amazing photograph, which depicted the *Starship Enterprise* from the American television series 'Star Trek'. He had been commissioned in the late 1950s by one of the Hollywood studios, to design and build the original model. Years later, when my son Jacob and I were visiting the Smithsonian Institute in Washington DC, we viewed this original model on display.

Volmer was in his seventies and knew all the designers and test pilots from the 1940s, 1950s and 1960s. These people were the legend of the 'right stuff'. I was 'his boy' at thirty-eight years old. Many of these characters gathered regularly to talk and discuss aviation. One evening I lectured at the US Sport Aircraft Association and met Irv Culver who was one of Volmer's closest associates. He had retired from Lockheed's Skunk Works, a name that he had conceived whilst working at the establishment. He had designed the wing aerofoil for the VJ-23, which had the unique drooped leading edge and a wing section that showed no sign of a defined stall, nor would it allow a spin to occur. Irv Culver happily told me he had no academic qualifications, yet he did much work at Lockheed on the U2, F104 and the Blackbird spy planes. I felt honoured to be accepted by the elite of the aviation profession. These old boys had witnessed the development of aviation from almost its birth to the present day. They liked me because I too had achieved without academic expertise and they watched in amazement at my flight routine in their design. I remember some saying, 'Gee, I didn't know it could do that.' –Well, I didn't know it couldn't! I knew exactly who these people were and what they had accomplished and felt very humble and privileged to be amongst them.

One of the group amongst our regular gatherings in the local restaurant at Glendale was Charles Tucker. He related an astonishing story – then told me to buy the Aerofax book about the Northrop F89 Scorpion jet that tells of this very tale. He said that in early 1950, he was scheduled to fly high-speed passes at the Hawthorn plant of Northrop Aircraft for the Air Force inspection team. It was Flight #102 of the XF89 prototype. During one high-speed pass, the skin of the tailplane peeled away, followed by the separation of the tailplane. The aircraft pitched up, losing a wing, and plunged into the ground at 500 mph. It hit an oil storage tank, causing one of the largest fires in Los Angeles that had ever been known. Tucker was somehow thrown clear but suffered many injuries. His parachute had a huge rip in its canopy, which meant his descent was too rapid to survive. His life was saved by falling into the one tree left standing in the remains of an orchard on land that was being cleared for a proposed housing project. The workmen were to have felled the tree that same day. The other crew member, an engineer named Arthur Turton, was killed.

Others amongst the group of ol' boys was ex-P38 Lightning pilot Jim Estronic who flew in Italy during the Second World War and had amassed 35,000 hours on aircraft. I dismissed him temporarily as a typical airliner type until he said his hours were mostly in Africa flying Invaders.

Volmer's VJ-22 was a two-seat amphibian aircraft for home-builders. I flew it from his local airfield at Sylma. On one occasion we tucked up the undercarriage (u/c) (landing gear to them), and flew to Catalina Island.

On the way, we passed over the centre of the huge LAX International Terminal of Los Angeles. This seemed unbelievable to me and I checked three times with Volmer that this was correct. I gradually realised that jet airliners coming in one end and going out the other, left a vacant central airspace – there was no way this would be allowed in England!

We landed in the water at Catalina. We lowered the u/c and taxied up a ramp to stop on dry land. I thought this was amazing – I think one has to do it to appreciate . . . land/water/land. Three large placards with instructions faced the pilot in the VJ-22. It was complex to transfer an amphibian to land/air or air/water or water/land because sometimes one system (wheels) was used when another was not or vice versa. We took off as a flying boat from Catalina through an inlet westwards. I couldn't seem to get it airborne; the chop on the water was increasing as the inlet entered the open Pacific Ocean. We were doing 70 knots and not lifting. I heard Volmer shout, 'China, here we come!' as I continued to fight this thing off the water. After a final bounce we made it and Volmer very sternly pointed at Placard No. 2 where it said 'raise steering rudder', which had been the cause of all the drag preventing us from becoming airborne. Checklists are there to be followed Mr Cook, I thought, mentally reprimanding myself for such an omission! I flew on and we then made a water-landing at Avalon, which was halfway down the island, and moored in a beautiful harbour, a haven of water surrounded by steep, craggy hillsides. What a long way from my little village in Suffolk, I mused as I absorbed my surroundings and the warm sunshine. A large pretentious house dominated the hillside. 'Mr Wrigley's (chewing gum) place,' remarked Volmer. Here, spread before me was the embodiment of the American dream, a Hollywood film set of heaven on earth!

The village of Thorpeness had been owned by one family, the Ogilvies. Mr Stuart Ogilvie still owned all the houses, golf club, beach, farms and boating mere. My father was his accountant/ secretary. There was a population of 200 locals in winter and 2000 rich holiday people in summer and a feudal system existed. This was not for me and I had left as soon as possible and joined the RAF in 1959, age nineteen – but I still loved the village. How different things appeared in America.

Our flight to Catalina concluded with a landing at the 'Airport in the Sky'. The runway cut across the narrow centre of the island, each end of which dropped 1500 feet sheer into the sea. 'Get it right,' Volmer said, 'and you will receive a special rookies' certificate, but you will go around again – all first-time people do.' He was implying it would take me more than one attempt to land. 'No I won't,' came my rather curt reply. The runway was not flat. Halfway down its length, the land rose then fell considerably, creating a hump effect, which gave the illusion on touchdown that the end of the runway was much closer than one would have anticipated, as one could not see beyond the top of the rise. I opened up the throttle and Volmer promptly closed it. We both struggled with this control, until I realised that I had been fooled like every other pilot attempting a landing for the first time. We made a normal landing and I was awarded my certificate from the

'Airport in the Sky', stating that I'd traversed the Pacific Ocean! I'd flown across 30 miles of water from the mainland in the most perfect conditions of visibility and wind in the amphibian, which could have landed on the water at any one moment, and was awarded a beautiful certificate! They ought to try it over our English Channel, I thought!

Whilst on the island, we ate buffalo burgers and drank real lemon juice – a new experience for me. The buffaloes had been put on the island in the 1920s by a film company. They thrived so well that the island is now overpopulated with the animals – hence the culling – and buffalo burgers! No one would pay for them to be transported back to the mainland it seems.

My trip was completed at low level, flying up the west coast of California – past the now retired transatlantic liner the *Queen Mary*, which was moored at Long Beach, along with Howard Hughes' *Spruce Goose*. We bypassed ex-President Nixon's home on the cliff top because the last time Volmer flew past the estate he was grounded for a month. Before we finally returned to the airfield at Sylmar, we landed in an isolated, elongated lake, bordered by the San Gabriel Mountains. This beautiful lake was surrounded by sugar pines, which intoxicated the air with their scent. These trees grew right down to the edge of the crystal-clear turquoise water and humming birds flitted in their branches. With the hatches open above my head, I climbed out and sat astride the nose of the VJ-22 and thought this surely must be paradise. As we sat there, I couldn't suppress my laughter when Volmer came out with the outrageous politically incorrect statement and said, 'I wonder what the poor people are doing?'

I have always loved trees and my two-acre garden contains numerous trees of varying sorts and sizes. Besides being living things of great beauty, they provide an invaluable source of food and protection for wildlife and, by their intake of carbon dioxide and their expulsion of oxygen, they are indispensable to the existence of life on our planet.

In California, USA, I was fortunate enough to gaze at the tallest growing trees in the world – the 300-foot high Redwoods. I was also able to marvel at the largest growing trees – the monumental sequoias at King's Canyon – one of which bore a plaque stating that it was 500 years old when Christ was born!

The oldest living trees are the bristlecone pines, which grow high in the desolate White Mountains of California. Access to see these wondrous trees, one of which is said to be 4000 years old, is severely restricted. This is disappointing, but is understandable when one learns that one of these historic trees has recently been destroyed by a chainsaw just so that its age could be calculated by counting its rings. How anyone could carry out such an act is beyond my comprehension. I was able to pass within feet of these extraordinary trees when I was taken in a Grob glider from the Tehatchepee Glider Port, which was situated near the White Mountains. It was a flight I shall always remember.

My pilot for that flight was the test pilot for the very secret stealth bomber B2. I discovered that in spite of this guy's status, he still turned up from nearby Palmdale to fly gliders during his free time. The attitude of 'I'm a pilot' in England just doesn't exist in America. Aero modellers are regarded with as much respect over there as the top test pilots. We have a lot to learn. It was aero modellers who first put turbulators on models that resulted in the 'trip' turbulators on the wing struts of my design.

SBAC FARNBOROUGH AND AIR DISPLAYS

I partook in many major air shows throughout England during that period 1978/80. I became a known quantity and with influence from Duckhams as my sponsor, I was entered in the SBAC (Society of British Aerospace Companies) Farnborough Air Show in 1980 and given the privilege of opening the show. I think there were 125 aircrew from all over the world taking part in this all day, week-long, air show. It was a very precisely organised event with timings outlined to the second. Duckhams paid me to undertake the event and covered the insurance for £10 million, which was mandatory. Harry Potter, my able assistant, and I would have to do our stuff here in front of 140,000 people who all knew about aviation.

Two days before display week, all pilots were required to show one's routine and timing. I was allowed six minutes – as much as McDonnell Douglas with their F15 and latest F18 fighters. My timing and routine were approved, but the question of my flying licence cropped up whilst booking in with Duncan Simpson on the SBAC Committee. He was one of our best test pilots with the Hawker Hunter. 'Where's your licence, David?' he asked. I mumbled and fumbled a bit and showed the hang gliding proficiency bit of paper, which meant nothing in reality, and said I'd been flying twenty-six years. To which he replied, 'I know that David, but where is your licence?' There were kindly sniggers from hotshot pilots lined up behind me and certain murmurings. I played this out whilst Duncan became increasingly irritated, before complying and showing him the right piece of bureaucracy. I don't know why aircrew play pranks, but it always happens – maybe it's to hide the realisation of the dangerous lives they lead.

Once lined up on the vast threshold of Farnborough runway, things were not so funny. Harry, helping me, had checked out the VJ-23E and we waited in our isolation for the correct time. It was so quiet and I remember John Blake (one of the best commentators in the business) on the commentary kindly saying 'How very lonely it must be for David out there.' I knew I would be making history by running down the runway to lift off, though I doubt if my type of running action was the original reason for the name 'runway'.

At one minute before the start and with my little McCulloch engine running, torrential rain began to fall. Rain was bouncing 3 or 4 inches off the tarmac. We sheltered beneath the VJ-23's wings. I felt utterly dejected. There was, with the greatest will in the world, no way of flying in those conditions. I felt I was letting Duckhams down, but mostly, I wanted to perform this opening privilege. Exactly six minutes later, the rain suddenly stopped – just like someone turning off a tap. A PIK 21 from Finland was waiting nearby for the follow-on slot. This was a powered sailplane, but the pilot waved off his chance to fly. I knew why, for we were in the eye of a thunderstorm. With our lightly loaded wings, we could be sucked up out of control into a raging maelstrom. It was windless, bright and clear and we obtained clearance to take the PIK 21 slot. I flew the full six minutes with the control stick forward in order to prevent the aircraft from being snatched upwards – the lift was violently sucking me aloft. Amusingly, I could see Concorde orbiting to the west, awaiting the end of my routine. How much fuel was that burning whilst I concluded my flight?

The following day at the pilots' briefing tent, (the word 'tent' is hardly befitting for the splendid RAF blue silk drapes that surrounded us) an impeccably dressed RAF Group Captain addressed us on the previous day's display. 'The Red Arrows – if you overfly the crowd once more you will be banned for the rest of this week. Will the Italian helicopter display team see me after this briefing?' The Airbus pilot then received a similar rollicking. We all sat in silence as these rebukes were made in a stern, but courteous manner.

'Will the powered hang glider pilot stand up?' I quaked with dread at the thought of being reprimanded in such company. 'Display of the day – well done!' The pilots all applauded. How did they know what I had done? Surely most pilots pull levers and push buttons, I thought – things that ace engineers and specialists had all worked out and pilots just used them. It seemed that this honour came from people who really did know about flight.

When talking later to Mr John Cunningham from the SBAC committee, he confirmed that, yes, they did know and appreciate what I had accomplished in those conditions, but warned me never to be influenced by pressure again. I had been driven by my commitment to Duckhams and the awesomeness of the occasion. (Mr Cunningham – 'Cat's Eyes' Cunningham – was the Second World War pilot who first used radar at night to shoot down German aircraft. The cover story for the secret radar was that he ate lots of carrots, which gave him night vision! He is the most deserving man I know who has never been given proper recognition.)

With Duckhams' sponsorship, I continued to give many appearances with the VJ-23E.

Sometimes these were private special events, where only I and Ken Wallis with his autogyro would fly. One such event was the

final of 'It's A Knockout' in Arundel, Sussex. Neither of us n
much space to become airborne, so when I found the only likely
take-off site nearby, he told me, 'I've seen a few places in my life,
but this one takes the cake!' He related to me how once, in Rio de
Janeiro, he had used the viewing area on top of the huge statue of
Christ as a runway. There was not enough room for the ground
run on this viewing platform, so he had blasted across its width,
hit the rim and was flying!

Ken Wallis helped my friend, Colin Buck, to launch me at
Arundel and paid for his kindness by falling flat on his face when
he couldn't keep up the required pace, but he was in his seventies!
As I wandered towards these 90-foot high oak trees, he apparently
said in his dry manner to Colin, 'Every monkey to its own branch,
I suppose'. The climb rate just allowed me to clear the tops of the
oaks, but even so I had to lift my legs as I scraped skywards.

The previous night, we had stayed at the Golden Goose in
Arundel and had been plied with plenty of really good red wine.
We were definitely rather worse for wear by the time we staggered
up to bed. Colin had somehow found the room and, when I
entered, I saw him splayed against the opposite wall. Wearing
nothing but his red underpants he was feigning being whipped
and shouting, 'Hit me – hit me!' At that precise moment, Ken
Wallis opened the door and, with a large grin (similar to Punch),
hoarsely whispered, 'Wrong room!' and vanished. 'That makes us
look really good, Colin,' I remember muttering. The final laugh of
the evening was that he and I had to share a double bed together.
As I switched off the bedside light, a voice from the darkness
droned, 'Don't you put your willy near me . . . !'

My other major flying appearances were at Biggin Hill, Fairoaks,
Halfpenny Green, Leicester, Teeside, Blackpool and many more.
Harry Potter accompanied me on many of these displays. He was
an ex-rugby player – large, bearded and ginger. Being an upfront
sort of person, he used to look after the ground side of things such
as rigging the aircraft and sorting hangarage if it was a two-day
show. He was always a receptive consumer of my complimentary
meals. He strode around the various airfields with an assumed air
of authority and importance that far outweighed the actual value

of our tiny, powered hang glider. 'We are the powered hang glider. Move that Mosquito out, so we can get in the hanger,' I once heard him say. I also saw him at Biggin Hill peering over the shoulder of Raymond Baxter during the recording of a TV video session. The session abruptly stopped, with Baxter greatly annoyed. He enquired of Harry, 'Are you vital?' 'I am to me,' came Harry's reply. But Harry proved his worth on numerous occasions. Once at Leicester Airfield Open Day, a helicopter persisted in landing too close to our very lightweight VJ-23E. Although the plane was well picketed to the ground, the downdraught caused us great concern. After two warnings to 'Please land a little further away' were ignored, Harry bounded over to the pilot in the helicopter, reached through his window and told him in no uncertain terms what he thought of his behaviour. This verbal onslaught was quickly followed by a wrenching of the pilot's helmet across his face to emphasise the point. Clearance parking followed.

In conditions of zero wind, we were still having launch problems. In 1979, even running at full pace and with a powerful thrust from Harry, we only just managed to get airborne as was shown on my first day at the Biggin Hill Pageant. We were undecided as to the wind direction. Tiny wafts of breeze alternated first one way then the other. In front of a large crowd, we eventually raced towards the beginning of the runway, as opposed to along it. I just managed to fly, crossed the boundary fence and the public road, and descended into the Biggin Valley. It was highly embarrassing. All that noise and racket from the McCullough engine and then I disappeared from view! I was being paid by the show organisers and Duckhams to put on a display by the first powered hang glider to cross the English Channel and I'd totally vanished for my allotted six minutes! At least all the other aviators present had a guaranteed lift-off – I had no such assurance of success! Scratching around the Biggin Valley, I was dealing with sinking air that exactly matched my full climb rate. Figuring that sinking air cannot go below the ground on the side of the hill, I flew closely to it, gradually gaining the 50 feet necessary to cross the road on return to the airfield. At least four of my six minutes must now be gone I calculated, but I managed to cross the road safely and wished I could have thanked the double-decker bus driver for stopping to let me cross his path! Nicely clearing the boundary fence, I unwittingly scraped over the Royal marquee of King Hussein of Jordan, who was sitting with his entourage, watching the display. Rather depleted, I completed my display, hopefully thrilling the crowds – who I am sure were only waiting to see my full-bore landing run.

During the afternoon, I was invited to meet King Hussein in his marquee, which was situated – as I knew – on the opposite side of the runway from the public. Security at the marquee was tight. After greeting and shaking hands with the King, I was moved to the viewing area of the Royal compound and introduced to the King! I thought I had already been introduced, but it had been his double. It was extraordinary that a double could have been found, for the King was quite small in stature and possessed a disproportionately large head. Harry was only halfway across the end of the runway before he was escorted back by the security guards. He hadn't been invited to meet 'His Royalness', but was probably already quoting; 'We're the powered hang glider . . . '

I remember at the Farnborough Show, the press were very interested to write about the VJ-23E, so I let Harry deal with them. He was delighted to expound the virtues of this unique aircraft, having never flown it! I am sure he talked for hours! Meanwhile, I slipped off to meet up with the Ranger of an RSPB area in Surrey that had several pairs of breeding Dartford warblers. I had not seen one before and it was to my great delight that we were successful in our quest.

The show most suited to the VJ-23E was at Old Warden, Bedfordshire, where the Shuttleworth Collection was housed. Only old and slow planes flew from this famous collection in its lovely setting. David Ogilvie ran the show there at that time and welcomed my little flying machine. He was the first person I'd met who thought similarly to myself. He said, 'Radio on your aircraft, David?' 'No,' I replied. 'Good,' he said 'Because that over there is a perfectly airworthy aircraft that has a radio, which is unserviceable, therefore the Civil Aviation Authority (CAA) rules say it can't fly. Have you ever heard anything so ridiculous?'

The Shuttleworth Collection subsequently had the VJ-23E on static display for a few years and it was then transferred to the Air and Space Museum in Manchester, where it still resides today.

VJ-24

In 1979 Volmer Jensen designed the VJ-24. This was a foot-launched glider with the engine etc. behind the pilot. It was built of aluminium tube, unlike the construction of the VJ-23. Irv Culver came up with yet another design for the wing and this section had the remarkable stall speed of 12 mph, which was lower than the 15 mph of the VJ-23.

In 1980, I went to see Volmer again in Glendale. In three weeks I helped him cobble together what was probably the world's first microlight. We mounted a Yamaha KT100 10-hp two-stroke engine on a mount in front of the wing and added a seat and wheels.

I flew this little aircraft with great delight at a very difficult site, which was surrounded by wires and trees plus the added hazard of a nearby river.

Operation from their previous flying area had been halted by the arrival of a police bike with its sirens screaming. The officer stipulated loudly that no flying was allowed. Our group comprised of four ol' boys over eighty and me, with a hopefully impressionable English accent. Volmer stood silent listening to the officer's tirade. Volmer informed the officer that I had travelled 6000 miles to fly this plane, but the officer was unimpressed. 'You can fly it, but I'll arrest you,' he retorted. One cannot help ask the question 'Is America really free?'

On my return to England, Steve Emmerson and I built the VJ-24, the second aircraft to be constructed in the confines of my base-ment. With aluminium tubes and pop rivets, this aircraft went together quickly and we were soon using it for air shows in the summer of 1981 as an attraction for people who liked slow flying machines. This little aircraft was right at the start of a new form of aviation – the microlight. Various types were emerging by the day. The VJ-24W was amongst the first generation of microlights (ultra-lights in the USA), but retained normal three-axis controls. Other types were weight-shift flexwings, which began life as foot-launched powered hang gliders but developed into a trike attached to a hang-glider wing.

The two-axis machines from America such as the Eipper Quicksilver and similar Rotec Rally were constructed of tubes and a single-surface fabric wing. The sport was on the move. The CAA in England put forward a specific set of standards for the construction of microlights called BCAR Section S. They also introduced a new 'D' category pilots' licence, which was less demanding in its requirements compared with the traditional 'A' licence needed by all pilots. This allowed many more people to fly, a sport that had previously been the preserve of the wealthy.

My little VJ-24W performed faultlessly for several years, but it was being outdated by better designs. Initially, it retired to Old Sarum, Wiltshire, where it hung in the roof of a hangar. It now resides at the Newark Air Museum as an example of the early microlight movement.

CHAPTER 2

Designs

MUSFLY

In 1979, my colleague Neil Moran and I worked out a design to win the Kramer prize of £50,000, to fly a man-powered aircraft over a set distance of a quarter of a mile in a figure-of-eight course. Neil is a brilliant mathematician and was also a draughtsman with me at Richard Garrett. He calculated the power required and I designed the airframe. We concluded that previous man-powered aircraft designs had followed the wrong path. They were designs that had very low drag and flew just 20–25 mph, but incurred too much weight.

Our design, called 'Musfly' (because we thought it must fly), was contrary to previous thoughts. We conceived a design with a very low speed – 12 mph – which would incur very little drag and possess a very low weight. It was a wire-braced wing with the head-on appearance of a gliding seagull, i.e. downturned wing tips. The span was 70 feet and the weight was to be well under 100 lb. To power the machine, we would use two people with treadles instead of pedals. The pilot would treadle with his feet and fly with his hands, using twist grips for roll-controlled ailerons and the pitch would have weight shift control by suspending the pilot capsule beneath the wing. The role of the second person would be to treadle with both hands and legs and be the source of the power supply; he could pull opposite arm/leg treadles for increased power output. This system produced far more output than had previously been possible. We became quite excited about our

30

design and applied for a grant from the Royal Aeronautical Society Man Powered Group. This group appeared to be headed by an ex-Squadron Leader who had previously flown a man-powered craft called *Puffin*, to some slight success. He was non-receptive to our ideas and refused our application for a grant on the grounds that he didn't like to see that much power being applied to a man-powered flying machine'! Surely, we thought, this was the area on which previous designs had failed. No grant, therefore, but we were recommended to the head of the Imperial College of Aeronautics London for a briefing with a certain Mr Irving.

Neil and I entered the Imperial College with some trepidation. What were we 'country hicks' doing in a place of such calibre? Mr Irving did not agree with any of our design philosophy. He ridiculed our downturned wing tips, which greatly reduced, if not entirely eliminated, induced drag (the highest of the drag forms for low-speed flight), even though Neil had not included the reduction of drag from them in his calculations. Irving called the tips theory 'witchcraft'. Maybe people would like to note the wing tip devices seen on airliners nowadays – I doubt if they are 'witchcraft'. For although they are in a different form, they are doing the same thing. Irving also did not believe the lightweight, low-speed theory to be credible. We left the meeting in a rather disconsolate manner. There had been so little appreciation given towards our design and theories.

I built the Musfly, mostly alone in a disused warehouse at the Richard Garrett works in Leiston, during my spare time. With some help from colleagues, I had almost completed covering the machine's wing with Mylar film, when the building was demolished. With nowhere to take it, low funds and low morale, the project was dropped and the airframe scrapped. I'd learnt a lot though. The Musfly was strong enough for flight – it weighed well under 90 lb and the power to the 11-foot propeller was exactly what Neil had calculated. We almost came to use my PADPROP. This was an amazing design for a propeller that not only rotated, but projected fore and aft at the same time. As the blade went forward, whilst rotating, it feathered. When going aft, the blade was flat like an oar of a boat. At a slow 60 rpm, this large diameter propeller gave a huge increase of thrust. If only the man-powered group had helped us with a little bit of funding, I'm sure with my slow-speed flying experience we could have achieved our goals.

It was ironic that the American Paul McCreedy not only won the Kramer prize money in America – with the aid of immense financial help – for completing the required course and distance, but also took my record of the 'lowest powered flight across the English Channel'. All in a man-powered aircraft that flew very slowly (11 mph) and was wire-braced for ultimate lightness, just like the Musfly . . . I really did begin to wonder whether people who were supposed to know what they were talking about, really did. I have never castigated anyone who 'did not know' – but I do not suffer these fools lightly.

My design theories for the Musfly did provoke a heated argument with a certain Mr Donovan – head of Raleigh Cycles racing department, at that time – who happened to have a second home in my village at Thorpeness. Whilst studying how to power the Musfly, I constructed an aluminium tandem bicycle using 1-inch square tube. The square tube seemed to possess more rigidity than the round and was lighter than the steel used in a traditional bicycle. I also noted that the treadle mechanism gave a longer power stroke compared with the rotating pedal. Using a tough plastic chain that free-wheeled back on the upstroke, it made me realise that the design of Mr Donovan's bicycles were almost exactly the same in 1979 as they had been eighty years before. When I confronted him with this fact, he naturally disagreed and we stood, two engineers nose to nose apart. I was beginning to think that what already existed wasn't necessarily always right and often the way forwards is not to be influenced by the knowledge of other people, but to believe in one's own ideas.

The Shadow

I was now beginning to think that the time had arrived for me to design my own aircraft. Although I was academically unqualified in aeronautics, I had been flying since I was fourteen years old, when in 1954 I had flown Auster Aiglets and Tiger Moths at

Ipswich Airport. I had initially been an airframe fitter on joining the RAF and, had later flown in many fast and big jet aircraft. I was an engineer and design draughtsman and also reckoned that I was capable of doing almost anything with my hands. All these combined attributes and experience at the age of forty-one, were contributing factors to enable me to do my own design, but to succeed in such a task required a burning personal drive and the courage of self belief, with total commitment.

The drive and instigation to do my own aircraft was born when Richard Garrett, the engineering firm where I was employed, went into liquidation. Seven hundred very skilled engineering people lost their jobs in a very rural area. This was an outright tragedy in 1981, but it provided me with the perfect opportunity now to focus my thoughts on creating an aircraft of my own conception.

During this period, Steve Emmerson and I built microlights for Blois Aviation at Cockfield Hall, Yoxford – a stately house some 10 miles from home. Steve Emmerson had been one of my apprentices in the drawing office at Richard Garrett and had become a fine engineer. He had helped me on many occasions over the last few years in my aeronautical projects. We assembled US imported Quicksilvers and Rotec Rally microlights. I then flew them and taught pilots to solo on these machines. For a year or so, Steve and I continued with this, but all my thoughts were channelled towards my ultimate goal of creating my own aircraft. The consequence of this was that I was often accused of rudeness, because of my apparent lack of attention when dealing with people. Steve and I worked well together. He rarely spoke, so my thinking was uninterrupted!

It was an extraordinary scene at Cockfield Hall with Rodney Blois gallivanting around with his aristocratic air. We constructed aeroplanes in the vast hall, surrounded by priceless furniture and paintings. Not really the norm for a workshop! There were drawers full of birds' eggs from the past and tiger skins stretched out on the floor. Once I put one of these huge tiger skins on and peered through its gaping jaws. Hiding in the poorly lit hallway, I was expecting to leap out with a huge roar and frighten Steve, but it was the Scottish housekeeper who became my terrified victim and I deservedly received a reprimand from Rodney Blois for the incident!

One of the many interesting people I met whilst working for Blois Aviation was David Clarke. He had been banned from flying in Jersey because he had violated the airspace over an International Golf match. He was one of those unique people who had the ability to fly anything and he quickly took over the instructional side of this little business at Cockfield Hall.

Whilst we all enjoyed aviation and became close friends, my real desire was to progress with my own design. It was at this point that I consulted with Neil Moran. I had the clear idea that with sufficiently lightweight materials, I could design and construct an airframe that would be inside the CAA's empty weight rulings limit of 150 kg (331 lb).

Neil and I visited Ciba Geigy at Duxford in Cambridgeshire. Their Bonded Structures Division representative met us by appointment and showed us all their composite structures. It was fascinating to see their strong lightweight materials, which were used in production on high-tech aircraft. For me, the composite that held the most potential was a material called fibrelam. This was a paper honeycomb structure sandwiched between two fibre-glass skins. Its main industrial use was for the flooring beneath the carpets on modern airliners. The engineering salesman David Southwell – himself a pilot – exuded so much enthusiasm for my project that he gave me two whole sheets of 10 feet x 4 feet fibrelam to take away and use as I wished. I learned about the special adhesives and the Chief Structural Engineer, George, demonstrated how to form and cut the material.

Following our informative day at Ciba Geigy, Neil and I immediately began work on a monocoque design using fibrelam as the elementary structure for the fuselage/cockpit, boom tube and main spar for the wing. Whilst Neil Moran worked his magic with the structures mathematics, Chris Tansley and I began building the aircraft in my basement. I decided it was to be named 'Shadow' 01 as I thought this name had appeal and would be universally acceptable. The existence of Lord Heskith's Formula 1 motor racing team called 'Shadow' assured me of this.

The fibrelam went together quickly and easily. The boom tube folded up from a rectangular section at the front to square at the rear from one piece and the main spar caps had to be laminated with uni-directional glass (fibre in one direction) as Neil calculated that the fibrelam was not strong enough in tension. The ribs were made of foam, the wing 'D' box was covered in fibrelam skins, and the rest of the wing was fabric-covered. For the rudder, I used the already proven design of the VJ-24.

To say the result was a failure is an understatement. I rigged the aircraft in my garden and after supporting both wing tips on stands, sat in the centre of the wings. The wing bent so much that all the wing 'D' panels 'oil-canned' because the deflection was so great. This would be no good at all. I could get hold of the boom near the tailplane and move it laterally several inches without any of the rest of the airframe moving! If it had flown, it would have been similar to flying a rubber band!

I immediately telephoned Ciba Geigy and talked to George, the Chief Structural Engineer.

'Your fibrelam doesn't do what you claimed – it's wasted a month of my time. The "E" value is low – it bent easily – but the "I" value is high,' I informed him – it won't break.

To my amazement, his reaction was disbelief! Within days, Neil and I transported the whole aircraft to Duxford and rigged it up outside Ciba Geigy's offices. With George looking on, I attached a spring balance to the end of the fibrelam boom tube and pulled 10 lb sideways – the deflection was 7 inches.

'I can't believe it,' he mumbled.

'And look at my sensitised face – your epoxy resin has made me look like a myxomatosis rabbit!' I said.

I was not running these people down. They really did want to help, but this was just another incident of people not knowing what they were talking about. For sure, they made and knew their product, but had they ever used it? David Southwell continued to be helpful and enthusiastic about the project. He told me of another Ciba Geigy department on the same site that made Araldite adhesive. This would also be suitable for bonding the fibrelam. But he was unable to contact them, as the two departments were not in communication! That advice could prove the solution for one problem – my sensitisation – but the structural use of fibrelam would have to be rethought.

By now I had unfortunately lost faith in Neil. With the help of Steve Emmerson, I set about doing a patch-up job on 01. Chris Tansley had left the country, delivering a yacht to the West Indies, so was now unavailable. The whole design was destined to be a trial and error production. I removed the wing 'D' box skins and uni-glass from the spar caps. Aluminium strips replaced the uni-glass and 1.2-mm plywood covered the wing leading edge 'D' box. Tests showed plenty of stiffness, so David Clarke and I took it to an old airfield to test-fly. The engine was an ex-snowmobile Kohler 35-hp twin-cylinder two-stroke. We flew it up and down the long runway at Flixton, Suffolk, and eventually David Clarke made one or two good flights above 500 feet. Problems emerged with boom flexing and flaps needed to be fitted to give high lift for landing. There were as yet no brakes and the ground steering was primitive – a makeshift screwdriver protruding through the cockpit floor from the nose leg tube! David Clarke found this unconventional method of steering confusing and was never quite sure which way to push the screwdriver!

I knew that some pilots always had problems when contending with unfamiliar control systems. When I was teaching on the Rotec Rally microlights, I noticed certain pilots had difficulty with pitch because the control stick hung from above and one pilot with 21,000 hours on airliners, put one of Blois's Rotecs on its back whilst taxiing. He even set up a rig in his garage to try to overcome his difficulties. The Rotec stick was just the same in pitch as any other conventional control, i.e. forward for down flight and back for up, but he could not compute the configuration. I had similar problems when I attempted to fly a weight-shift trike or hang glider! Their controls are the reverse of those in orthodox aircraft and I had great problems, the result of which was a broken arm!

The death of Shadow 01 occurred at Flixton airfield on the day David Clarke observed a small silver object falling away from the plane as he flew. The engine immediately stopped. Using great ingenuity and skill, he glided the aircraft back to earth and was, thankfully, unharmed. The silver object, I discovered, had been the propeller-retaining washer. The whole plane had proved unsatisfactory in every aspect of its life. I made an instant decision. 'That's it,' I said, 'I've had enough.' And with that statement, I took out my lighter and set fire to the aircraft and burnt the whole damned thing!

I was depressed and frustrated. I had used all the expert knowledge and advice that I had been given to produce Shadow 01 and had failed. The solution seemed clear. I would do it all myself. No one in the future would divert me from the conviction of my thoughts. This would come straight from my heart and mind and would, I hoped, be a leap forward in the world of aviation design.

I had lived and studied aeroplanes for a large part of my life and numerous aspects of existing aviation design bothered me. For example, why were there so many aircraft designed with such a poor field of vision for the pilot – surely the most basic requirement for flight. And why were prototype aircraft produced that failed in so many obvious ways, needing constant correction and modification? Why weren't these unsuccessful features perceived at the conception stage?

I was determined to think my design concept through in every detail, including the structure, the aerodynamics, the material usage (knowledge from 01 had already showed that total use of composite materials was not the ultimate way forward). I would create an aircraft that fulfilled and encompassed all my thoughts.

The following weeks were spent deep in thought and intense concentration. Each night I considered and resolved all the points and problems of a different design feature, until I had finally formed the definitive vision of my aircraft. I was passionate to succeed.

I was consumed with an overwhelming drive, which forced me forwards and fired me with energy and enthusiasm. This was an attitude forged in childhood from my South African-born father, who had always instilled in me that to be first was the only acceptable position. One didn't win silver – one lost gold!

Design Concepts

'Get it wrong at the start and it will be wrong at the finish' is a maxim worth contemplating when creating an aircraft.

When I initially met Volmer Jensen, one of the very first remarks he made to me was, 'What did you alter when you built the VJ-23?'

'Nothing,' I retorted.

'Well, you're the first guy who hasn't thought he's better than the designer,' came back the reply. 'Alter one thing and you alter a hundred others.'

Consider the Spitfire aircraft of the Second World War. Of course I love the Spitfire – who could not? But why was this plane and others of that era, designed so that the pilot at the critical moment of take-off, was unable to see the runway and had to fly blind until the plane had reached a speed of 60 mph and the tail lifted. Would we drive a car with no forward vision until we reached a speed of 60 mph?

And why did these designers put 90 gallons of high-octane fuel in front of the pilot, knowing he would be going into battle? How many brave pilots died through being burnt by flaming petrol because of the bad positioning of the fuel? The first Hawker Typhoon had an entrance door hinged from its front edge in the event of having to bale out. Imagine 300–400 mph of air pushing against the door; to open it would have been impossible combating such forces. The reason for many of these faults is that the designer does not actually fly himself, and is thus unaware of what is required. Ever heard of a musical composer who didn't themselves play? It's all obvious to me, when I think about it. It doesn't make me right, it makes them wrong! If the designer puts a two-seat design side by side, then invariably he has to position the wing either above or below these people for balance (centre of gravity) reasons. This restricts the pilot's view either upwards or downwards. Why put the engine at the front? The propeller blast alone puts 200–400 mph of air skin friction drag over much of the airframe. It is far better to have the engine/propeller behind as a pusher configuration for efficiency. Designers usually stick wings onto the fuselage sides. This causes interference drag between the two – is it better to lift the wing above in clear air?

Thus, the design concept of Shadow 02 was pulling together. I also wanted the design to look aesthetically pleasing. Most aircraft look awful – especially microlights. I envisaged a smart, sleek-looking aircraft enclosed from the cold and wet and with all the 'proper' controls for the pilot – brakes, flaps, in-flight re-start, a second seat for the passenger, and very quick rig and de-rig so it could go in a trailer and be taken home. These were the design concepts of the proposed Shadow.

Materials

All materials have properties that can aid the construction of an airframe or degrade it. This is why I can never accept the designer who basically uses only one type of material. Airframes are invariably all wooden, all metal or all composite materials – the designers never seemed to cotton on to the fact that they all used rubber tyres because that was the 'best material for the job' it was doing. Consequently, these one-material concepts are heavier than they need to be. Already the fuselage/monocoque was going to be fibrelam and used in a way that kept changing shape and direction – this way, its lightness and properties gave the best stiffness. The monocoque design incorporated the seat shapes; thus saving the weight of two seats. Ciba Geigy used an aluminium insert that bonded in from each side as an interference fit with a $\frac{3}{16}$inch diameter hole, which could be drilled out to ¼-inch diameter. Each insert had 1100-lb shear and pull-out strength. They could be positioned in the fibrelam wherever required, unlike a tube space frame where every 'hard point' had to be designed in from the start. The second seating area was only for an occasional person, similar to a sports car's rear seating. The rear bulkhead of fibrelam was also the firewall between the passenger and engine. This type of crew monocoque has a distinct safety advantage over tube space frame assemblies because in a crash situation, broken or bent tubes are not there to injure the crew. A complete monocoque would weigh 16 lb and would be bonded throughout with an Araldite grade strength of 4800 psi. Some joints at 90-degree junctions would have special fibreglass angles to back up the strength.

I knelt on the floor in my living room and designed and drew this complex shape and all its parts in a week – there are a lot of hours in a week at over twenty a day. I could hardly stand up sometimes from my piece of chipboard, which I used as a drawing board.

But what was bothering me greatly was the wing – its aerodynamic section and its spar.

The essence of an aircraft is in its wing. It provides all the lift and most of the stability and agility. Yet, it has to have great strength. First, what section was the aerofoil to be? My book of aerofoil sections showed hundreds of differing shapes and their various characteristics and speeds, but absolutely none showed anything like the speed range of 20–100 mph. My envisaged microlight was to be the fastest and best in the world, within the confines of the regulations defining a microlight. Existing micro/ultralight in the early 1980s just buzzed and floated around fields – none of them was capable of seriously leaving its area and cruising cross-country.

It became obvious that I would have to develop my own aerofoil. Using the format of Irv Culver's drooped leading edge 'D' box shape, I drew this up and projected the ribs to the trailing edge. I believed 90 per cent of the lift came from the forward part of the wing and that the other 10 per cent just streamlined the air. Lots of the lift was actually formed in front of it, rather like the bow wave seen in the water in front of a boat (dolphins can be seen using this). Aft of the 'D' section the wing was to be fabric-covered – there was little point in trying to hold a precise section aft of 30 per cent chord, anyway. I struggled with this section, eventually working out the co-ordinates by percentages. Some academic training would have been an advantage I know, but I got there. It took just over two weeks.

The main spar followed quickly. It has been said that theoretically a sheet of paper standing absolutely vertical can support an infinite weight. The trouble is of course that it doesn't freely stand – it needs support. I used a shear web of 1.2-mm plywood and kept it vertical with numerous nose ribs made from styrofoam, then clad it all in the same three-ply 1.2-mm plywood. The spar caps were a top hat section of aluminium as used on 'white van' interiors (Luton vans). This stuff was the right shape to bond and rivet and, amazingly, the right grade of aluminium, HE30. It was also mass-produced and cheap. A complete 'D' section of one wing weighed 22 lb and was 14 feet long. My knowledge, gained from Ciba Geigy, allowed the bonding of differing materials – in this case aluminium/plywood. There were also back-up aluminium strips bonded and riveted. The wing planform was tapered and the thickness tapered, making it very pure for lift distribution. The 30-mm thick styrofoam (used mostly for the lining of cattle or pig sheds) was available at most builders' merchants. It had a weight of 2.2 lb per cubic foot, and was quite light but very good in compression. The whole leading edge assembly was a big torque box. It was strong and light. I made the wings detach from a 4-ft centre section, which remained on the fuselage. It was quickly detachable, with each wing having two large, vertical retaining pins. When, later, during a structural analysis Paul Owen was assessing the Shadow for compliance to BCAR Section S, he congratulated me for getting the wing 'break' disconnect to within $\frac{1}{16}$th of an inch of the optimum place. He was convinced I was a genius. I told him to look at the main wheels' distance across and he would see it was also the same. 'That was really so I could get it out of my basement doors,' I laughingly told him, but he thought I was merely being modest not honest!

The trailing ribs I covered in glass woven mat using epoxy resin, as polyester resin 'ate' the foam. Bits of uni-glass were placed at key stress points to assure structural integrity. The complete wing was then proof tested – off the airframe. Steve and I loaded the wing and it produced a strength/weight ratio of 50:1 without failure. The wing attachment point to the centre section had 3600 lb force going through it at 6 g and this joint had a running strength of 15,000 lb. This was some structure! I had achieved great strength with low weight. The whole wing only weighed 100 lb. A Light Weight Structures friend, upon hearing the 50:1 strength/weight ratio, said he didn't believe the figures. If I could have achieved 30:1, I'd have done very well. I told him this was proven by physical tests and that he should revise his structure to my type of 'I' beam for his proposed design for the cover of the stadium at QPR football ground.

I rejected the previous fibrelam boom tube and decided on a 5-inch diameter 18-g aluminium tube used for irrigation on our local fields. The material of these tubes, which were normally used for pumping water, was corrosion resistant. The tubes also had the added bonus of being fatigue resistant to enable them to withstand the rough handling of farm work. They are produced in France and although I managed to get the correct specification, it was not that impressive for an aeroplane. I had used 4-inch diameter similar tubes for both VJ-23 and VJ-24, but they were delicate slow aircraft that would not endure hard 'g' forces or certification. Also, these were rolled from sheet and then machine-welded along their whole length. Later the CAA told me they liked this because not only was the weld constant (from a machine), but the thickness of the tube was standard – unlike a drawn or extruded tube where the inside diameter could be slightly non-concentric, therefore varying the wall thickness.

So towards the end of 1982, Shadow 02 was being conceived. I had no work income, but a wife and two young children to support. We lived off my funds saved from the air show contributions. I had saved all the income from sponsorship and displays, except for that which went as thank-you pocket money to colleagues who had assisted me. This situation was about to change, for one day two local retired businessmen appeared unexpectedly at my home saying, 'We watched you struggle David and work hard at your enterprise. As we have retired and have plenty of income, we would like to give you £5000 towards the cost of your project and we wish you the very best of luck!' They were Mr Dennis Brett and Mr George Ireland from Thorpeness. They became the true Godfathers of the Shadow. Their kindness and generosity enabled my dream – Shadow 02 – to be born. I allowed myself £25 per week and Steve Emmerson gave me his time whilst on the dole. In the 1980s, there existed a wide-ranging variety of work skills amongst the local population. If I needed anything to be machined or welded, pressed, cut, etc. that was beyond my available facilities, all I had to do was call a friend locally and the job could be done. How different it is now, when most people's skill is pressing computer keys, which, I may add, produces nothing.

The airframe came along easily, with its mixture of materials combining their assets for the job they were performing. Steel had to be used for some things, whereas aluminium, foams, wood, ply, glass fibre, honeycomb, fabric and all manner of other materials made this airframe. I used inch series hardware, i.e. bolts that were the unified standard (this was a standard devised by the UK and USA during the Second World War, so that aircraft produced were compatible). Commercial nyloc nuts were much cheaper than 'aircraft' nuts and could be used on/off at least twenty times. The aluminium grade was H-30 to a British Standard but 'uncertified'. Prior to purchasing the aluminium, I visited a manufacturer and discussed the advantages and disadvantages of the aluminium I was to buy. They showed me two 1¼-inch tubes – one had been tested by them and certified as being of a certain hardness and defined tensile strength. The other tube was from the same batch but hadn't been tested. It was identical but a tenth of the cost. To produce a 'certified' aircraft, it had to be constructed with 'certified' materials. Microlights are not certified but 'approved' by the CAA. Therefore, this type of aluminium was allowed in manufacture. This was the CAA's way of keeping down the cost of this sport and for this they should be applauded.

By the beginning of 1983, 02 was almost complete. A friend called David Raeburn visited frequently at this time and did a lot to help sort out the wheels and brake systems. He had been trained in mechanics in the RAF so was able to work unaided after an initial explanation of the design. I had only produced drawings for the fibrelam monocoque and the wing section. The tailplane size I decided by laying out tubes on the floor and rearranging them until the overall appearance 'looked about right'. My assessment proved correct for the tailplane has never been altered after twenty years of production. Eyeball engineering is not a skill one possesses at twenty years of age – it comes with experience – something we all have to wait for! My eye for the right size or thickness for the job it is to perform is also usually spot on – although after a decision is made I often then calculate the configuration using my adequate GCE 'O' level maths. I could see I was accurate at guessing the size of things when in tension, but not so good when estimating size in compression.

The reader may wonder if this is the correct way to design something as potentially dangerous as an aeroplane, but I always backed my theory by physically testing pieces and assemblies for their strength. Calculations weren't infallible. I often wondered about bonded joints. It's all very well saying there's one square inch of bonding between these two pieces, which represents 4000 lb of strength capability. Would one hang from a helicopter at 1000 feet relying on this bond? I wouldn't, but I would if there was a ¼-inch diameter bolt through this joint as well! This method, 'old engineering' I call it, was used by me throughout the design of Shadow. It combined the excellent stress distribution of a bonded joint, which a bolt doesn't give, with the assurity of mechanical hold!

The undercarriage construction might sound amusing because although the main tube beneath the fuselage was proper chrome-moly steel, the shock loads were taken by flag pole rods of 1-inch diameter. These fibreglass solid rods were called pultrusions and involved uni-glass fibres compressed into the circular rod shape, which gave excellent stiffness, but took out the shock of landing loads and drag forces from braking. To get the really strong $1^1/_8$-inch diameter chrome-moly steel tube (4130) to shape, I had to have it formed on proper equipment. I therefore went to Aldeburgh, 2 miles down the road to Reade's builders, and asked Lenny Strowger, their storeman, if he would help.

Lenny, like most people in the area, knew me, not because of my Channel crossing, but from school and the engineering works at Richard Garrett, where most of us used to work. Added to which I had become well known, having been on local TV quite a bit which, to the local population, obviously meant I was a millionaire! Not much happened in East Suffolk and if one achieved anything, the word soon spread! Previously, Lenny had found in his words, 'the best bit of wood in Aldeburgh' when I had needed to build the 57-inch diameter propeller for my VJ-24. 'Yes Dayverd,

I will bend this bit of tube for you,' Lenny replied to my request in his perfect Suffolk twang. I had come fully prepared and produced a plywood template to measure the correct angles. He set to work on the plumber's forming equipment, grunting with effort and grumbling. 'What the hell kind of steel is this?' I kept quiet. At the precise moment he finished the second bend, the whole lot of former and stand shattered into pieces, such had been the effort needed to form this tube.

'Well, in't that a bloomin' rum'n, that former has worked for the last 150 years here and that took Dayverd Cook to come from Aldringham to bloody well wreck it. Whatever am I goin' to tell the plumber?' I quickly grabbed my bit of steel tube (perfectly formed) and unobtrusively made my exit!

With the aid of Messrs Brett and Ireland's money, I was able to purchase a Fuji 50-hp twin-cylinder two-stroke engine to power 02. This had a reduction ratio of 2.5:1 for the propeller. It was easier to buy a 52-inch diameter propeller than to make one and probably cheaper too as regards time and effort.

The glorious day arrived when Shadow 02 was finally finished. I had painted and doped everything to my best standards. There was no fuel can hanging off with hurried connections like on 01. Everything was to be perfect.

Dennis Brett had purchased an old caravan to convert into a trailer for the Shadow. He had stripped its interior and I had sawed the back end off the caravan so that when de-rigged, the Shadow would fit perfectly inside. My plane was now moveable!

I transported it first to our local cricket field at Thorpeness for a photo session but sadly, after taxiing around for a considerable period, the nosewheel succumbed to the roughness of the ground and broke. This would have to be redesigned with suspension to enable it to cope better with non-flat surfaces. I designed an efficient piece of value engineering for the nose leg with minimum parts. I incorporated features such as suspension, a caster, a swivel, safety wire in case the suspension bungee broke, and an inside retaining wire that would adjust friction to prevent the wheel shimmy – all retained by one bolt. 'Now, let's see if the damned thing will fly,' I thought.

At Flixton's disused airfield near Bungay, Suffolk, I thought that prior to attempting flight, it would be prudent to discover if the ballistic parachute fitted to the aircraft would actually work. The sole purpose of this piece of equipment was to save the aircraft and pilot if there was a structural failure in the air, by lowering both to the ground beneath its canopy. Taxiing fast down the runway past our camera, I pulled the pin of the ballistic parachute. Immediately the parachute exploded out from its container, blooming behind the Shadow and bringing the plane to an abrupt halt. The device was a success, now I could test-fly the aircraft with a slightly easier frame of mind.

Many enthusiastic friends had gathered at the airfield to help in any way they could and to witness with mounting excitement what we all hoped would be the Shadow 02's first flight. One of these friends, David Raeburn, gallantly volunteered to repack the parachute. The job took the best part of an hour, such was the force required to get the 'chute back into its container. He was a big and powerful man and when I had been test-flying Shadow 01, he used physically to stop the plane as it rolled by on landing – 01 having had no brakes if you recall!

I tentatively flew up and down the runway, many times, gradually gaining confidence in the handling and feel of the aircraft's controls. The Shadow 02 proved a delight to fly. It was really easy to handle as with the CG (centre of gravity) and the neutral pitch correct, I progressed to gentle climbs over the runway and glide touchdowns. It was perfect! Now for the moment of truth: the first circuit . . .

Another good friend, Terry Aspinall, had his flexwing trike ready to act as chase on the first circuit. He said he was willing to crash his trike to reach me if anything went wrong, which was greatly reassuring at such a tense time.

Terry was an ex-Marine Commando and a remarkable fellow. He had walked from John O' Groats to Land's End and swum the English Channel to raise money for charity.

One of his most memorable tales concerned the state funeral of Winston Churchill. He had the great honour to be chosen as a pall-bearer and on the day prior to the funeral, a practice of their duties took place. The Marines were waiting in position, bearing the correctly weighted coffin, at the exact spot where they would then carry it from the gun carriage to the waiting boat on the River Thames. It was at night, raining and the pallbearers were standing on wet cobblestones, wearing their parade boots, which were fitted with steel studs. 'Suddenly,' he said, 'whilst standing at attention holding the coffin, we were on the move! Our shiny steel studs were sliding us uncontrollably down this road to the Thames! None of us dared to make a move to stop and we were on our way boy – still at attention!' Of course, the boots were changed to rubber-soled footwear for the following day's State Funeral, but the story certainly showed the value of a rehearsal. It would have been tragic if they had inadvertently launched Winston Churchill into the Thames.

The first flight of the Shadow 02 was a success. Everything went well. Although I was rigid throughout and hardly moved any of the controls, all my fears proved groundless and later we all celebrated the day with a great deal of beer, well into the night.

Numerous flights were made in the following days of April 1983. I allowed David Clarke to fly the plane a couple of times, whereupon he was overflowing with enthusiasm.

'It was showing over 100 mph when I buzzed you all!' he had shouted once on landing. This isn't fast for an aeroplane but it was double the speed of any other microlight on the market and I was getting a climb rate of well over 1000 feet per minute, which is a wonderful performance in any civil aircraft. I just knew I had created a winner.

Whilst developing the Shadow, I had heard that Colin Chapman, the head of Lotus cars, was proposing to produce a microlight using an engine of their own design. (Jim Clark, the Formula 1 racing car driver had driven for team Lotus and Colin Chapman had been his closest associate in the racing car world. I think every fellow has a hero, someone they admire and think, 'If I was him I could do that too!' and Jim Clark had been mine. His premature death in 1968 had upset me greatly.) The Lotus Works at Hethel, Norfolk, was fairly local, only 48 miles away, so I arranged to meet Chapman at his home one evening. I had always admired and respected his imaginative and progressive engineering ideas. I thought that as he and I were of like minds in the engineering world, he would be sympathetic to my design concepts and would maybe consider using the Shadow in conjunction with his new engine.

After studying the photographs of Shadow 02, Chapman swiftly dismissed my proposal, stating that he was about to commission a microlight design from Bert Rutan in the USA. I argued that all Rutan's designs had a canard wing in front of the aircraft, which restricted the pilot's view and would also cause problems in wet weather – canards being renowned for their loss of lift in the rain. Another distinct disadvantage would be Rutan's total use of glass-covered foam throughout as a building material, which would make the finished plane too heavy for the required category limits of 150-kg empty weight.

Chapman would not accept any of the points I put forward and our talk concluded with a heated argument over the usage of materials and frustration on my part, with his lack of foresight and appreciation for the design principles of the Shadow.

History proved me correct. Rutan's design was constructed using his standard fibreglass-covered foam. It did have a canard wing and it was too heavy and didn't give the performance quoted to Lotus. The design was a 'lemon' and Lotus had paid $30,000 for the taste.

The Shadow made its first public appearance in the spring of 1983, at a microlight fly-in held at Woburn Abbey, Bedfordshire. On seeing the plane emerge from its trailer, Catherine remarked that it resembled 'a beautiful butterfly appearing from its chrysalis'. Gleaming white with a green strip, it looked sleek and streamlined with its canopy-covered cockpit. It was a moment to cherish. The vision that I'd had for so long in my mind was now revealed to the world. The Shadow was so different in every conceivable way from any other microlight available at that time and it caused a sensation at Woburn, winning the 'Concours d'Elegance'. The only disappointment of the day was that after flying a couple of circuits, the support bar across the top of the undercarriage broke. But the Shadow was not alone in this; several other microlights suffered the same fate due to the rough surface of the take-off area. However, I managed to get the undercarriage welded at the local garage during the lunch break and the plane became serviceable once more. I later replaced this steel bar with a multi-strand wire swaged at both ends, which was made up for me by the engineer Peter Wilson at the Aldeburgh Boat Yard.

The flying of the Shadow continued throughout the summer of 1983, with it consistently showing good airworthiness and strength. One of the features about the wing was that it was inherently strong. This was due to its cantilever structure and with the addition of struts its strength was doubled.

01 had a cantilever wing, and although strong enough, everyone questioned this fact so when it came to designing 02, I added struts to waylay people's fears over its strength.

Another characteristic of the Shadow was that it possessed an amazing speed envelope ranging from 20–100 mph and seemed to have no perceptible stall break. The top speed of other microlights of this period was on average 60 mph, so I began to consider attempting the 3-km microlight category speed record.

Enquiries showed that no national 3-km course existed. After eighty years' of aviation, Britain did not have one. In the US, every state has at least one such facility. Not to be outdone, and with much help from my friends, I established a 3-km course. One of my friends, Peter Lucas, worked at the BT research centre at Martlesham and arranged to borrow, for a weekend, all the necessary electronic equipment for surveying two points 3 km apart. The equipment was worth at least £10,000. My best friend, Mike Hilling, happened to be a hydrographic surveyor and he threw his expertise in to mark out the co-ordinates to within 0.5 inches by using laser technology, even taking into account the curvature of the Earth.

The course was marked out along the shore between Eastern Bavents and Cove Hythe, Suffolk. I would fly its length over the sea at the stipulated 100 feet so as not to contravene 'air law', which is a minimum of 500 feet vertically or horizontally from any person, building and or structure. All the stipulations were laid out in the FAI (Fédération Aéronautique International) Sporting Code based in Paris.

I purchased two identical digital stopwatches and had them issued with accuracy certificates. The run would be calculated from elapsed time. The course had to be flown twice in each direction and then the speeds averaged to make a final figure. On the designated day and with the assistance of a considerable number of people posted along the route, I took off from Flixton airfield, flew to Cove Hythe and opened-up along the 3 km course. I held 02 back slightly in case someone in future just pipped my effort, but they never did. Over the four runs, I averaged 126.36 kph, which upped the existing record held in the US by 40 per cent. The FAI were presented with such overwhelming evidence, that even without any official observers, they issued me with a true FAI world record. The Shadow had made an historic start. Shortly after, that particular record for Class C-1-a/o (A/C less than 300kg) was deleted for safety reasons. Therefore, Shadow 02 will hold that world record for ever!

A problem evolved with the drive reduction system that I had designed. After approximately ten hours of flying, it regularly failed due to fatigue. I was getting quite jumpy in the cockpit with propellers flying off and having to glide into fields, making dead stick landings. During one dead stick landing, the 3-ft high crop of rye brought me to a halt from 40–50 mph in 15 feet. I must have suffered at least 15 negative 'g', for I lost consciousness. I slowly regained awareness to find I was submerged in an unrecognisable world of green. For a few seconds I wondered where the hell I was! I slowly realised that I was staring through the base of the crop and that the plane must be minus its nose leg. I never did get on top of this piece of basic engineering. It was probably because the whole construction was too light.

The Fuji engine that first powered 02 was used for almost a year. The propeller was quietest and most efficient at about half the engine revolution, so a reduction gear and toothed belt had to be used. My system, I thought, could make it lighter than that of the engine suppliers. I was wrong, so resorted to fitting the proprietary system with its toothed belt. However, this reduction system also failed very dramatically on 02, when I was flying near our CFM factory in Leiston in 1984. The whole lot sheared off, with the propeller exploding like a 40-mm shell behind me. I was quite low at 500 feet with the engine screaming unloaded at +20,000 rpm. I immediately turned the ignition switches off to no avail and it was only when I selected full choke that the engine finally came to a stop. This was followed by the flap handle, which fell onto my shoulder. Obviously this system had been shattered. Worse was to come, I instantly knew that there was no response from the elevator or rudder. The curse was that of all the directions the propeller and reduction drive could have gone, they just had to fly upwards into the aircraft structure above. Moving either of these controls would have been foolhardy, as I realised that terrible damage had occurred behind me. The ailerons mercifully were still working, so with very slight and gentle banking, 02 descended in a controlled way towards a cropped field below.

Praying fervently for the height to decrease, we finally reached 50 feet to my intense relief. Hopefully I would now survive, even if the whole aircraft around me collapsed. The plane landed lightly, in line with the crop and into wind – perfect. I tentatively climbed out and took a deep drag on my pipe, thankful to be alive, and watched in horror as the aircraft instead of sitting back onto its tail skid as it should, remained on its nosewheel and the whole of the boom and tail crashed to the ground. The boom tube had been almost completely smashed through. Had I used the elevator or rudder, the whole lot would have departed in the air.

A breathless Colin Buck arrived from the factory. He had raced through hedges, fences and over the top of sheds to reach me and was undoubtedly relieved to see me sitting there calmly smoking, but was totally astonished at the state of the Shadow. As an engineer, he soon discovered the fatigue failure of the main reduction toothed gearwheel. He was all for suing the company for this failure, but as the engine world developed, Rotax engines from Austria produced a reduction gearbox as an integral part of the engine and this resolved such problems for the foreseeable future. From then on the production aircraft had an armoured structure built into the centre wing above the propeller arc to prevent the reoccurrence of this type of accident.

An initial characteristic that puzzled all of us about the Shadow was that it was taking about 100 yards to lift off. Most microlights in the early 1980s were usually airborne in 20–30 yards. It wasn't until I accidentally broke the tailskid off when over-rotating, that we realised it had been preventing a high-enough angle of attack at take-off. A quick modification shortening the tailskid, allowed take-off distances to be reduced to about 40 yards. It seems that sometimes the simplest cures can solve what are perceived as complex problems.

Another 'strange' characteristic, but one that didn't concern me much, was that the Shadow wouldn't naturally, by itself, become airborne. A positive rotation was required; otherwise it would happily blaze through the hedge at the end of a runway. Some time later, Brian Harrison took me to Glasgow University of Aeronautics, where I met the professor and some of his staff. Explaining this characteristic, I was interested to hear their views on the subject. I laid out the wing section drawing for them in the professor's office and they peered intently at it for a long time in complete silence. I began to feel slightly uneasy, but at least I could say it was proven and did fly. To the contrary, the professor's comments were complimentary.

'If British Aerospace had generated this section, they would have taken a thousand hours and maybe achieved only 10 per cent more.' I was being praised!

'I took about 170 hours and thought that was for ever!' I replied.

The assistant then asked, 'You also did the whole of the rest of the aircraft?'

'Yes, of course. Don't you work on the whole aircraft?' I enquired.

'Oh no, I only specialise in the first 2 feet of a helicopter's blade!'

These people were very pleasant and helpful to Brian and me. They certainly made me feel good. I didn't get an adequate answer to my rotation characteristic query, but as this was also true of the B-24 Liberator used in the Second World War, which was produced in tens of thousands, I haven't let it bother me.

On 1 January 1984, the CFM factory was initiated in Leiston for the production of the Shadow Series B. Four of us, Steve Emmerson, Colin Buck, Brian Harrison and I, started the intense work rate needed to get production underway. I have never counted, but someone said 11,000 parts made up a Shadow and a lot needed drawings. We employed a couple of apprentices and later that year John Wibberley joined us.

All the required jigs were designed and built by Colin and Steve. Manuals, registers and drawings I did with help from a lot of my colleagues. It was helpful to have been a draughtsman and design engineer. 02 was used as an example aircraft with production methods built in. The front cockpit was lengthened and many awkward items sorted out by John Wibberley.

Combined with just getting into production, came the time-consuming job of gaining the CAA factory approval and CAA certification called 'Type Approval'. It is impossible to describe the enormity of these tasks and it would take well over a year, a year of relentless hard work, stress and frustration, before the factory would be able to sell aircraft in the UK. Meanwhile, the only income made was from selling the first batch of five aircraft to overseas customers.

Our example Shadow for certification was 09. To allow Type Approval, the CAA assessed the design through 'Structural Analysis' – both theoretical and practical loading. Aerodynamic theory analysis and extensive flight tests were followed by 'sound' certification (noise levels). If the aircraft and factory gained these approvals, then the design was 'frozen', i.e. all following production was to the same standard. Any alterations or modifications to that frozen design had to be approved by the former process. The CAA does not easily give approvals but once the certification is made, then the CAA will stand by the design in case of lawsuits or compensation claims, as long as that aircraft has been made to the approved example. In rough terms, these qualifying approvals cost the company £30,000 by 1985 – plus one hell of an effort.

Structurally, the design analysis completed by Paul Owen was, he said, a revelation and showed reserve factors of plus 20 in many cases when 1.5 or 2.0 would have sufficed. He told me it had been a pleasure to work on the structural and aerodynamic analysis for the Shadow and this clever aerodynamicist made no charge for his work.

I have no idea how the suggested load figures are arrived at by an approving organisation, but in many cases I fear that aerodynamic theory is 'best guess'. Certain standards exist from the past, which then had to be applied to my design. The first killer blow to my design was that it had to be tested as a two-seater. This was of course correct, as the CAA said, 'If two can get in then it's a two-seater'. The Shadow therefore was to be tested with the equivalent loading of two 90-kg crew and not one. With a requirement of +4 g and –2 g limit loads (everyday flying loads) and +6 g and –3 g for ultimate strengths, it pushed the final wing load with an extra 90 kg x 6 (540 kg) more than I had originally planned.

02 was used for structural certification purposes, as production aircraft were ordered and produced for individual customers. This was a very stressful time for myself as well as 02. I had a beautifully working aircraft that may well be destroyed by load tests six times its AUW (all up weight), which comprised the aircraft weight, maximum fuel and two 90-kg pilots. The empty weight was a fraction under 150 kg, so the 6-g ultimate load was 2088 kg (4602 lb). This was all on the wings of an aircraft, which must not weigh more than 150 kg (331 lb) – a hell of a requirement. I remember that after 02 held these loads whilst being inverted in a farmer's shed, Elton John's current song 'I'm Still Standing' had great significance.

I used 50-kg agricultural seed sacks spread along 02's wings. The fuselage was loaded to 6 g, whilst the wings were supported – this was not outlined in the requirements, but was done for my confidence in the design. Amazement grew as 02 showed no apparent deformation.

I queried the nose leg requirement of 1600 lb when it started to be overstressed at 400 lb. The Shadow was not going to comply.

'But surely this applies and was written into BCAR Section S to prevent the ankles of flex wing "trike" pilots from being exposed to damage in the event of nose leg or wheel failure?' I put to the CAA.

They would have none of it and pursued the line; it's down as a requirement, so the examiner must write a tick of compliance in that box on his form. I demonstrated to the CAA examiner how 02 would take off and land without even the nose leg being fitted. So why did I need to comply with this requirement? A new beefy nose leg would tip the AUW over 150 kg. No! They still wanted a little tick in the box on the form. I knew then I would never fit in well working for a bureaucracy. Another manufacturer told me the CAA guys dreaded coming to CFM. I was in their court but if they ignored engineering sense then they were told exactly how I felt. To their credit, most of these people weren't 'the CAA'; they were nice people and one even told me the Shadow had some of the finest engineering he had ever seen on an aircraft. But I still struck out against foolish requirements.

Another test was to drop the aircraft from a certain calculated height to prove the undercarriage. It wasn't very high, but I thought the impact would exceed +3 g and result in the wings shearing off. I was assured the impact would not exceed 3 g, so I dropped a 'g' meter onto grass from the correct dropping height several times. Each time it showed +9 g. With the wings removed and their weight added to the cockpits, we dropped 02 from a hangar roof, following which I sent a photograph to the CAA showing the 'g' meter fitted to the cockpit dash panel reading +9 g! No comment came back . . . Someone unkindly said to my wife, 'How ever do you live with a person who is always right!' This is not a true statement, but in engineering I can see when something is rubbish at first sight.

Even before the flight tests began, the standard aerodynamic calculations showed that the Shadow's tailplane had to take a maximum load of over 300 lb. As it only weighed 9 lb, I could see immediately that it did not have a strength/weight ratio of 34:1 and thus was not strong enough. In tests, Steve Emmerson and I saw deformation on the tailplane that made the elevator non-functioning at 130 lb.

Tim Hardwick-Smith, from New Zealand, joined the factory about this time. He was a Mechanical Engineering graduate and very much needed. Tim devised an ingenious mechanical load device that showed tail loads when in flight. It could be calibrated on the ground by pulling the tail down with a spring balance at 10-lb intervals. This had to be invented because the 'brains' at the CAA would not accept strain gauges that had shown maximum tail loads of less than 70 lb. We were told that due to 'electronic delay' these results were untrue. (Electrically, signals go at a speed fast enough to circle the Earth seven times a second don't they?)

John Wibberley carried out this test by flying 02 and applying instantanious full back stick throughout the speed range up to 108 mph VNE (Never Exceed Speed). He should have been given a medal for courage. The maximum tail load shown on Tim's gauge was 78 lb at 70 mph. Interestingly, as the speed increased to more than 70 mph, the loads decreased. The graph produced was fascinating to look at and confirmed that the boom tube was deflecting with strain and lessening the tailplane load. I suppose the original requirement of 300 lb was calculated with a non-deflecting fuselage-to-tail structure.

The question now arose concerning the boom tube strength. I tested two boom tube examples in the factory. They were set up exactly as fitted to the airframe. Both failed at 600 lb when loaded at the tailplane. One completely sheared, going off like a gun, and the other collapsed, producing bending. I was confident that when the tailplane was at maximum load (78 lb times 1.5 factor = 117 lb) and with the knowledge that deformation only started at 130 lb, that the tailplane was well within limits if someone was foolish enough to apply instantaneous full back control stick at any speed.

Tim also did a lot of work on the wheel and brake systems. He removed the hydraulic/disc set-up on 02 and used a Honda moped front drum brake. This system was a very practical alternative because mopeds, unlike aircraft, frequently use their brakes, so this system should last for years. I mused whether in this computerised world, if at some future date after some 350 aircraft had been produced using their respective 700-odd brake callipers, Honda would find these figures suspicious, suggesting perhaps a fault with this item and consequently change the design.

An item used as a filter inside the fuel tank also caused concern at the local Mace shop; namely a plastic tea strainer, which with its handle removed was attached over the fuel outlet. The shop assistant could not make out why the factory used so many tea strainers!

Tim also revised the ailerons as used on the first eight Shadows. These revised ailerons were not only self-balancing, but lighter than the originals and did away with the necessity for a mass balance.

Flight-testing had shown the Shadow to be so passive that I asked my friend Peter Troy Davies to fly and write up the air tests. It obviously wouldn't be right for me, the designer and pilot, to claim such benign characteristics. A manufacturer has to demonstrate speed at much more than the stated VNE (108 mph in this case). A dive speed approaching 125 mph had to be shown but kept 'in-house'. Peter did witness aileron flutter at this speed, whilst diving from 8000 feet.

Watching his dive from Flixton airfield, I saw and heard it happen. I found myself praying he would get down all right as the height slowly decreased. He was flying gently, putting no strain on the airframe, and thankfully landed successfully, but 02 was not in a happy state. Peter, white-faced, looked impassively up at the wing centre section, which showed it had split right across and at a weird angle. 'How ever strong is this aircraft?' he muttered.

02 was mended within a week and the ailerons modified, but further tests with John Wibberley flying, demonstrated the flutter reoccurring. John landed safely without damage to either him or the airframe, but the flutter nearly broke his flying wrist. Luckily the problem was cured by the addition of full counter-balancing. As said previously, Tim Hardwick-Smith redesigned the ailerons for production.

The flying compliance testing continued. When the reports were completed, the non-stall, non-spin characteristics were queried by the CAA. To have characteristics so different from normal had to be investigated further. Of course, it was the wing profile with its drooped leading edge that was the key difference. I knew from my VJ-23 days that the profile did not let go and stall, but I didn't know until now that it was also anti-spin.

The CAA sent two of their test pilots to Suffolk to investigate my claims. Daryl Stinton was their foremost investigator pilot. I found him a bit overbearing, but I knew much less about flying than he did. I wondered if he had ever designed, built and test flown his own aircraft; then put it into production and then had it come under scrutiny? Looking at 02, he pompously said to me, 'So it doesn't stall hey? Well it's stalled now isn't it!' It was like his foot was across mine – an immature attitude I thought. A delay was caused when I asked what would happen if they crashed or damaged 'my' aircraft – who would pay? There appeared to be no answer and an awkward silence ensued. Stinton blustered something about the fact that he had flown so many hundreds of different types and I asked him what happened when he had put one of the world's only Lysanders on its nose recently? There was an air of hostility between us. A few 'phone calls to the CAA solved the awkwardness shown at CFM. But I couldn't get them to put anything in writing. The trouble was this was not going to be normal flying; it would be flying that would purposely attempt to upset the claimed flying characteristic, with a possible dangerous outcome.

These two hotshot CAA pilots threw 02 into impossible manoeuvres – pitching up vertically, and crossing the aileron and rudder controls whilst cutting power. One pilot tried for thirty minutes to try and make a spin or departure. 02 would have none of it; even when pitching over vertical it still pitched forwards just like it was following a book of orders. The most either pilot could get from the Shadow 02 was half a spiral turn followed by an automatic recovery. Stinton then asked me to fly whilst he acted in the rear cockpit as second pilot. We flew for forty minutes and I followed his instructions throughout this flight, nothing too dramatic thankfully. On returning to Parham airfield, the CAA test pilots had changed their previous attitudes completely. They were pleasant and enthusiastic, and Mr Stinton even said 'Well done'. Officially, they would only allow me to state that Shadows were 'stall and spin resistant'.

Following CFM's claims concerning the docility of the aerodynamics of the Shadow, one prominent magazine editor posed the question whether the Shadow may be a danger to pilots who went on to fly other aircraft types. Would they be caught out by the nasty characteristics expected in normal aircraft? I didn't see this as CFM's problem if the Shadow made other aircraft seem less safe.

The situation at CFM was becoming desperate. We had now been waiting for over a year for the CAA to approve both the design and the factory. We were still not allowed to 'trade' until released by the CAA. The amount of work was staggering. After all the flight tests and structural proofs of this design were completed, many manuals had to be written up and 'approved': the Pilot's Notes, the Service Manual and Drawing Register. There seemed an endless list of compliance, all to be done by a very limited number of people. The factory approval was an entire entity in itself, being based almost exactly as though CFM was operating under the same basis as British Aerospace – but we were without the resources or personnel to carry out all the necessary requirements. We were 'green' to this system, with the Area Surveyor from CAA Stansted stoically sticking to his systems and trying to bully us into shape. The finances had all but gone and a 'Rights Issue' had to be asked of the people who had kindly put money in to start the factory. All my air show savings were gone. The bank overdraft was at its limit and the bank's faith in the venture was beginning to waiver. Yet still the CAA prevaricated for no apparent reason. CFM had to pay £90 per hour for the privilege of being investigated. I was on the edge of despair. The strange thing, to me, was that nothing had failed so why was the aircraft still not approved?

Catherine, who had witnessed all the stress involved, even wrote to the Prime Minister, Margaret Thatcher, asking for pressure to be put on the CAA. Catherine had contended with my home-building for years, often having to retrieve from our base- ment her kitchen utensils, such as the bread knife or iron (covered in glue or dope), plus the noise beneath her kitchen of the occasional engine run, with associated fumes. After Catherine's letter to the Prime Minister, things did progress. I have no idea whether this was because of the natural order of events, or whether it was pressure from above that moved the CAA. I'm sure of one thing though, that these well paid people can have no idea of the pressure that small companies have to bear whilst not being able to trade. I'm sure I was very wound up on several occasions when I had to confront our Area Surveyor as to why, for instance, trace-ability was so necessary, which meant that every item on the aircraft had to be recorded with its own batch number, stating how many pieces were in that specific batch, etc. When the day finally came that I had these Approvals, the whole factory went out that evening and celebrated. CFM's Shadow was the first three-axis microlight in the UK, or anywhere else in the world, to gain 'Type Approval'. This was highly valued and was the ultimate reward for all our exhaustive work.

Aircraft could now be built and released from CFM. Customers, who had kept faith in us and had put down deposits, received their Shadows. At last the factory was on its way.

Production of a part involved making every item identical and I soon discovered that even though the factory possessed much engineering skill, the parts would be better if they were made by specialist companies. A sheet metal company would tool up for each specific piece and produce identical parts, as would welding and glass fibre specialists. The factory bought a lot of equipment from Euro-Wing, a company in Scotland, run by Brian Harrison. They had previously been the manufacturers for the Goldwing microlights. Brian had been at CFM from the beginning. He was one of 'the original four', the other three being Colin Buck, Steve Emmerson and me. Brian Harrison's skills were associated with glass/form composites. He made the plug for the nose cone, the moulded wing tips and his knowledge of using glass fibre was a great asset in the building of the aircraft.

Reliability became a really good asset with our production aircraft. Everything worked as it should, with very little mainte-nance as the design was based on sound engineering. The factory was regularly checked every few months by the CAA, for minor modifications on the aircraft. I always stated that none had been made, which of course did not prevent the minute survey under-taken by the inspector engineers. However, no modifications were ever found.

STREAK SHADOW

One of the anomalies in the UK is the hierarchy created in the flying world through the graded licence system, which restricts the types of aircraft one is permitted to fly with a certain form of licence. There exists a slight feeling of snobbery from those who fly Group A aircraft. In general, they consider microlight pilots a lower breed and an A licence pilot is rarely seen flying these types of machine. I was sure that many Group A private pilots would have liked to have owned a Shadow, but it seemed beneath their status. All aircrew, whatever their licence, take the same tests and examinations for Air Law, Meteorology, Technical and Radio; the only differences are in the qualifying hours. A Microlight Group D licence requires twenty-five hours and a Group A forty hours. Also, the medical for a Group D licence is less demanding.

In an attempt to erase the boundary between these two classes of pilots, I redesigned the Shadow in June 1988 to become a Streak Shadow Group A aircraft. It made sense when doing this to use as many parts of the production Shadow B Series as possible. The only changes I made were to the size of the wing, which as an aeroplane rather than a microlight, was not required to have a square metre of wing area for every 10 kilograms of the overall weight. The engine was altered to a 64-hp Rotax and I reduced the tailplane incidence slightly; the rest of the airframe remained the same as the Shadow.

The 64-hp Rotax is produced by an Austrian factory. These were excellent twin-cylinder, in-line, two-stroke engines. They were fitted with a reduction gearbox, which had alternative ratios to select and were liquid- or air-cooled depending on the model. Later versions included electronic dual ignition and separate from the fuel oil-injection. The Streak was intended to be a kit-produced aircraft, as the regulations stipulated that aeroplanes be built to a higher standard than microlights, i.e. in the using of certified materials and engine. Thus, it was submitted to the Popular Flying Association (PFA) for approval.

Later, an odd incident occurred when the CAA requested me to attend a meeting at their headquarters at Gatwick, concerning the design of the Streak Shadow.

I duly attended the meeting and sat before a panel of four engineers. The question put to me was both short and brief. 'Why was the wing less thick than on a Shadow?' My immediate answer was 'Because it is shorter. A wingspan of 28 feet instead of 32 feet can be less thick in depth but have the same strength.' Thus one statement apparently sufficed, as after a moment or two the meeting closed and I returned to the factory – a round trip of 240 miles! I never did know the reasoning behind this meeting, but it seemed that I had said the right thing. In all, it was a very strange affair, as the CAA usually leave homebuilts to be handled by the PFA, a self-governing organisation.

The wing design of the Streak had less thickness, which made a thickness/chord ratio of 12 per cent as opposed to a Shadow wing ratio of 15 per cent. As stated, the span was reduced to 28 feet, using the same flaps as previously but shorter ailerons. The wing tips remained the same as on the Shadow. These wing tips were intended to delay the ambient air pressure beneath the aerofoil from easily reaching the upper surface where less pressure existed. The result was that the wing behaved as if it possessed a greater span than its true dimensions. This had the effect of producing a higher aspect ratio (chord to span) wing and increased its efficiency.

The proof of all this had emerged sometime before when I was checking out a new Shadow 03 due for immediate delivery to Norway. Because the wing tips had been delayed in production, I had to check out the aircraft without them (noting speeds and all other data). The aircraft was then completed with wing tips and I was able to recheck the previously recorded speeds and data. With the wing tips fitted, 03 flew 7 mph faster, proving my theory to be correct.

With a Permit for Test Purposes issued by the PFA, I flew the first Streak Shadow from Eye airfield – a former B-24 Liberator base dating from the Second World War. The aircraft, #108 G-BONP, was painted a stunning brilliant red, which was known 'in house' by the factory as a 'wodge of red'.

I was investigating the streamlined wing struts, which incorporated turbulator strips. The only flight fault revealed from the initial test flights was that these wing struts vibrated at speeds above 80 mph. This was cured by adding jury struts for support. Otherwise, the flight characteristics were outstanding. The design revelled in its power-to-weight ratio (8.5 lb/hp). Climb rates were up to 1800 feet per minute with an acceleration of 0–60 mph in 3.6 seconds. I could attain an altitude of 1000 feet from standstill in 38 seconds with 10,000 feet showing after 8 minutes 40 seconds. This performance was very exhilarating for the pilot. The Streak worked perfectly after the addition of the jury struts.

With a level speed of 121 mph and using a system of factors applied for Never Exceed Speed (VNE) and design speed, I calculated that the Streak had to be demonstrated at more than 200 mph in a dive to obtain its certification. An aeroplane can, of course, exceed its level speed by diving. Thus, for structural reasons and concerns, all aeroplanes show a never to be exceeded speed on the airspeed indicator (ASI). However, manufacturers have to test aircraft a certain factor faster than VNE. These very high speeds were causing me concern – not only for myself for I was to demonstrate them, but also for the design. The Streak was based on a microlight and I could feel it did not want to do these speeds. A large amount of pressure was needed to keep the control stick forwards when diving, whilst the aircraft was trying to pitch back upwards.

I was so concerned about these high speeds that I wrote about them in a letter to Mr Walker, the chief engineer at the PFA, when I sent the submission for approval. At a subsequent meeting in Shoreham, PFA headquarters, he suggested to me that it would be much safer to 'fix' the VNE myself at what I considered the correct speed, rather than by using the factors of the level speeds. I immediately suggested 140 mph and felt exceedingly relieved that I would not have to demonstrate a proof dive of 200 mph. This suggestion was pure common sense and was the response from a senior engineer who had got some 'time in'. I welcomed this greatly, as I'd seen precious little from the CAA on many occasions. The Streak Shadow #108 G-BONP gave thousands of demonstrations over several years, mostly to potential customers, but also at air shows and many places all over Europe.

My colleague Pat White and I usually trailered the aircraft to its intended destination, as this allowed us to demonstrate the quick rig and de-rig time of six minutes from the opening of the trailer doors. I have to admit to boredom when flying cross-country and my navigation is far from conventional. Also, towing by car allowed us to return home without having to extend our stay in a place we didn't wish to be because of poor weather. When a long distance flight of two to three hours was necessary, I used to get a proper pilot with a GPS (Global Positioning System) to lead the way in a similar Shadow or Streak aircraft. This took away the pressure of having to navigate myself to remote farm strips and was a plus, if anything, in front of potential customers; showing two aircraft must be better than one.

The updating of my licence to Group A, the legal requirement to fly an aeroplane rather than a microlight, caused great amusement to my instructor. He said I was the only 'student' he had ever taught who arrived at the licensed airfield, in the aircraft in which he was to be instructed! I actually arrived with a legally weighted microlight that had insufficient wing area when two-up and thus became an aeroplane. This shows the absurdity (or loop hole) of some regulations, doesn't it? Military-taught aircrew were not qualified to fly civilian aircraft. I know of a brilliant helicopter pilot flying professionally for film work, who had left the military after operating helicopters but then had to re-qualify to fly an identical machine for civilian work. This entailed flying the statutory hours before he could be passed. It is a ridiculous situation. During his training, he used to fly solo from the airfield and when out of viewing range, park on a hill with the engine running and read a book for an hour before returning! The daftness of these bureaucratic rules shows no bounds with instances such as these.

My unconventional navigation methods did have room for improvement, although my instructor had to admit they worked. My methods do away with many of the intellectual attributes, called brainpower, that pilots use. The radio was another of my hates. A radio is unnecessary if flying outside controlled airspace in the UK. The essential requirement of a pilot is to be vigilant and always on the lookout for any other aircraft or hazard in his flight path. It is a constant source of amazement to me that so many pilots fly totally by their radio instructions and instruments; they fail to use the view from their cockpit and by so doing, often miss the obvious. Of course, electronic equipment provides a vital safety feature in difficult weather conditions, but one should never underestimate the value of one's own eyesight. This is why I designed the Shadow with an all-viewing cockpit canopy. Occasionally, I used to tune in on my radio and hear traffic controllers informing other aircraft about a 'rogue aircraft' (with reference to myself). I was not a 'rogue'. I was not illegal – I was just not under his control. To me, the USA has evolved an excellent system to be followed by a pilot when approaching an airfield. The pilot announces who he is and what his intentions are. A mute controller at the airfield monitors the announcement without comment; he just stands-by in case requested. The arriving pilot can hear calls from other active aircraft and only has to join in as appropriate.

As can be noted, much of my flying philosophy is very different from most pilots. It drives me mad to sit motionless on a cross-country flight, just flying straight and level (one might as well be sitting on a bus). I enjoy turning, diving manoeuvres, experiencing the feeling of freedom, executing perfect turns without slip or slide and rolling above or around those thick, pure white glorious summer cumulous clouds. I suppose demonstrating the factory aircraft, combined with performing at the occasional air show, made me disinterested in leaving the immediate area for any other purpose. I would have made an absolutely hopeless airline aviator, flying straight and level for hours on end. Testing original proto-types and checking-out first flight production aircraft is my area of interest in aviation.

I became so precise and technically correct after flying up to three times a day for years, that when assessing different equip-ment to improve our aircraft, I could fly from a standing start to 2000 feet altitude to within one second on consecutive flights. Thus, I could make a meaningful technical assessment of any data collected, for instance when testing a new type of propeller or from altering the pitch of the propeller blades. For absolute maximum efficiency or performance, these types of tests did not necessarily always suit what a customer required. Shadow owners most often wanted a high cruise/low fuel consumption performance. My philosophy did not always coincide with requirements.

People want extras for their planes just as they do for their cars, but the extras don't necessarily improve the aircraft's capabilities. A car uses more fuel – fewer miles per gallon – when fitted with power steering, alloy wide wheels or air conditioning. Facts like that are not usually known or appreciated. An aircraft that weighs more will be disadvantaged by longer take-off runs, lower climb rates, and greater fuel consumption. The addition of an electric starter necessitates a battery – a total weight of 25–30 lb (11–13 kg). Wheel spats were a particular hate of mine, but they were provided for the owner if requested. The aircraft's performance, though, was certainly not improved by the addition of spats – a fact I proved one day by holding a wheel assembly fixed to a device outside the window of a car, whilst it was being driven at 60 mph. With a spring balance attached, the drag could be measured with and without wheel spats and the drag with the spats was greater! An improvement on wheel spats was shown by Brian Johnson, when he enclosed the outside of his main wheels with a flat disc!

Originally I had fought ounce by ounce to keep weight down on the airframe and, to me, it now seemed ridiculous to add all these extras that people felt they needed but it was me thinking as an engineer and not as a businessman. I've never been business orientated; other people at CFM handled the finance. I found it too intimidating.

IMAGE

The Streak Shadow was selling well as a kit. Licensing agreements had been set up for production in New Mexico, USA, under the name of Laron Technologies and in South Africa as Shadowlite. I began to consider what design could follow the previous successes. My designs had broken new ground in aviation, with their safety features of non-stall/spin and in their construcuon, which used materials best suited to the job for which they had to perform. Priorities had been pilot view, side control stick and bond, plus mechanical structural integrity. The microlight area of design was going nowhere for me because the Shadow had reached the boundaries of microlight definition. Being limited to not more than two people, defined by maximum weight rules and minimum wing area rulings, I could not upgrade or better the design.

As some movement in all up weight (AUW) was later approved by the CAA for microlights, I was able to uprate the B series Shadow to C series. This would help flying training schools with the addition of a 50-hp engine and streamline struts. Helpfully, the B series owners would upgrade their aircraft to C series with a modification kit from CFM.

The only design area remaining was the kit market for pilots with full licences, namely the PFA in the UK and the Experimental Aircraft Association (EAA) in the USA. I concluded that there must be hundreds of ex-military pilots around the world who no longer flew aeroplanes. These would be very capable pilots with no aircraft to fly that could simulate the high power-to-weight ratio of their previous machines. Some of these chaps had purchased vintage ex-Second World War fighters such as P51 Mustangs or Spitfires at great personal expense. These Second World War aircraft have, as a high priority, fabulous acceleration and climb rates that alternative General Aviation (GA) aircraft do not possess. In fact, the GA aircraft such as Cessnas and Pipers etc. are so hopeless in performance that occasionally after releasing their brakes, at full throttle, I have been left wondering if the brakes had been released. This was clearly demonstrated to me soon after I had left the RAF, when my best friend Bill Smith let me take control of a French Morane-Saulnier Rally Club. I pulled up to a climb and was told to decrease the angle immediately. I'd been used to going up when desired and had to realise only 350 feet per minute was available. I thought it all rather tame and my interest in flying civilian aircraft ceased until I saw that VJ-23 of Volmer Jensen. I still consider it very clever to fly slower than 20 mph. My friend

Bill was burned to death in a Tiger Moth, trapped by the engine after a crash. Petrol poured down on him from the fuel tank, which had been designed into the wing above the pilot. Never let anyone try and convince me of the attributes of a Tiger Moth. I learnt to fly on these things in 1954 – no brakes, no ground steering and who decided to put that fuel tank there?

It was becoming obvious to me where the opening lay for a potential new aircraft in the market. This aircraft would possess a very high power-to-weight ratio. Second World War fighters such as the Spitfire culminated with ratios of 4.5 lb/hp. The Streak's best power-to-weight ratio was 9 lb/hp. If I used a 100-hp engine, then the AUW of this design would have to be no greater than 450 lb. If the pilot weight and fuel weight were deducted, then the airframe must not exceed 220 lb. It looked difficult to achieve. The Shadows were originally built to 331 lb (150 kg) maximum empty weight rules but these were two-seaters. It would take a lot of deep thinking to create an airframe with that lack of weight. The conclusion I arrived at was simply to omit some of the airframe. In fact, a flying wing seemed to be the answer – this has no tail empennage. I recalled a classic statement made by the flying legend Howard Hughes when designing his aircraft. 'What ain't there don't weigh nothing.' He was right. The fascination of creating a pure wing aircraft has lured many an aircraft designer and now it was to become my train of thought.

Brian Johnson, on knowing that I was in the throes of conceiving a new aircraft, bought me a wonderful book about the German design called 'Nurflugel' (only wing). I had admired the German Horten brothers Reimar and Walter for many years; their expertise extended from gliders to jet fighters and they had designed and built many flying wing aircraft before and during the Second World War. My design, though, would possess fins as I didn't believe satisfactory crosswind landings could be performed without them. Therefore, the new design now named 'Image' was to become a tailless aircraft.

I am not one of those designers who falls into the trap of spending years in the drawing and building, only to discover after so much time and effort that the design fails to work. The 'concept'

Image would certainly prove if the aircraft could be built to such a low weight. But I was definitely not going to waste time on developing a retracting undercarriage and proper finish effects on the creation of an unproven theory. The wingspan would be only 22 feet and the empty weight not much more than 220 lb. (We would paint the aircraft matt black when complete; mostly to hide the poor finish of the joints and canopy!)

Work quickly commenced. Brian obtained a MK9 Spitfire canopy, which when reversed from its normal placing, made a super streamlined covering. This I saved for the building of the series Image. One big problem with the swept-back wing was holding the centre of pressure at $1/3$ chord. The Hortens used washout (twisting the wing leading edge downwards at the tip) and created a bell-shaped lift distribution.

During one of my frequent visits to Volmer in Glendale, California, I was taken to meet Irv Culver – the ex-Lockheed aerodynamicist. He had always boasted that he had no academic qualifications and had used his own formulae. When I showed him my design of the Image I told him of the Horten bell-shaped lift distribution. I was certainly taken aback when he responded somewhat bitterly, 'Goddamn Kraut horse shit!' Volmer, who had apparently only ever been heard to swear once in his life – and that was when he had hit his thumb with a hammer – nearly passed out on hearing this statement and quickly withdrew. Irv continued, 'And why isn't the airfoil upside down at the wing root? I did that twenty-five years ago on airliners.' True enough, I have since found that on looking at airliners' wings, the section is upside down at the root. Irv was the top man of aerodynamics and if I was as Volmer called me, 'his prodigy', I had better do more. I told him I'd guessed the washout at –6 degrees, which is a lot, and received no comment; perhaps this was satisfactory. All in all, it was not a successful meeting.

One benefit I received as the designer of a tailless aircraft, was that I was allowed to enter the Chino Air Museum free of charge when I visited it with Volmer. Not many people in the world had designed, built and flown a tailless or flying wing and I viewed some actual Horten airframes at Chino. The staff were so accommodating that they would have lowered the airframes from their hanging cradles if I had so wished.

Several reviews in aviation magazines had profiled the Image along with its progress. Amazingly, I received a telephone call at the factory from *Herr* Reimar Horten, calling from Argentina.

'So you are stymied with the airworthiness people, hey?' chuckled a deep, guttural Germanic voice.

'Unfortunately,' I replied and quickly added, 'Can you tell me what the washout on the wing should be?' lest this key man should ring off before I had the chance to ask him for this vital piece of information.

'What do you think it should be?' he asked.

'I guessed 6.'

'You know something,' he said and laughed.

I never did get an answer from *Herr* Horten, but was staggered that not only was he still alive, but he knew of my Image. I realised now just how interested the aviation world was in flying wing-type aircraft. The Image looked similar in some aspects to the Chance Vought F7U Cutlass used by the US Navy during the early 1950s because I had always thought this aircraft looked exciting. On completion, the PFA required an in-depth aeronautical report to be made by a specialist. I found a willing engineer, but at a price.

Eventually, a physical assessment by the chief PFA engineer took place; the only criticism was that the fins were shaded from the airflow if a spin occurred. I argued that this design format in the past had shown that tailless aircraft were not capable of getting into a spin (autorotation). How could this criticism arise for a pure flying wing aircraft that has no conventional fins and rudders? It was to no avail. The Image would have to have fins and rudders below as well as above the wing before a Permit for Test Purposes (PTP) could be issued.

I was really fed up with having to comply with opinions other than my own and other people messing with my design. Against all UK legislation, in an act of defiance, I needed to prove that my concept was correct. I took the Image to a disused airfield and flew it. A friend, who had the experience of flying many different types of aircraft, flew the Image over forty flights that day. Initially, up and down the runway, a take-off and landing. Then close, inside the airfield boundary circuits. It went like a rocket even though the engine was an old Rotax 532 with just 65 hp. I chased and videoed the aircraft from standstill to flying speed (in my TWR V-12 Jaguar). The Image was getting to 90 mph in four seconds such was the good power-to-weight ratio. The Jaguar had no hope of staying with it at take-off, but we still obtained some excellent footage. The characteristics were different from a conventional aircraft; there being no normal rotation at lift-off. Upon reaching flying speed, the Image seemed to pop vertically several feet for its separation from the runway. We also watched a 180-degree manoeuvre that took some believing. Banking at 90 degrees, the 180-degree direction change took place in a flash. The 'g' force must have been extremely high, but as it was only for two to three seconds, it did not affect the pilot. It reminded me of the Folland Midge, forerunner of the Gnat at Farnborough 1954, when it performed a 180-degree turn in an unbelievable short time and space. Agile jets of the 1990s are not agile compared with my memory of that manoeuvre.

I duly complied and modified the fins and rudders to extend below the wing, as requested. This stipulated modification by the specialists changed the appearance of the design and, after being issued with a PTF, totally changed its flying characteristics. Try as we might in this legal form, the Image did not fly properly again. Phugoid oscillations occurred in the air, which resulted in the damage of the undercarriage and wings on several occasions.

The final flight occurred after lift-off down the runway at Bentwaters. The aircraft careered violently up and down and eventually smashed heavily into the runway. This was probably going to be the end of the project and nearly the end of my son Jacob, who in his haste to reach me, had to be prevented from leaping out of the chase car whilst it was still travelling at 40 mph. I was unhurt but shaken and very sad. My dream was to have been rocketing up at +4000 feet per minute at that moment, not being helped from the wreckage of the Image, which had consumed two years of my time and effort.

Since this dramatic crash, I have concluded, on reflection, that the control stick should have been tensioned with a bungee chord fore and aft. This would have stopped the pilot chasing the sensitive pitch phugoid oscillations, which were associated with tailless aircraft that were closely coupled. (Aircraft that possess a short distance from the nose to the tail.) Unfortunately, convention rules the day in aviation, which is why so many aircraft for sport use are still side-by-side seating, high or low wing types, and all look like Cessnas or Piper Cubs. It's a shame because my design ideas were to move aviation forwards. It is also a fact, I remind myself, that there are no flying wing airliners. I had been looking so forward to fabulous climb rates and cruising at 250 mph for so much less than it costs to run a P51 or Spitfire.

The life of the Image concluded when people from the Inland Revenue visited the CFM factory for the purpose of sequestering assets in lieu of tax payments. The Image met with their requirements. The present tax situation originated from the fact that CFM owed me royalties for my design. In the early days of the business, 'Godfathers' Messrs Brett and Ireland had looked far ahead and had written into the Company Agreements that the company was to pay me a royalty for the sale price of each aircraft, less the cost of the engine and propeller. Over the twelve years, this royalty had accumulated to a sum of £40,000. Due to the financial state of the company, I had never drawn any of this money. But the tax people saw the whole situation in a different light and even though this royalty only existed on paper at CFM, they decided that I had to pay tax on my royalty amounting to £21,000. My suggestions of cancelling and annulling the agreement were dismissed. I was to pay the tax on money I had never received. In the end, the Image was not sequestered, as I informed the Tax Authorities that it possessed no intrinsic value as an unproven machine and the money had to be found. This whole episode was very painful and left me with a sense of outrageous injustice.

The final, ironic, sequel to this saga was yet to come. Following the attempted sequestering of my Image, it was moved for safe keeping to the storage of a presumed friend; a friend to whom the company provided a lot of subcontracting work finishing and spraying our production aircraft. Completely unbeknown to me, he later took it on himself to sell my privately registered aircraft and trailer (which did not belong to me) to a broker – apparently for the reasons of so-called storage fees. Years later, in a stranger than life coincidence, the broker, totally unaware that I was the actual owner and designer of the aircraft, contacted me and offered me my machine for £3800.

TETRAPLEGIC

A completely different sort of challenge was presented to me when a tetraplegic, called Trevor Jones, arrived at CFM. He literally rolled into the factory in his sophisticatedly engineered, self-powered wheelchair. He announced that he would dearly love to possess his own Shadow and fly solo, although his disability prevented the use of his legs and hands. My immediate reaction was that this was a total impossibility, as there was no way a man in his situation could fly solo. Reading my thoughts, Trevor led me outside to where his vehicle, an American-type equivalent of a Ford Transit, was parked and proceeded to demonstrate how he was able to drive. Operating controls from his wheelchair, he electronically slid open the side door, whereupon a ramp unfolded and he drove straight into the car and manoeuvred into the driving position. Climbing in beside him, he then drove around our industrial estate with great dexterity. I was impressed. On our return, Trevor looked at me and half whispered, 'It's only technology, David.' He was right and I felt rather embarrassed by my initial thoughts of dismissal. I had just witnessed the impossible made possible for his independence on four wheels, so why not in the air? Perhaps it wasn't such a farfetched dream after all for Trevor to fly his own plane. We took Trevor to our local airfield and placed him in the front cockpit of the Streak and I flew the aircraft from the controls in the back. Anyone who has seen the joy of a disabled person realising their freedom in the sky cannot fail to shed a tear of compassion.

Trevor's disability was the result of a tragic skiing accident in which he had suffered serious back and neck injuries. He had been a helicopter pilot flying in the Falklands war and had also, it transpired, been the pilot of the rescue helicopter that had lifted Richard Branson from the Irish Sea after his transatlantic balloon crossing.

I really wanted to help this man fulfil his dream, but how? The phrase 'it's only technology David' hammered persistently in my brain. I spent the following days and nights in a ferment of mental turmoil. How could I adapt the Shadow's controls so that they could be operated by a person with such a severe lack of mobility skills?

Gradually, the impossible began to become possible in my thoughts. There would be no rudder pedals in the front cockpit, only in the rear. After all, Trevor could not operate his legs but a passenger in the back with normal controls might be mandatory. A special bracket with two uprights could be attached to the control stick. This would enable Trevor's wrist to be held in position whilst his hand was placed on the control grip. A similar control stick with wrist-holding bracket could be substituted for the throttle lever, which would still function as an engine throttle with full power forward and back to idle, and by moving this same control stick laterally, the rudder could be operated. This same method of control was to be copied in the rear cockpit. So with the use of his arms rather than hands, the three-axis control could be achieved. Right arm – pitch/roll. Left arm – throttle and rudder. The rear cockpit could be used conventionally but would have the opportunity for the accompanying pilot to lift his feet off the rudder pedals and teach himself to use the throttle stick as a yaw control.

One big problem remained and that was the braking system. Normally, two levers are located on the conventional rudder pedals, one for the left wheel-brake and the other for the right. This is termed differential braking. The nose wheel castors freely. I decided to ask Rex Garrod, a local friend of mine. He owned a Shadow, and as a profession designed 'special effects'. If anyone could resolve this problem he could.

It wasn't long before Rex had thought of a feasible way to control the brake and steering in Trevor's Shadow. He invented a pneumatic-powered system, which could be operated by a pad behind Trevor's head. It is complex to explain but was easy to understand when seen working. If the throttle/rudder control stick was neutral and at idle, the pad, on being operated, would brake both main wheels. If this control was to port or starboard, it operated the brake only on that side – but the control would not have to be at idling throttle. Thus, taxiing could be achieved braking port or starboard. Only when the throttle was closed would both brakes operate. A tiny compressor would keep the system charged; the reservoir for air being a small ex-fire extinguisher bottle.

The tetraplegic Shadow had become a possibility and Steve Emmerson, Martin Blowers and Jacob began work on the build in the factory.

The Shadow's naturally gentle flying characteristics would be a tremendous asset in aiding to build confidence in a disabled flyer. For CG reasons, solo flight could only be performed in a Shadow with the pilot in the front cockpit. The crew in the rear cockpit was situated at the aircraft's point of neutral CG. Therefore, it was irrelevant to the trim of a Shadow whether the rear cockpit was occupied. So we test flew Trevor's aircraft with Jacob in the front cockpit, acting as ballast, whilst I flew the aircraft conventionally from the rear. I then took my feet off the rudder pedals and learnt to use the throttle/rudder control stick. This seemed perfectly manageable, so after a while we landed and swapped cockpits. Jacob was now in control in the back. Using the conventional system, he took off and after gaining sufficient altitude, I took over in the front cockpit and taught myself to operate the aircraft with the controls adapted for Trevor's benefit. Everything functioned satisfactorily so all that now remained was for me to fly solo using the redesigned system from the front cockpit.

The knowledge that the adapted control system functioned perfectly did not totally erase my feelings of anxiety prior to that first solo flight. This time there would be no reassuring back-up from the rear cockpit if things did go wrong. It was a very cold day I remember, but as I taxied to a halt after the successful flight, my face was bathed with perspiration caused by the acute concentration that I had needed to fly by the unconventional method. Taxiing had proved the most difficult task of all to accomplish, but more importantly we now had a working aircraft that would be feasible for Trevor to fly.

Trevor was contacted and arrived in eager anticipation to test-fly his plane. After being lifted into the cockpit by the huge, tough, David Groves from the wing department and then receiving a preliminary talk through explaining the control system, he was raring to go. I, of course, had to accompany him as cover pilot on that first flight, but he was most competent and flew with great skill. It was to his advantage that he was used to dealing with unconventional controls on his wheelchair, etc. The adapted system on the Shadow posed no problems.

It was a thrill for everyone present to witness his joy on landing after that first flight and we were jubilant that we had succeeded in making the impossible possible and he was able to fulfil his dream of flying once more. As Trevor relaxed in the cockpit, I was allowed to enjoy a moment of light relief operating his £5000 high-tech wheelchair. Like a delighted child with a new toy, I set off down the runway at what appeared an amazing pace for a wheelchair. It was a great shock therefore, when I realised I was being slowly raised skywards as well as still going forward at speed! Frightened out of my life, I frantically went through the selection of controls, to try and return myself and seat to the body of the chair but to no avail. Thankful that at least I had an accurate working knowledge of the braking system, I returned to Trevor in my new, elevated, position and humbly begged for instructions so that I could descend to earth!

We could all see that the aircraft could be safely operated by Trevor Jones. Naturally, he needed assistance for fuelling, starting and getting in and out of the cockpit but, fundamentally, he was his own man once the flight commenced. The aircraft now had to be finally approved by the CAA. It had been a protracted struggle from the outset, trying to cope with the CAA's demands for this adapted machine. An aircraft for a person such as Trevor, could not by its very nature comply in the same manner as a standard machine, as it was individualised to his requirements, but it still had to meet with the Airworthiness standard. One of the CAA criticisms was that there was no provision made for the fuel cut-off. How was one to design a fuel cut-off control that could be operated by a person with no ability to use their hands?

Rex Garrod resolved the problem with a switch that operated an electric on/off valve. He had been rummaging in an aircraft scrap-yard and discovered this device, which had previously been used in a F4 Phantom. The CAA seemed somewhat reluctant to accept this solution and asked for a guard to be placed over the switch and for a wiring diagram of the electric valve. There was obviously no way I could write to McDonnel Douglas in St Louis, USA, for this information, so a bit of creative drawing from Rex was submitted to the authorities to enable the aircraft to receive the correct tick of compliance in its associated box on the sheaves of airworthiness paperwork. Typically, it is only the UK regulations that require this fuel on/off system in microlights, which, to my knowledge, has never had to be used in the eventuality of fire.

Eventually the day arrived when all the requirements demanded by the CAA were met and all that remained was for Trevor to demonstrate to the flight department of the CAA that he was capable of flying, in order that he could be issued with a special limited flying licence. This meeting with the CAA left him exhausted and mentally broken. In my opinion, the officials were far too harsh in their manner and made no allowances for the physical state of Trevor in their handling of the situation. I must admit my exasperation with the CAA was frequently brought to breaking point. In no way would I wish for a state of no regula-tions to exist in the sport but I couldn't help feeling that on many occasions the CAA possessed and, seemed to delight in, an attitude of obsessive nitpicking.

The actual costs of the aircraft in terms of time and money had been great but because of Trevor's outgoing attitude and com-mitment against all the odds, the company decided to sell him the aircraft at the standard price. Rex Garrod also refused any payment for the huge amount of work he had done resolving the fuel cut-off and braking system.

Later, Trevor led a celebratory flight across the English Channel, accompanied by a large formation of other aircraft. What an achievement!

As a result of this, an APT (Aviation for Paraplegics and Tetra-plegics) school was set up at the Shadow Flight Centre, Old Sarum, using modified Shadows similar to Trevor's machine. This was financially backed by the kindness of Mr James Edmunds. James owned a Streak Shadow and had made an epic flight from Salisbury, Wiltshire, to Beijing, China, an outstanding feat for an aircraft of this type.

Many paraplegics consequently learnt to fly at APT and some even built their own Shadows to the modifications of the trail-blazer for the disabled fliers – Trevor Jones.

'D' Series and Korean Side-by-side

Continuation of the current designs could only last for a limited length of time. The buying public generally aspire for the 'new', often with irrationality. It is a condition that has been promoted by the car industry, which, invariably, produces a 'new' model for each successive year. At CFM, we found this sales play a problem. It was difficult to update the microlight category Shadow, which already possessed such outstanding characteristics. The type had to be built to a formula and modifications involving the authori-ties were very expensive to a manufacturer. There were no basic faults or weaknesses to eliminate in a Shadow, so modifications were not necessary.

Over the years, different designs from the United States came onto our UK market and I became bemused that we lost orders to non-progressive aircraft. One such design that acquired well over a hundred orders was the 'Kitfox'. It was a similar story for the Rans S6 and the Australian 'Thruster'. These designs were out-dated looking aircraft and contributed nothing to the field of aviation design. Not only had these machines a poorer per-formance than the Shadow, but they also lacked safety features such as non-stall/spin characteristics. We could only conclude that there were over a hundred aviators in the UK that did not want to buy British and only desired designs that reflected the past. I did ask a Kitfox owner once as to why he had chosen this aircraft and couldn't resist enquiring if his choice of car was based on the same principle – did he perhaps drive a 1930s Austin 7?

The extent of design modifications that had to be made to other homebuilts was noticeable, including Airworthiness Directives (ADs). Only one AD has ever been issued for CFM designs. This was ruthlessly jumped upon by the relevant aviation authorities, it almost seemed with satisfaction, and resulted in all the Shadows being grounded for inspection. The fault occurred in only one aircraft and was caused by the owner's abuse of his machine rather than a failing in the design of the plane. An expensive modification was subsequently put in place even though the model had had years' of safe operation and thousands of hours' service. These latest 'new' designs had a relatively short shelf life and quickly lost favour once they failed to live up to their owners' expectations. After their initial burst of sales, they would be overtaken by the next 'newest new' design to hit the market. And so it continued . . .

The only adaptation that could be made to a Shadow was to increase its cockpit width and make more room available for the passenger, and this we did with the 'D' Series Shadow. The Streak offered PPL (Private Pilot's Licence) 'A' licence holders an alternative and it subsequently progressed to become the StarStreak. As the market seemed to dictate side-by-side seating as a necessary requisite in an aircraft, I realised I would have to design a Shadow with this configuration, though the sale of over 400 tandem CFM aircraft worldwide was not exactly a failure of type! The side-by-side configuration goes against all my principles of design. Nissan from Japan had already, in the past, requested such a model from CFM, an undertaking that I had declined for the same reason. It was, as it transpired, very difficult to get Nissan to accept our refusal. A few months later we were contacted again and informed that all other manufacturers had been eliminated and CFM was their final choice to design a side-by-side microlight! . . .

It was about this time that Laron Technologies (our licensees in the United States) showed me a design called the 'Twin Shadow', which they had received from Korea. CFM had sold many

Shadow/Streaks to Korea and the Aeronautical University of Seoul had produced a side-by-side version using the technology of my design and direct copies of the majority of CFM Shadow piece parts. Initially, it looked good. I studied what they had done and came to the conclusion that it could be improved. This Twin Shadow was a double-boom aircraft and even though it had the crew sitting beside each other, they were positioned ahead of the wing, thereby eliminating one of my foremost gripes, which was the lack of up or down pilot vision caused by the conventional side-by-side seater designs that had the crew placed either above or below the wing. This conventional type of aircraft design was due to the fact that the CG spread was less when the crew weight was close to the aircraft's CG. By positioning the crew ahead of the wing, large tail surfaces were necessary to equalise the aircraft's CG.

An amusing aspect of this design was in their study of my wing section. The conclusions of the aeronautical research study made by the Korean University was that the Shadow/Streak possessed a 'Volmer' wing section. This was obviously a misrepresentation of the truth to divert attention from their blatant cloning of my design. The wing section that had been used on the Twin Shadow was identical to the wing section of the Image that the Korean, Mr Park, had viewed when visiting the CFM factory, a wing section that had obviously, to his way of thinking, been developed from the previous Shadow/Streak models and must therefore be the best. He was unaware that actually I had used an NACA profile for the Image, which was specifically for a tailless design and which would suit its performance envelope! The Far Eastern mind did not seem to have the innovative process for such a train of thought but they were very good at copying!

The hardest part was always the first line on the blank piece of paper. And so, because of the market requirement, construction of my side-by-side Twin Shadow began at CFM and Lola Composites was asked to produce the honeycomb/glass monocoque tub.

A few months later I visited the Laron factory in Portales, New Mexico State, to see and fly the Twin Shadow, which had recently arrived from Korea. Flying a new aircraft for the first time was always a nerve-wracking, stressful experience and the Twin Shadow proved no exception to the rule. Almost immediately, the impressive latest high-tech, digital-read-out instrument panel went wrong. Every instrument that gave invaluable information to the pilot went blank, which meant that Harlow Wise (one of Laron's founders) and I had to fly the plane 'blind'.

I intensely dislike many of these so-called electronic improvements. A basic old-fashioned round instrument with a needle is far more meaningful to read. Too much reliance on electronic devices is not a good thing and can lead to the detriment of a pilot's basic aviation skills. The value of using the traditional map and compass and actually looking (weather permitting) at the landscape below should never be underestimated. GPS systems are not infallible.

Apart from the instrumentation failure, the Twin Shadow flew well enough. I reminded myself that the airfield was nearly 4500 feet AMSL (Above Mean Sea Level) but when landing, the aircraft dropped like a brick. There certainly weren't many 'Shadow' characteristics in this machine. Its appearance was smart and neat but I feared the overall production costs of the machine would be too expensive. For example, the flaps were operated by an electronic motor used from the seat adjustment of a Mercedes car and the hydraulic brakes were from a modern motorcycle. Impressive stuff, but this was all going to make the price to the customer too much for the performance given.

After this visit to the States, my interest in the side-by-side seater began to dwindle. My thoughts were reaching out into the distant future for an aircraft that maybe would be a class winner, progress aviation and could be produced at minimal costs – the equivalent of a £50,000 aircraft for £8000 – but more on this theme later.

CDG Glider, Microlight Regulations and Airworthiness

One of the subjects discussed during this visit to Laron in the States was the requirement for a cheap trainer glider – a glider that when cable-launched could glide within the confines of the airfield.

On my return to England, I soon converted a C Series Shadow

into a glider. Minus engine, fuel tank and fuel system, nose leg and with only one central wheel for towing and landing, the production costs would be very low.

To keep the costs at a minimum, I decided to design the tow-release mechanisms. Not knowing the slightest thing about this subject, it would be a challenge to see if I could produce a device that would be as effective as the existing design or maybe even better. I based my idea on the simple catch system used on all household doors, which have been proven worldwide to work without fail. Having successfully completed my design, I allowed myself to then read a thesis study by students from Cambridge University, on this subject. It seemed that the best release system available functioned correctly only 60 per cent of the time, so my humble door catch mechanism with its 100 per cent success rate, low weights and low costs had more than exceeded expectations.

The CDG (C series, dual control glider) was finally completed with a coat of bright bubble-gum pink paint, a colour that provoked many caustic comments when the glider made its first appearance at Wormingford Airfield, near Colchester, Essex. People had failed to realise that by being this colour, it would be easily visible to those in the air and on the ground. Conventional gliders are only white because of their glass fibre composite construction. White reflects heat from the sun and by doing so, prevents the composites heating up, thereby weakening the plane's structural ability. The performance of the cable-launched CDG was not outstanding. After testing, I realised that I should have based the glider on the StarStreak wing and increased its span so that the aspect ratio was much higher. The glider's best feature was that it had a sink rate of only 200 feet a minute when it flew at speeds of 45–50 mph. The lift/drag ratio was quite poor, though at 15:1 it certainly fulfilled the requirement for a learner glider, which was only intended literally to hang around the airfield. Other than this, the CDG was going nowhere. The most successful aspect of this CDG was my releasing mechanism, but because of its innovative styling it was suffering the usual fate of non-acceptance in the aviation world where convention rules the day.

Often, I found, my ideas were better than the accepted norm, but

I knew that each new design of mine would entail an endless confrontation with the authorities to gain its approval. Take the simple case of aircraft metal locking nuts, for instance. The adage in the aviation world was to use once and discard because the nuts lost their grip after being used half a dozen times. Why use these when commercial nyloc nuts had a much longer life and were so much cheaper? I demonstrated to the CAA Area Surveyor that I could successfully wind a standard commercial nyloc nut twenty times on and off a bolt and it still retained its grip and could not be loosened by hand.

The fabric covering on the Shadow wings was another example. Why use aircraft polyester or Dacron at enormous expense when the commercially sold equivalent is ten times cheaper and just as effective? I contacted Coulthards Materials, sending a sample of aircraft covering material, and requested a sample of a similar weft and strength. This they did and the aircraft wings were covered with polyester dress-lining fabric! The material was then attached to the wings and flying surfaces with clear household Bostik glue. The aircraft surfaces that were to be covered were first given two coats of Bostik, which were allowed to dry. Fabric could then be positioned at one's convenience and the mere wiping action of an acetone-soaked brush over the fabric would immediately produce the required bond. Aircraft glue was not a necessity for this job. Besides being more expensive, it was messy to use and, more importantly, it did not give as good a bond.

In the majority of conventional wings the fabric was wrapped completely around the wing when covering. Our fabric was bonded onto the plywood wing 'D' box with only a one-inch margin. This provoked the customary CAA reaction; they insisted on a strength test to prove it was a satisfactory method. The reason for this traditional method of covering was that most wing ribs were constructed of metal tubing, which offered very little area for bonding, but the Shadow wing ribs were constructed of 1¼-inch flat-topped styrofoam covered with glass fibre and were therefore ideal for the Bostik bond over the large area. The strength test was to see if the joint of the largest area wing panel would fail under the pressure of 4 x the normal wing loading. As the test proved a success with the bond showing no signs of failing, I progressively reduced the bond line depth to ½ inch on the 'D' box. On testing, this, too, successively held under the 4 x normal wing loading conditions!

Another bonding process I tried to simplify was the bonding of the aluminium strips that were used on the wing spar booms. So it was with great interest that I pursued the possibility of using a new type of double-sided structural tape produced by 3M Scotch that would eliminate the current lengthy process of degreasing, abrading, priming with Accomet 'C' and, finally, bonding the aluminium with Araldite adhesive secured with pop rivets. Samples were subsequently set up for viewing and testing but the ever cautious authorities would not even consider the substitution of the tape for the current process, until the samples had had four years' of full exposure to all weather conditions prior to testing. Needless to say, this idea progressed no further.

In my opinion, the airworthiness rules in the UK are excessive, which, consequently, leads to inflated costs of aircraft. We have the absurd situation existing where every country possesses its own differing levels of airworthiness regarding microlights or homebuilts. For example, in Germany the flying of ULMs (Ultra Light Machines) is allowed only from specified designated areas and then flying is only allowed if the sound levels of the engine are the equivalent of the sounds emitted from a country meadow in summer! Initially in Australia, microlights were not allowed above 400 feet altitude and were banned from crossing any highway. In the US, microlights don't exist as a separate category of aircraft; they are incorporated with the homebuilt machines. The only airworthiness rules in America are that the new type of aircraft should have completed twenty-five fault-free flying hours. No structural assessment, aerodynamic analysis or design submission is required by the authorities. This is in complete contrast with the UK system, where, as well as the twenty-five fault-free flying hours, every conceivable test, aerodynamic analysis and submission has to be completed to the authorities' satisfaction before permission to fly is granted. Whereas, to me, the US regulations are insufficient, the regulations in the UK are excessive and too restrictive and tend to smother any form of creative thought. To my thinking, the South African approach seems the most logical and sensible. The South African authorities carry out an eyeball engineering assessment of a new type, which if successful, then allows the aircraft to fly within certain areas for a proving period.

It was a complicated and time-consuming task, trying to grapple with all these differing airworthiness regulations so that the Shadow would be able to fly in all these countries. This was just one of the many aspects of my work at CFM. There was the constant pressure of work on new models and their associated approvals, demands of demonstration flights to potential customers (which amounted to over 500 a year), air show displays and business visits abroad. But above all, there was the ever-present burden of financial problems. The hard reality was that the Shadow was a beautiful, outstanding aircraft that took too many man-hours to build and was, therefore, not a moneymaking product. The CFM aircraft had to be under-priced. Price-wise, they were already at the top end of the market but we feared a drastic drop in sales if we increased the selling price still further. It was a risk we could not afford to take, even though we knew our monetary incomings just failed to meet our company outgoings. It was all a tremendous strain. Often Pat White and I, as the directors, would forgo our salary to enable the employees to receive their wages. We were forever striving to resolve the monetary situation in numerous different ways but, basically, it was to no avail as the failing lay at the very heart of the matter in the complexity of the Shadow's construction.

Promoting the aircraft through record attempts was always an advantageous exercise, as none of our competitors could match the aircraft in performance. It was to be years later before the trikes fitted with huge four-stroke, multi-cylinder engines and dual ignition attempted long-distance flights. These trikes were, by then, costing as much as the factory-produced Shadows.

GLINT

Ideas for my next design project were always forming and fermenting in the back of my mind. I was aware that several American designs, in the homebuilt category, had made leaps forward in the performance of light aircraft. Invariably, these designs were conceived around side-by-side seating and airframes based upon glass or carbon composites, using honeycomb sandwich techniques. I knew any design of mine would never be to this formula.

Back in the 1970s, a man from the States, called Bede, had produced an attractive aircraft – the BD-5. Its pleasing, smooth lines were so admired by one American journalist at the time, that it had been termed as 'sexy'. I've never quite understood the use of such a word with regards to an inanimate object but that's probably because I'm English and not American. Anyway, the description did wonders for the advertising of the aircraft. Bede received so many $20 deposits for the BD-5 kit, that he gave up producing the parts and quietly disappeared into the depths of South America with the money. Aviation comprises all sorts!

I also admired the design lines of the BD-5 but, to me, it had the basic fault of being too tiny in its overall dimensions. The engine was situated behind the pilot in the fuselage, driving a pusher propeller via a shaft to the tail. This concept was the result of good, logical thinking and I could envisage a larger-sized aircraft based on the BD-5, but with the two seats in tandem and using 200 hp for the power. The engine used by Bede was only 40–60 hp but it still gave 150–200 mph performance.

Not knowing what to name my new concept, as I was constantly having to refer to it, I temporarily called the plane the Glint, after the cancelled 'black' American project of that name.

To enable a high power-to-weight ratio, so that the aircraft could give a military-style performance, a ratio of 5–7 lb per horsepower was required. My Streak aircraft possessed a ratio of 13 lb per hp; the tailless Image had a ratio of 4.5–5 lb. I even considered a lengthened version of the Image, fitted with a Formula 1 Cosworth engine that could take part in the American Reno Races, with an estimated performance of near 500 mph! Perhaps this was idle dreaming, as the design never came to fruition, but success was so close.

The Glint was to have the conventional layout with tailplane and fin and a sleek, curvaceous shape. Marketing a new aircraft had previously shown that beautiful (sexy) lines would be successful – remembering Bede's BD-5 – so style and line, combined with progress and affordability in aviation, were my aims.

Many American designs cost between $40,000–$70,000 and were too expensive. A major part of this cost was the engine. Makes of engines such as Lycoming and Continental were overpriced because of low production rates and, in my opinion, were non-progressive designs based on old ways of thinking. Great advances have been made in the construction of automobile engines, which have ensured a far better reliability rate and at far less cost. The old principle of pistons travelling all the way to TDC (top dead centre), stopping and then descending to BDC (bottom dead centre), as used in the first petrol engine cars, was successful, but engine design has progressed since then. To me, it seemed wrong to still be using engines such as these in aircraft, when there were so many better models on the market. Mazda had a rotary engine, which was used in their RX-7 car. This rotated with a double rotor based on the Wankel type developed in Germany by NSU. Unfortunately, the engine still bore the stigma of early failures with the sealing rings, which were originally encountered by NSU, but Mazda had resolved the problem. Thus, I perceived that it would be ideal to use a 200-hp Mazda car engine for the Glint, as this engine rotated in the same direction as the propeller and basically consisted of only two moving parts. My excitement mounted when enquiries showed that second-hand engines of this type were available, with a two-year guarantee, at the unbeliev-able price of £700. Apparently, a law in Japan states that car engines are to be replaced after certain periods and so the world market was flooded with perfectly good engines of all types.

The fundamentals for the design were in place. My starting point was the balance of weight so that the wing could be positioned. As the engine was amidships just aft of the pilot, all the major moments were excellently together and the drawing rapidly took shape and became the form of a sleek aircraft.

It is not necessary to be trained academically to design an aircraft. If the size of a rudder was required, I looked at the fin/rudder ratio of previous successful designs and a ratio soon became apparent. The same applied for calculating the tailplane size compared with the wing area, etc. What was important to me was that the end result was not founded on ancient concepts that produced aircraft of similar appearance and mediocre performance. One can only assume that copycat designs were produced by the big manufacturers, with merely profitability in mind. The idea of creating a design for aviation enthusiasts at a really economic price, whilst still progressing aviation design, was what I was trying to achieve. To be wealthy was not of paramount importance in my life.

The fuselage of the Glint was such that its shape would have to be constructed from honeycomb sandwich composites, so I contacted David Southwell, who had given me invaluable assistance in the past with his knowledge of composite materials. He had now left Ciba Geigy and was working in engineering sales at Lola Composites. Lola manufactured all the monocoques and Formula 3000 tubs for the Indy cars, which were raced on the US circuits. Naturally, as in modern thinking, these were all built exclusively from carbon fibre. But I did not want to use carbon fibre for the fuselage, it was far too expensive, so I asked if it was possible for them to produce some samples made up of cheaper composites, for my examination.

David Southwell was right on the ball. He designated the lowest-cost aluminium honeycomb to be sandwiched between the cheapest glass fibre cladding, which was then dyed black to resemble carbon. The samples were then autoclaved. I was delighted with the results, the pieces formed seemed indestructible. A curved sample showed an amazing strength-to-weight ratio of 2000:1.

My entire fuselage cost in material and the rest of the aircraft including the engine as a kit, could be estimated at £8000 in 1996 prices. This was an exceptionally low price compared with kits of other performance aircraft, which were in the realms of £40,000 – five times that amount.

The Glint's wing would differ from conventional aircraft in that it would be a hollow plywood construction, which would also serve as a container for the fuel tank. As the Glint was to have a range of 1000 nautical miles, plenty of fuel space was needed. The two main spars would comprise my well-proven aluminium caps, bonded and riveted to the plywood. The wing would feature anti-stall drooped leading edges and split flaps, and the undercarriage retracting mechanism would be via a simple lever operation. The interior surface of the wings would be sealed from fuel leaks, by coating it with a special type of marine varnish. This method was used regularly by aero modellers and the varnish was easily available. I made up a test sample box of scrap 1.2-mm ply, painted its interior with the marine varnish and then filled it with petrol and left the box to stand. The system worked perfectly; in fact a year later there were still no signs of fuel leakage!

After I had completed my design work on the Glint, Brian Johnson and one of his colleagues in the special effects world, produced a twenty-second video of the Glint in flight, based on my three-view dimensional design drawings. I was then able to view my forthcoming creation when, in reality, it did not exist! Brilliant!

There appeared to be one glaring error. The rudder area would have to be increased by two-thirds.

It was interesting to engineer the drive from engine to propeller. These two items would be 6 feet apart. A silent triple chain would take power from the engine output shaft to a propeller shaft. This would have to rotate inside a Kevlar tube in case of failure. As the pusher propeller would be vulnerable to damage when on the ground – either by the airframe tilting back or by over-rotation on take-off – an airbrake-type skid would lower whenever the under-carriage operated to the down position. A liquid ring and rubber damper would isolate the engine harmonics from the drive chain. The Glint sadly never came to fruition. It remained a dream, unproven on the drawing board due to increasing financial problems in the company.

DESIGN PROPOSALS

In later years, the biggest order for microlights ever placed in the UK from overseas, came from India, who found the perfect aircraft for the basic training of their Air Force personnel in the Shadow 'D' Series.

Over the years I was inundated with various flying proposals and designs from different people. I was not the lateral thinker that people seemed to assume. I considered myself as a logical-thinking engineer and it was difficult to respond to most of these, sometimes outrageous, ideas. One of the most bizarre proposals was from the fellow who imagined leaping out of an aircraft on what he described as an aerial surfboard glider. To me, this appeared horrendously hazardous, especially when it came to landing.

Another idea, the wing-in-ground-effect (WIG) was of much more interest, but Mike Plewman (joint MD) insisted I stuck to my job. This proposal was to have me build a boat that would fly sufficiently fast to lift off from a sea or lake and only to have enough lift to rise a few feet above the surface. The request was to build a two-man prototype. The full-size machine would be to fly containers between Caribbean islands. Much later, we saw that the Russians had developed WIGs of fantastic proportions for civil and military use.

One chap, who became a close friend, was Jack Pedersen. He said he had head-hunted me after he'd seen my Shadow at Farnborough. I'm not permitted to print where he worked, but he was probably one of the top brains in England. Jack wanted me to develop a pollution-free engine, which he'd designed. The principle was that it could be made in any size to drive anything from a power station to a model aeroplane. It was based on a Wankel-type trapezoidal eccentric rotor, using a water seal as a liquid ring. This engine was going to 'save the world'. I did a preliminary amount of design on the engine, but CFM really didn't have the time or resources. One of our original apprentices, Patrick Robinson, carried out tests and minor development to see if it was practical and we did gain a SMART Award from the DTI (Department of Trade and Industry) for Stage One development.

But, really, the whole thing needed proper funding. There have been many very good alternative power units designed by individuals, but they often end up lying dormant, due to lack of investment from established companies. Imagine Ford or Nissan being interested in a really good environmental engine for their vehicles, when they have just invested £1 billion in the latest models of their range. No way!

This was always a long-term fear I had with Jack Pedersen's liquid ring and eventually this imaginative idea, too, was sadly dropped.

CHAPTER 3

Shadow Achievements, Records and Awards

DISTANCE, NORFOLK AIR RACE, ENGLAND TO AUSTRALIA, EVE JACKSON, INDIA, SEAGRAVE TROPHY

02 was used as the customer demonstrator, although its front cockpit was shorter in length than its production counterpart, the cockpit on production models being lengthened slightly to prove more comfort for taller pilots. The positioning of the control stick at the side also gave more room than in a traditional-style cockpit and the uninterrupted wide-ranging view from the Perspex sailplane-like canopy contributed to the feeling of spaciousness.

Peter Troy Davies looked pretty squashed sitting in 02, but he had never complained, calling the cockpit 'snug'. Peter had often driven long distances to help me and had courageously flown all the air tests for the factory without any monetary reward, due to the poor financial state of CFM. He was a first class pilot, my skills rated very low in the ability scale compared with his. As a way of thanking Peter, I offered him the Shadow to attempt a Flight World Record, whereupon he decided to try and double the existing FAI distance record of flying in a straight line between two points.

Consequently in April 1983, he took off in 02 from Parham

airfield and flew to St Just airfield at Land's End, Cornwall, and succeeded in more than doubling the World Record for type C-1a/o category. He was in the air for over six hours, but he achieved his World Record.

Two years later, two Shadows flown by Peter Troy Davies and Brian Milton completed a flight from Hurn airport, Bournemouth, to Kirkwell airport in the Orkney Islands, some 600 miles non-stop, which is still held as a UK record distance flight.

These FAI records were recorded in the *Guinness Book of Records*, even though I had refused permission to print when it had been requested. I had no desire for these truly deserving records of the Shadow to be published alongside such frivolous feats as the greatest distance achieved by someone's nose pushing a pea along a road. To me, these sorts of activities were not worthy of record claims.

An FAI record is gained only by strictly adhering to a documented set of rules regarding each discipline. I met an American once who claimed twenty-four World Records in his aircraft. It made my official FAI World Record for speed over 3 km appear insignificant, but in reality what he had done was set himself the task of flying from one city to another – any city, any distance great or small. Simply because no previous record of that flight existed, he had claimed them as 'World Records'. Of course, these were not recognised by the FAI, so the truth of the situation was that his words were meaningless bluster.

A year after the Speed and Distance Record had been obtained, CFM entered two Shadows in the annual Norfolk Air Race. David Clarke flew 02 solo and Peter Davies and Eve Jackson flew in Shadow 007 – the first production aircraft. The two Shadows averaged 77 mph over 150 miles, coming home first and second within two minutes of each other. Their performance completely outstripped all the other microlights. The loud protests from manufacturers of flexwing trikes led to class categories being formed for competitions from then on.

The Shadow design was updated to full dual flying controls with the addition of brakes in the rear cockpit, ignition switches, an electric trim switch and airspeed indicator (ASI). The design could now be used as a trainer for flying schools and Peter Troy Davies and Fiona Luckhurst bought 027, one of the first CAA-approved kits, to build themselves for the purpose of training pilots.

I had observed that the major fault with company-built aircraft was that they were non-profit making because too many hours were involved in their building. A kit version, on the other hand, took far fewer hours to produce and would therefore be profitable. Approval for the Shadow kit caused no problems with the CAA as they could see that the primary structure of the wing main 'D' box was factory-built. The fibrelam monocoque was self-jigging with all welding done and parts ready for assembly. In all, a kit version of the Shadow took 500 fewer hours of work than to build a complete aircraft.

1986 was an eventful year for CFM. Eve Jackson flew her B Series Shadow 007, *Gertie*, from Biggin Hill, England, to Sydney, Australia. Without sponsorship and in her own time, she achieved many firsts for microlighting.

During her stay in India, she was based at an airfield called Safdarjung, which was next to the sprawling New Delhi metropolis. Unable to progress to Thailand, due to her permit to fly expiring, she arranged with Pan Am airways to fly me out to India to inspect and flight test her plane and renew her permit.

When I arrived, Eve had already carried out a planned engine service, which had involved the engine being returned to England, and was now busy replacing the serviced engine. I have always had feelings of unease when working with foreign air traffic controllers and my experience when testing the plane reinforced this state of mind. The air test brief was: not over 1000 feet above ground level (AGL). I also requested the flight to be inside the airfield boundary with tight circuits. When airborne however, the controller pushed me way out from the airfield, right over New Delhi, because a priority military flight was inbound for Safdarjung.

I was now several miles out and only at 1000 feet. There was the horrid sight of New Delhi below, horrid because there was nowhere to land safely in an emergency. There were no school playing fields, football grounds or waste areas; it was a complete urban sprawl. The temperature was well over 30° even though it was late afternoon with hazy inversions and a lot of pollution in the air.

Suddenly the engine lost power and stopped, completely seized up. My worst fear had happened. I remember being completely rigid, but could hear myself shouting at my stupidity for allowing this situation to have happened. I was going to have to land without the remotest hope of finding a suitable landing area and would probably die slammed up against some building below. All I could think of was that I'd survived all these years of flying and now I was about to die in some sodding place like this. I was totally distraught. Tears of frustration filled my eyes as I silently lost altitude, realising my fate was to come in less than five minutes. I have always fought when in trouble. Dad drummed into me, 'Be the best, No. 1, never give up.' Being sad and having to accept the inevitable was alien to me. The gripping fear normally associated with this type of situation was less than expected, for subconsciously my brain was working hard.

'Look at those huge vultures ahead. They're not flapping their wings, they must be soaring. If I joined them and tried to soar . . .' I headed towards the birds and started to circle with them – 650 feet AGL suddenly I wasn't losing height. The vertical speed indicator (VSI) showed level flight instead of 250 feet per minute down. Like a miracle, the VSI twitched to 100 then 200 feet per minute climb. It wasn't much, but a glimpse of salvation had appeared with these birds. This huge type of vulture with their 10-foot wingspan seemed to accept the presence of the Shadow circling with them in their orbit. They defiantly eyed this massive white 'bird' with its 33-foot wingspan as we flew only yards apart. We all climbed back past 1000 feet AGL, but it seemed agonisingly slow.

Staying with the vultures following the weak thermal, I gained enough height till I was able to see Safdarjung airfield once more. I gave a pan-pan call to the air traffic controller; it should have been a Mayday, but received no response. 'Who cares?' I thought. I couldn't care less about priority military flights inbound or their air law. I had been given a slight chance of getting out of this alive! Patience was difficult in this situation. 'How long would the lift last? How much height do I need to be able to glide back?' I was in a high state of tension, almost without hope and then given a possible chance. Safdarjung beckoned, so I peeled off out of my vulture thermal and flew the Shadow at its best glide angle and hoped to get back. Just before the threshold of the runway, some idiot planners had built a dual carriageway fly-over construction; this was the notorious fly-over that killed Premier Ghandi's relative when he struck it in a Cessna. I aimed to one side and touched down in silence on the runway, rolling to a halt. The radio startled me just as I was thanking 'Big G' in my thoughts, with the air traffic controller announcing that I was ' . . . clear to backtrack'. With no engine running? No acknowledgement of the pan-pan call? I turned the radio off, somewhat bemused, and didn't bother to reply.

Accidents or crashes always seem to happen at the end of a sequence of events. In the previous scenario it was the usual three events – not being over 1000 feet, being told to fly away from the airfield during a check flight, plus an engine failure. Thankfully, after the initial shock, I did not seem to be particularly affected after this potentially fatal event, probably because I was too pleased to be still alive!

Eve's solo flight to Australia was a magnificent achievement and effort, which quite rightly gained her the Segrave Trophy and myself, the Segrave Medal. 'Behind every great woman is a great man,' stated the announcer as I was informed of my award. This award is only presented when an outstanding feat is achieved on land, sea or air. It is not awarded lightly, nor annually, being distinctly different from film, TV or pop scene awards, which appear to be continuous and often bear little resemblance to distinction.

Even in aviation, I have seen awards given without proper merit. The Royal Aero Club (RAC) has Gold, Silver and Bronze medal awards and the Bronze medal that I was awarded for the 'Lowest Powered Crossing of the Channel' was equal to the worth of my achievement. A Gold is reserved for outstanding aviation feats, such as first to fly the Atlantic or step on the moon. Consequently, I was astonished when attending my presentation ceremony that Prince Charles on behalf of the RAC awarded the Gold medal to two balloonists who had attempted to cross the Atlantic Ocean and had failed! I distinctly remember being held back by Catherine and the President of the BMAA (British Microlight Aircraft Association), Ann Welch, from going up to the podium shouting, 'How could a failure be awarded?' All that's wrong with the competitive spirit in England was revealed in this presentation and I was disgusted at such a decision.

During my intense flying time at CFM, I averaged over 600 flights a year for nine years. Due to the immense number of flights there were, inevitably, bound to be incidents, which usually amounted to three per year. It isn't necessarily always the pilot's fault. Aviation is the most unforgiving of all sport, one cannot afford to make any errors. But these 'events' can be caused by factors such as the weather, structural failure, mid-air collisions, engine failure or disorientation of the pilot. All one can do is to try and forestall any potential 'event' by planning and thinking ahead as much as possible. If one is prepared, a chain of 'events' is less likely to happen. Being aware of these potentially hazardous factors, it is possible to out-think the odds. Combined with a certain amount of luck along the way, these attitudes have served me well over my forty years of flying. But I do realise that a totally unforeseen incident such as a large bird flying into a wing can wreck an aeroplane. An example of one such unforeseen incident happened to me one day. I was searching the distant sectors, whilst flying over Parham airfield in Suffolk, when I noticed a small black dot on the horizon. My altitude was less than 1500 feet and as I watched, the black dot seemed to get larger. I guessed what it might be and as I dived vertically towards the ground and levelled off at 100 feet, an F104 Starfighter screamed overhead at about 1000 feet, flying at 600 knots.

Although I didn't see the Starfighter coming, I'd correctly assessed the black dot to be the trail of its smoky exhaust aimed directly towards me. I hoped this sort of awareness made me a better pilot, or at least one that could outwit or out-think the odds.

Being a good pilot is different from being a good driver – an attitude that most people think they have when driving a car. The
latter is rarely true, however, as most drivers on a skid-pan quickly
discover.

Pilots can be split into several categories ranging from the
professional airline or military types, through to the amateur
private aircraft owners; all possess their own level of skills and
relevant abilities. I would rate myself as a reasonably good
'flyer'. In flying 'circles', it is easy to see someone who can
handle an aircraft better than you. The realisation is there for all to
see who fly. Just ask a pilot if he can recover from an inverted spin.
There will be very few who can.

DAWN TO DUSK

David Southwell, the chief sales engineer from Ciba Geigy at
Duxford, and I had become close associates. He was also a pilot
and his enthusiasm for the Shadow had grown since he had been
given the opportunity to fly my aircraft. He had helped me
immensely at Ciba Geigy, by getting a computer disk produced so
that our production fibrelam monocoques could be produced at
Duxford. This suited CFM, for if mistakes were made using this
expensive composite honeycomb, then the mistake was with them,
not CFM.

In the spring of 1986, David suggested to me that we should take
part in the international Dawn to Dusk competition. I readily
agreed as any venture that would promote aircraft sales would be
a worthwhile challenge. (The idea behind this competition was for
individuals to fly and achieve any set task of their own choice that
extended from dawn till dusk on a set day of their own choosing,
which fell in the stipulated period during the height of summer.)

He proposed that we flew to all the 8th Air Force bases used by
the Americans during the Second World War in East Anglia. There
were sixty-seven! Most of them had been dug up, abandoned or
returned to farmland. It was a daunting task.

As I was too involved with the running of CFM to undertake
any of the competition planning, David took on all the prep-

arations for charts, course changes, headings, timings and the radio, and also organised a charity collection connected with the flight.

We planned to fly at 60 knots, which would be, in navigation terms, a nautical mile per minute. This would ease our task with the stopwatch.

So it came to pass that at dawn one day in June 1986, we prepared to commence our flight in my original Shadow (02), at Bassingbourne airfield (USAF 91st Group). The whole world was enveloped in a fog, which had not been predicted by the meteorological office. Consequently, it was nearly 10:00 hours before we could depart.

Our flight would entail having to pass through several restricted and controlled areas of airspace. To enable us to do this, we had previously arranged clearances and our allocated call sign of SHADOW 91. As our only aids for navigation were a compass and map, the Shadow was restricted to Visual Flight Rules (VFR).

The flight commenced with a take-off into a very low cloud base, coupled with the added hazard of rising ground. Both of us must have had eyes like saucers as we probed the murk for the two high radio masts that we knew were in the vicinity. We zoomed past one mast within feet, at about half its height, so I calculated we must have reassuringly missed the other, which was close by.

David handled all the communications to air traffic controllers. He navigated by informing me over the intercom of the next compass heading combined with the number of minutes it would take before we reached the next field, which left me to set the heading and the stopwatch and fly the aeroplane.

Thirteen airfields later we refuelled, having been airborne for one and a half hours. The weather was now sunny and clear but with a variable 20-knot wind. We felt pleased with ourselves so far, but realised that we still had to undertake yet another five similar stages and each stage was a distance of around 80–95 nautical miles. A photograph was taken of each airfield from low altitude, even if there was little evidence of its previous existence, so that we had proof of our flight for the records.

This was practically eyeball navigation for nine hours. The wind didn't help either, changing through 90 degrees twice and building up to 25 knots. Our log shows we averaged 58 knots (67 mph) for 501 nautical miles (576 miles) in 8 hours 58 minutes. The Shadow averaged 29.5 miles per gallon and used 2.1 gallons per hour. The various air traffic controllers were most helpful, instantly recognising our pre-arranged call sign. We did have to miss two old airfields in the Thetford army training area, due to the military firing live ammunition, but we reckoned this omission would be acceptable by the judging committee! Our original plan was to 'touch and go' at all possible airfields, but as the start had been delayed we just didn't have sufficient time.

During the day, two memorable events occurred concerning other aircraft. As we arrived over Honington, my old V Bomber base, the tower called saying there was a fast military aircraft on a reciprocal track and height. Would we call when it was sighted – we never did. The other incident was when I spotted a Harrier less than 300 feet away to our port, heading straight at us. I instantly dived the aircraft and closed my eyes awaiting the impact, but we resumed our course seconds later, thankfully still intact! Poor David in the back had had no sighting or forewarning of this Harrier – he had his camera, log and pencils fly all over the cockpit but managed to restrain his reactions to 'What the **** are you doing?' I don't expect for one moment that the pilot of the Harrier had even seen us.

We returned to Basingbourne just before dusk, feeling almost punch drunk. David was later to comment that he could not hear properly for two days following the flight.

After a lot of detailed work on our submission to the Dawn to Dusk committee, we felt we had a reasonable chance of winning, if only through the effort and the input required to fulfil the task. Several months later, the invitation to the Royal Aeronautical Society in London came to all participants. To our utter amazement, we had been judged the overall winners. We were awarded the Duke of Edinburgh Trophy and the Precision Pilot's Award by the Duke and Duchess of York. Never before had a microlight become the winner of this competition where originality and considerable aviation skills are prime requirements.

John Farley, a test pilot for eighteen years, was one of the committee members and was one of the many interesting people we met that evening. He entertained my wife and me by verbally demonstrating how deceptively simple it was to undertake all those impressive manoeuvres, flying vertically and hovering in the Harrier.

DESIGN AWARDS

In many ways 1986–7 were memorable years for the Shadow. Besides winning the prestigious Dawn to Dusk international competition, the aircraft also gained a British Design Award and was one of the four finalists in the BBC Design Awards competition.

As a winner of the British Design Award, we had a highly polished gleaming Shadow on display at the Design Centre, London, where His Royal Highness the Duke of Edinburgh was to present the awards. When the Duke of Edinburgh saw the plane, he actually commented on its appearance and enquired how we had achieved such a high gloss finish on the wing's leading edge. My retort of 'Elbow grease?' gave rise to some amusement on his part.

The Duke of Edinburgh's personal choice of the award winners was a stamp-sized computer chipboard containing 13 million transistors – an amazing piece of electronic engineering. Unfortunately, the creator rather spoilt himself in my opinion, by openly flaunting his design to me, until I reached the point where I couldn't resist remarking, 'Aah, but can it fly?'

The BBC Design Awards presentation was held in one of the large studios at the BBC Television Centre in London. Amongst the finalists was the newly designed Jaguar car, which was not yet in production. This £50,000 machine had the humiliation of having to be pushed out of the building, as its highly computerised technical systems would not allow the, by then, frustrated technicians to remove the filler cap to pour some fuel into its tank, the car having to be drained of fuel as a safety precaution before its stay in the studio. The thought came to me that perhaps sometimes the latest technology was not necessarily an improvement to the working of a machine – the screw-top on the Shadow's filler cap was very simple, but at least it would always work. Maybe this was such a case of over-design on this particular layout, for I have always been an admirer of their superb engineering skills and have owned a Jaguar V-12 XJS for fifteen years.

I was very proud to have gained these Design Awards for the Shadow, but did find in some cases the decisions by the judges difficult to comprehend. For instance, in the BBC Design Awards, the overall design award went to the manufacturers of a set of ceramic bath handles and fittings. Without wishing to appear begrudging and condescending, I cannot possibly see that the design content of these articles is comparable with the complex design concept and work in the Shadow aircraft. But then, how can an aircraft be compared with a computerised chip, an ice pick and bathroom fittings?

In all, I was to meet the Duke of Edinburgh three times that year. The second time was at the winners' only meet held in the Stationers' Hall, London, for the Dawn to Dusk competitors, whereupon he said on meeting me, 'Not you again!' I then managed to make a complete fool of myself in front of the Duke of Edinburgh, by mistakenly presenting David Southwell's wife Heather as my wife Catherine, who I thought was standing behind me. The Duke was greatly amused and as I desperately tried to resolve the situation, told me to make up my mind as to which was my wife! So much for my correct behaviour confronted by royalty! Personally, I cannot be overawed by the presence of such people and consider that perhaps thinking about the occasion from a different angle, they are fortunate to meet people who are achievers in some field.

This was evident on another occasion at the Great Eastern Agricultural Show near Peterborough, where we had a Shadow aircraft on display. I was not actually present, but Pat White, my associate from CFM, later related to me how the Duke of Edinburgh broke away from his courtesy route. He scrambled down the side of two closely parked caravans to reach the displayed Shadow, informing his alarmed security men that he wanted to meet some real people!

THE LONG DISTANCE TRAVELLER

In September 1987 a hang gliding colleague from my past, Brian Milton, turned up at the factory to purchase a Shadow. He was proposing to fly from England to Australia, emulating the flight of the Vickers Vimy, which took part in a flying competition held in the early days of aviation. He was planning his arrival in Australia to coincide with the bicentenary celebrations.

He did his flight training with Pete Davies and flew some very long practice flights prior to leaving from London's Docklands airport *en route* to Australia. Brian Milton is a 'hard hitter'. I admire the drive and single-mindedness of people such as him – they are not always the most gracious of people, but they achieve.

The progress of his flight was followed with interest as he made regular reports for the TV news, then one day I received a call from him after his Shadow was overturned on the Greek island of Kythira. The aircraft had been blown over in 50+ mph winds and was, by the sound of it, totally wrecked. It didn't seem entirely his fault, as this airfield was at an altitude of 2000 feet with winds so gusty that when he arrived to land the small air traffic section had already gone home as the scheduled Twin Otter flight from Athens had been cancelled. Conversing through his HF (High Frequency) radio, I tried to calculate the spares he would require – an almost impossible task in the circumstances – and then flew out to Athens to confront the situation.

Our CFM storeman, David Foster, had made up various packages of parts, but the Greek customs officials proceeded to tear them all apart to investigate their contents. They were rewarded for their efforts when they discovered a bottle marked 'Dope'. 'What's this?' demanded a stern-faced customs officer, presenting me with the offending object. Somehow I managed to talk my way out of this embarrassing situation and eventually arrived at a cold, bleak mountaintop airfield on Kythira.

The Shadow's damage was bad – I would have written the plane off, but Brian insisted that it must be mended, as he was heavily sponsored and needed to arrive for the Australian bicentenary. My response was that a matchstick can be broken into a hundred pieces and can be mended, but would it then possess any strength? The job on completion was so rough that I even asked Brian to sign a document that stated 'David Cook didn't do this'! He signed.

Major structural items had been smashed. I mended an aileron push/pull tube that had been snapped by inserting a piece of rusty iron rod (concrete reenforcing rod) into each side of the break and riveting it together. A six-inch nail was driven through the boom to secure the tailplane. I don't want to talk about hanger tubes to fibrelam or boom tube to broken front spar, but all the repairs were done at a frantic pace in the open, working for two whole days and a night. Mike Atkinson, with Brian as backup, helped me, to the roars of collective laughter at the wizardry of the bodged engineering.

I test-flew the Shadow down the main runway. I expected it to fly like a broken claw. At 90 mph close to the runway, I pulled up hard in a maximum positive 'g' manoeuvre, immediately pushing over and down for maximum negative 'g'. Not even completing a circuit, I landed and inspected and declared the Shadow 'airworthy'. Brian took off that morning, flying into a 30-knot wind, heading out over mountainous seas for Crete. It was raining hard. I thought how very brave to put oneself in that situation.

With his single-minded determination and after surviving several other incidents, Brian Milton succeeded, reaching Australia for their bicentenary – a great achievement.

Following the two flights to Australia by Eve Jackson and Brian Milton, flyers often chose the Shadow for long-distance flying. Amongst the notable flyers was the Indian businessman, V.P. Singhalia from Bombay, who flew from England to India. He was made an honorary Air Commodore by the Indian Air Force upon landing. V.P. gave me an inscribed gold watch bearing an image of his Shadow on the dial – one of only four made – which I still wear to this very day. Thanks V.P.

Andy Nightingale, an RAF fast jet pilot, flew coast-to-coast in the USA in his Shadow, ending his flight at Kittyhawk, where the Wright brothers first flew a heavier-than-air machine called an aeroplane.

Another huge project, well backed by personal finances, was the flight by James Edmonds from England to Bejing, China. This flight was a major achievement, for to pass through Russia and China with the authorities' permission was nigh impossible. The Shadow had certainly proved itself and earned the name 'The Long Distance Traveller'.

ALTITUDE RECORD

In early 1990 it was back to earth – or should I say a long way from it? The idea was to promote the factory Shadows and Streaks by attempting to gain an altitude record. If this could be achieved, then my design would become the only type in aviation history to obtain the big three – speed, distance and altitude – within its own category of course. This category states the AUW (All Up Weight) was not to exceed 300 kg (600 lb).

Altitude flying requires a distinct skill, as I found when studying many of the written records of flights. I had to my advantage, the skill of flying low-powered aircraft, having crossed the English Channel using only 9 hp on my powered VJ-23. A great deal of skill was needed to have only gained 300 feet after flying 27 miles!

At the limits of an aircraft's natural ceiling, the power left from the engine is almost exhausted and steady flight is difficult. The RAF definition of an aircraft's ceiling is when the climb rate is down to 100 feet per minute – that's 10 minutes for 1000 feet. I learnt that with determination and with a delicate touch, altitude can be increased above the ceiling to the point when you reach 'coffin corner'. At this height, the aircraft will fall – maybe for thousands of feet. You may recall in the film 'The Right Stuff', when Chuck Yeager says 'Oh God' and falls to earth in his F104 Starfighter at the top of his climb to 104,000 feet. Well, that was when he had reached 'coffin corner'. The falling aircraft could be in any position and will continue falling below its ceiling whilst descending. None of us knew how high a Shadow could climb, so it was going to be a very exciting project.

I spent a day at Boscombe Down research airfield to discover how I would respond in a decompression chamber. Normally, civilians have to pay a nominal £100, but I was slotted in with another aircrew military type.

'You don't have to pay, David,' the RAF medic kindly said. 'You are one of the few people who does things right.'

I was astonished, as I didn't realise anyone had heard of me outside our own little circle of aviation. When the decompression chamber indicated the equivalent height of 30,000 feet, I had to remove my oxygen mask and place varying shapes into their respective positions on a board. The intellect level required would not have confounded a four-year-old but the effects of reduced oxygen had me fighting with the last shape, unable to complete the task. Several times, the medic in the decompression chamber, who was still on oxygen, told me to stop and put on my mask. Finally, he had to do it for me as I was so determined to finish the task and, by then, I had very few brain cells functioning correctly to think or act! Afterwards, I remember the medic saying that the object of the exercise was not that of a test to be won but one of experience. Recovery was swift but I recall an indefinable taste within me of something totally unknown but one I would recognise again only too soon.

One of our esteemed customers from Scotland was businessman and friend Tom Palmer. He was very keen for his Shadow (#106) to be used for an altitude record attempt, as it would be good for his company's promotions. So a special 150-kg empty weight Shadow was built with this purpose in mind. This airframe was very similar to Bob Bridgland's World Cup winner of 1989, but trimmed in bright orange for visibility reasons. The powerplant had no altitude compensation device, so I fitted a smaller main jet in the carburettors and omitted the air filters. By doing this, the air/fuel mixture would be weaker in rarefied air conditions, which would normally cause an engine to run rich and lose power.

Initially, I decided to do a series of climbs with a view to bettering the UK record of 19,000 feet, held for many years by Bob Calvert. He had used an engine with an output of 75 hp – just about double the power of a Shadow. The second attempt would be in another category C1 a/o for aeroplanes, which would be done in our factory Streak Shadow. This would be to better the 25,940 feet attained by American R. Rowley in a Mitchell U2 ultralight and the third attempt would be with Tom's Shadow microlight upgraded to 'C' series.

Studying the oxygen requirements for the human body and the accompanying complexities of the varying systems available to deal with this problem at different altitudes, soon becomes a sobering experience. Above 20,000 feet, humans live for only a few minutes without taking extra oxygen. A 'constant flow' system, which I would use, is sufficient to approximately 25,000 feet; above that, conditions get serious and a 'demand' system is then necessary. I would have a gauge to show the total amount of oxygen available and a flow gauge to assure me that it was functioning correctly. If one is lacking oxygen it is not, as has been seen in the decompression chamber, that apparent to oneself. One has a feeling of well being, even confidence. But I had devised a simple way of checking on my condition – I would count (in my subconscious) to nine, both adding and subtracting. I intended to do this the whole time whilst altitude flying. It was a simple method and it worked. I deduced that as soon as I made an error I would need to check my oxygen flow.

A visit to Ipswich parachute club confirmed that most 'chutes will tear to shreds if deployed when falling from heights above 10,000 feet – only high-speed specialist 'chutes can be opened above that height because the speed of the fall is much increased due to the rarefied atmosphere. I borrowed an unused 150-knot parachute from a Shadow owner, Patrick Wilkinson. This 'chute was rated for a pilot weighing 254 lb. As I weighed 140 lb, I reasoned it would be good for 180-knot deployment.

I found out from USAF Bentwaters that permission from the CAA was required for everyone climbing above 24,500 feet in the UK. The CAA man in the General Aviation department was very helpful.

'We are the department that likes to say yes,' he said. Good – that makes a nice change, I thought. 'Permission though is only granted for weekends and Bank Holidays – April 1st to August 1st.' This time scale suited me fine.

During the attempt, Eastern Radar would cover me, keeping any airliners in the proximity at bay. With great affection, the fellows from Eastern Radar who sit all day in a darkened room staring at radar plots, keeping our skies safe, sent a small plaque, which they wanted me to take aloft so that it could then be inscribed for their wall to hang beside trophies commemorating other aviation achievements.

The day was 7 April. The weather was clear, all systems were serviceable, but with an annoying 25-knot wind at ground level, and I was going to attempt the UK national altitude record. An electronic barograph went under my jacket because it would stop reading at temperatures below minus 20 degrees. There was a lot of equipment as I did up my seat harness. I was wearing a high-tech suit, for warmth, given by Tom Palmer. I also had the backpack-type parachute, a life vest (due to our proximity to the North Sea), my bone dome with radio connected, and oxygen mask and oxygen bottle placed alongside me, positioned on the airframe. Many would have been overcome with claustrophobia when the canopy was closed and I did wonder how some people would have fared under these circumstances.

A number of people had previously telephoned or written to me at the factory, suggesting themselves for this record altitude attempt, claiming they could reach a height of 30,000 feet at the very least, having had no previous flying experience above 2000 feet. One caller even expected the factory to give him an aircraft because he claimed to have medical knowledge on altitude flying. I don't think people realised the knowledge that is needed before one can make a viable attempt at a flight such as this. Altitude flying is a whole art in itself and requires immense study of the chemical compositions of the varying layers of air and their associated effects on the human body and an aircraft's behaviour when attempting to gain altitude.

Not particularly liking heights much above 1000 feet, I was not going to be comfortable with these altitude attempts. This was being done purely to promote the Shadow for sales purposes and to get Tom a record with his Shadow.

Shadow #106 climbed away steadily and was soon past 10,000 feet. I climbed at 60 knots, remembering to deduct one knot every

1000 feet for the true airspeed. Thus at 10,000 feet, the airspeed read 50 knots. I noted the outside air temperature (OAT) was –10°C on the gauge; at 19,000 feet the OAT showed –28°C and we were still climbing but only at 350 feet per minute. The climb time was extending. Over 20,000 feet the cold began to bite even though I was in an enclosed cockpit. The sun felt quite warm to me, shining through the canopy but my feet and legs were cold.

The Shadow started to feel a bit wobbly at 22,000 feet then suddenly it dropped – it fell 'off the edge'. It was just like someone pulling a chair from beneath me – I was quite surprised but the Shadow behaved perfectly. Falling with wings levelled at 30 degrees nose down, I held full back on the stick with full power still on – airborne time was now 57 minutes. Gradually level flight was regained somewhat lower so I tried climbing again. The ascending rate was poor, but remarkably I discovered that by flying full speed without deliberately pointing the nose of the aircraft upwards, I could achieve a reasonable rise rate of 200 feet per minute. It seemed an eternity before I attained 23,621 feet above sea level, but it was in reality only 25 minutes. The flight had lasted 75 minutes in total and it was time to come down. I descended at 90 knots with the engine set at 3000 rpm to keep it warm in the cold conditions. Notes showed the exhaust gas temperature (EGT) was 1100°F and cylinder head temperature (CHT) 300°F at maximum altitude – 6000 rpm. At sea level these readings were of course much higher – EGT 1400°F and CHT 450°F, rpm 6600. All these figures showed how amazingly tolerant the Rotax engines were even without carburettor compensation mixture. I had not wanted to equip my aircraft especially for altitude. All the records held by Shadows were on standard production types that anyone could purchase. My rapid descent was normal until down to 3000 feet. Here, some warmth was apparent in the atmosphere again but the pressure increase was too great to maintain a descent of 2000 feet per minute. Swallowing continuously, I still had to decrease the descent because the pressure on my eardrums was intense and it felt like they were gong to burst. I landed without any problems but the ground crew were incredulous at the quarter-inch layer of frost on the oxygen bottle and the glazed ice over the extra fuel tank inside the rear cockpit. Lessons to learn, but the UK National Record had been achieved.

Being the best in the UK is a source of great personal pride but to be the best in the world entails beating everyone. It is another level altogether.

CFM's Streak Shadow was fitted out incorporating the oxygen system with only the air filters removed. I was sure that another adaption would be necessary. The Streak Shadow, categorised as an aeroplane – rather than microlight – would attempt a record in class C1-a/o for aeroplanes weighing less than 300 kg. Fully equipped and with less wing area than a Shadow microlight, I did wonder if the Streak would even reach the previous Shadow record. It did have a liquid-cooled Rotax 532 engine of 65 hp – 20 hp more than the previously used engine. The Streak had a very high-sustained climb rate. I felt confident that red #108 would burn through the attempted altitudes. My take-off, like the previous one, was to be 40 feet above sea level from the cricket/recreation ground at Thorpeness.

On 28 April the right conditions occurred and the world record attempt was begun. Almost immediately my radio failed to receive transmissions, despite the fact that it had worked faultlessly on the ground. Perhaps I had inadvertently knocked out a jack plug on my bone dome. I failed to solve the problem in the climb, though it later turned out that my transmissions were strength 3–4 until 18,000 feet, after which the ground crew could not hear my reports. However, the time for take-off had been cleared with Eastern Radar twenty-four hours before. No horrid little radio (which I hated anyway) was going to cause me to abort after all the weeks of preparation. There was quite a build up prior to attempting the world record. The barograph had to be hired – a specially certified type to trace the altitude and time of the flight. I used an electronic type that would nullify the trace if it were opened, to stop false recordings. 'Cheat proof' is the proper phrase.

Within 30 minutes I was at 20,000 feet, still climbing at 500 feet per minute. I changed the oxygen system from medium output to high flow, and checked the flow meter. The engine rpm was 6000, and the engine temperature read 40°C rather than 80°C. It was cold outside, −30°C in fact. The rate of climb steadily decreased after 23,000 feet and the usual frost formed on my canopy. I scraped at it with relief when I found that it was inside the cockpit and not outside, but it quickly re-formed. I assumed that it was my exhalation from the oxygen mask. I was able to see forwards and upwards but not too well on either side. The climb rate at 26,000 feet was only 150 feet per minute – not good. I had the sensation that the Streak was balanced on a large ball – liable if balance was lost to topple at any moment. My neck ached from the weight of headgear and the high angle of climb that I had been maintaining for the last hour and a half. Although this was around the height to claim a new record, the previous one had to be bettered by 3 per cent, which in this case was 26,718 feet.

The long wait for edging higher had now to be endured. I took a photograph of the dash panel instruments and one of the area below, where I lived, which was to my detriment as the Streak wobbled precariously from side to side and I chased the ailerons for a whilst before managing to steady the plane once more. This must have been way above my 'ceiling'. Checking every ten minutes or so I saw the amount of oxygen left in my cylinder was down to a third of its total capacity. I must not let it drop much lower – yet I was so close to the record. At a reading of 26,500 feet on my altimeter it seemed to take an endless amount of time just to gain another 100 feet.

Finally I decided to set a few minutes ahead on the clock and told myself then to descend. Otherwise, Cook, you would not be going to survive for another go. But I hated giving up at this point. It had been such a massive effort, let alone the suppressing of my fear of heights, and I hated the thought of disappointing my expectant friends waiting 5 miles below. I then tried some of the most delicate flying I had ever done. Different techniques such as lowering the flaps 15 degrees, then 30 degrees, but to no avail. There was no increase in the climb rate. I tried different angles and speeds – the ASI was now showing 40 mph so perhaps flat out and level would work as it did with #106. The Streak flat out and level only reached 50 mph – true airspeed 76 mph. The engine temperature gauge showed no reading. The air-cooled engine in #106 did better temperature-wise than this Rotax 532 with its liquid cooling. I needed radiator blanks to raise that temperature. The EGT was also low, implying I should have made smaller main jets to weaken and help the air/fuel ratio.

As I checked around the cockpit, I glanced at the clock and saw to my horror that it was two minutes past my deadline for descent. I must have been so close to my goal – maybe failing the record by only 100 feet. I had to descend. I was so cold there was almost no feeling in my legs and feet. I reduced the power to the engine – it had been at full bore for nearly two hours, but as I nosed the aircraft over to commence a dive, the engine immediately gave a great shudder and stopped. There was total silence. As I gazed out I could see I was higher than the airline contrails lying to the south. I quickly glanced over my shoulder to check the oxygen bottle and thought it was nearly empty. Well, one thing was for sure, I would certainly have the longest time for a pilot in a powered aeroplane to find a suitable place for a dead stick landing!

Getting the Streak to descend rapidly proved difficult. The pitch trim for the elevator was set for full climb when the engine stopped. So as it was electrically powered, it now had no power from the alternator to change its position. I could not dive steeply without using two hands on the stick to force it forwards. I wanted and needed to come down as quickly as possible, as I was only too aware that I had been above 25,000 feet for some time. Silently, I dived the plane vertically. The airspeed indicator indicated 120 mph, which I calculated was probably a true airspeed of 150 mph.

The effort of pushing with both hands on the stick must have used up all the remaining available flow of oxygen because suddenly I could not breathe. No one ever remembers their last breath – only the moment when the next one becomes impossible. My immediate thought was that the oxygen bottle must have run out and there was no oxygen outside. I was passing through 22,000 feet when my head started to swim. I felt very giddy – you've done it this time, Cook. You're in real trouble and before you pass out you'd better get out quick. Almost involuntarily my hand went for the canopy latches. A steady, cold appraisal of the necessary procedure (latches, radio connections, oxygen tube to disconnect, unfasten seat harness, then over the side) went through the last few brain cells that were functioning. It would be preferable to be unconscious hanging from a parachute, than inside the aircraft diving vertically at what was now a true airspeed of over 200 mph. As my hand reached for the canopy latches, I heard in my mind 'two and seven is nine'. Right, it seems that I was not finished yet, even though that horrid odour inside me had reoccurred. I began to gag for air, so I purposely decided to stop trying to breathe for a trial period of fifteen seconds. As I looked at the oxygen bladder in front of my chest, I saw it expand slightly – the oxygen was not exhausted as I had previously assumed. The altitude was reducing at a rapid rate, judging by the speed of the pointer on the altimeter. I ventured to sip a tiny breath of oxygen. By regulating these sips until the dizziness faded, I found that I could breathe very slowly and quietly.

By 15,000 feet, I was still dropping vertically and became aware that the tremendous noise behind me was not as I feared, the tailplane breaking up due to the speed, but the propeller rotating in the airstream. I decided I would try to reignite the engine as the ignition switch was still on, so I selected full choke. To my immense relief the engine burst into life but this had the effect of accelerating the Streak even more, so I then reduced the throttle as I careered downwards even faster. Cutting back the throttle caused the engine to stop yet again. It seemed I was going to have to make a dead stick landing within the very tight area of the cricket pitch.

On the ground, Brian Johnson, my boys and Catherine were watching and waiting in silence, as they had had no sight or sound of me for over two hours. The VHF radio had failed to transmit my calls. Jacob heard the Streak first as it was passing through 8000 feet. He said there was no engine noise but a sound of air being ripped apart, such was the speed of the descent. The canopy was still in place, so he knew I had not baled out, but there had been no response from their radio calls, which had given rise to great anxiety. Brian had noted that the engine was out and that the wind direction for my approach had changed, so he had quickly organised a small fire to be lit to enable me to see the direction of the smoke. I saw the smoke from 5000 feet. It was typical of him to perceive this situation and I really appreciated his foresight to thwart a potentially hazardous landing.

I brought in the Streak, dead-stick, into our 150-yard cricket pitch, missed the electric wires and hedges and banged it downwards onto the grass. Frantically, I tried to apply pressure on the brake pedals with my frozen feet and legs and I narrowly ground to a halt within 10 yards of the hedge. An unbelievable wave of exhaustion, elation and pure joy that I had survived swept over me. At this point I think I nearly collapsed because my two boys then tore off my bone dome helmet, oxygen mask, disconnected the parachute and lifted me out of the plane. I will never forget my appreciation of the beautiful warm grass as I lay there – it was so wonderful to still be alive.

Brian checked that the sealed barograph had been working correctly. It showed an altitude of 8250 metres (27,066 feet) – a record surely. We later learned that Australian Scott Winton in his own design had achieved 29,000 feet in the microlight category R1 but it had resulted in his death. The FAI based in Paris decided in their wisdom to combine both categories R1 and C1 a/o, consequently his flight claimed the record even though this was not actually so. The French are apt to act like this as in their forgiveness of a Crime of Passion. So I was deprived of my world record claim but the flight achieved its purpose and gained much recognition, and I had learnt the hard way just how difficult it was to attempt an altitude record.

Time to Climb

In May 1993, we decided to attempt a 'time to climb' record as our next publicity project and beneficially it would be an inexpensive venture to carry out, an important consideration for any CFM event. The FAI's 0–3000 metres (10,000 feet) record was currently held by two Frenchmen who achieved the climb in 27 minutes. The rules stipulated that the plane must be carrying two people, so I nominated my son Jacob to fly Shadow 02 with the CFM storeman David Foster (who was the lightest of all the employees) to be the passenger. To make the aircraft as light as possible, David Foster had nobly volunteered to fly naked but I thought this might not be too helpful if the plane was forced to make an emergency landing away from the airfield! An official observer was required by the FAI sporting code to witness the event but, as I already held a certificate for this position, this would not be a problem.

We fitted out 02 with the engine from our factory Streak Shadow, as this would give 64 hp rather than 40 hp. This complied with the FAI definition of a microlight although it was, at that time, in conflict with the current CAA regulations. It was not till later that permission was granted by the CAA to use a larger size engine on a microlight – our 'D' Series Shadow being a result of that decision. Trials had shown that extreme thermic conditions resulted in the quickest altitude gain, so the weather on the day would be a critical factor in the gaining of the record.

A warm, breezy day with plenty of potential thermic activity and a 'buoyant' atmosphere was chosen and Jacob and David Foster roared off in 02 from Thorpeness cricket pitch, the sealed barograph to show the time against altitude positioned safely in the cockpit. An excellent result of 11 minutes 2 seconds was recorded; less than half the time of the current record.

To our dismay, the FAI rejected the claim on the grounds that I, as the 'official observer', was related to the pilot. Quite how this fact could alter the sealed barograph reading was not made clear and the official world record remained in France with the two Frenchmen.

CHAPTER 4

Overseas

Zimbabwe – World Wide Fund for Nature

A local admirer of the Shadow was the ex-Liberal Party leader Jeremy Thorpe. He could foresee many possible uses for the aircraft in Africa and he eventually tied up a deal in 1987, combining the World Wildlife Fund (WWF) with the Goldfield's Trust as sponsor, to provide a Shadow for the Zimbabwe Anti-Poacher Squad (APS).

The President of the WWF was the Duke of Edinburgh, who, on completion of the aircraft, came to present the Shadow to the head of the WWF at our factory. I was very proud to have the 'King' coming to my factory in Leiston. The Duke met all my crew and I then flew a display, using the aircraft that was to go to Africa. Due to the importance of the occasion, I was suitably dressed with shirt and tie and for the first time ever, flew my display routine encased in the restrictions of smart clothes. It was a beautiful hot summer's day, but the combined factors of heat, pressure of a royal onlooker and dignitaries with non-flying clothes, resulted in my appearance being somewhat less smart on landing. As I was red in the face and perspiring heavily, the Duke questioned me about wearing a tie but then had to laugh when I told him I'd had to as the King was coming!

It was through the WWF-sponsored aircraft for Zimbabwe that I met Susanne Campbell Jones, a film producer who was making a film for the DTI illustrating the uses of microlights and their role in aviation worldwide. The film would then be available at British Embassies throughout the world.

Selsey Birdman Contest 1975.
Left to right in mid-air: David Cook, pilot, Robert Jelliff, Chris Tansley and Bob Kent.

Selsey Birdman Contest 1975.
Flying more than 50 metres.

VJ-23 gliding flight along the Suffolk coast.

VJ-23 foot-launched hang-glider flying in a 30 mph wind over 50 foot high cliffs at Minsmere in Suffolk.

VJ-23 in 1975 flying along the coast at Minsmere.

The British Open Hang-gliding Championship in 1976. The winner VJ-23 seen in a 45° banked turn.

VJ-23E in 1977 with a 9hp 123cc McCulloch 101 power plant.

Seen here in the early powered flights, VJ-23E with David Cook flying is launched with the assistance of Chris Tansley into 'Almost Flight' in 1977 with 50lb engine thrust.

Off to France in 1978. Brian Pattenden (left) and John Wells help David aloft from the beach between Walmer and Kingsdown in Kent.

After the crossing, David is seen here on Bleriot Plage in France in May 1978.

The original *Starship Enterprise*, as used in the TV series Startrek, seen here in 1958 with its creator Volmer Jensen on the right.

The amphibian homebuilt VJ-22 seen in Baja, California.

David flies Volmer's VJ-23E during 1978 in California.

Volmer Jensen – 'Genius'.

Tense moments seen here in 1980 before David's first flight in VJ-24W.

VJ-24W – California 1980 First Flight. Airborne with a passer by left,
Catherine Cook, Mick Jocelyn, John Underwood and Volmer taking photos.

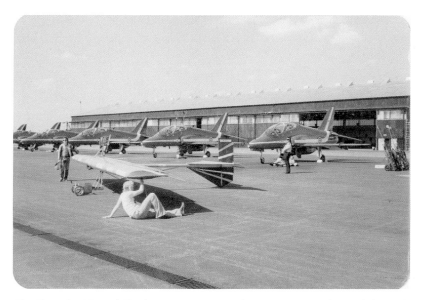

The First Act! David Cook, Harry Potter and VJ-23E wait in front of the Red Arrows at the start of the SBAC Farnborough Air Display in 1980.

A self-portrait of David flying VJ-24W over California in 1981.

MUSFLY seen under construction in Garretts' workshop in Leiston during 1979.

MUSFLY – the wing under construction for this man-powered aircraft.

'A'-Series Shadow in the sky in 1982.

The CFM Shadow 001 takes to the air with David Clarke flying at Flixton, Suffolk.

The CFM Shadow 001. Note the Fibrelam boom and shear web.

The first flight of the CFM Shadow 002 in 1983.

Jacob Cook in Shadow 002 when he gained his flying licence at the age of 17 in 1989.

The CFM Company works Streak Shadow on test over the North Sea in June 1988.

Streak Shadow #108 G-BONP shows an impressive climb rate and angle!

Ex-RN pilot Trevor Jones visits CFM to inspect his specially adapted Shadow during building.

Shadows in production at CFM's factory in Leiston.

David Cook being presented the Medal of Aviation Achievement by HRH Prince Charles in 1978.

The Duke of Edinburgh presents the 1987 British Design Award to the Shadow's designer, David Cook. Christopher Meynell (left) was the Executive Director of CFM.

David Cook and David Southwell were the outright winners of the 1986 Dawn to Dusk Competition. The trophies are the Duke of Edinburgh Award, the Precision Navigation Award and the Microlight Award.

HRH Prince Philip chats to David during a visit to the Leiston factory in 1987.

The presentation at the Royal Aero Club of the magnificent Segrave Trophy to Eve Jackson for her outstanding solo flight to Australia in 1988.

HRH the Duke of York presents the Dawn to Dusk Awards of 1986.

David's son Jacob helps his father prepare for an altitude record attempt in 1990.

The Streak Shadow at 26,000 feet. Note the airspeed 45 (71mph corrected), RPM 6,000, engine coolant temperature 0° and a climb rate of 200 feet per minute.

David poses with the works demonstrator G-BONP on Thorpness Beach.

Shadow at sunset – a very safe aircraft.

The President of the World Wildlife Fund, HRH The Duke of Edinburgh, hands over a Shadow for work with the anti-poacher squad for black rhino in Zimbabwe.

Zimbabwe – the Shadow being inspected by the locals.

Glen Tatum – head of the anti-poacher squad.

A day off for David and friend Saffron Cambell-Jones at the Victoria Falls.

David with his pal 'Special' at Charles Prince Airport near Harare.

Tim Hardwick-Smith's Shadow flies over his farm in New Zealand.

Dr. Ian Ferguson's Shadow at Yabba Point, Australia in 1988.

Using the road as a runway in Australia.

Laron Streak Shadow at 'Sun 'n Fun' in Florida in 1991.

Shadowlite aircraft line up at Cato Ridge in South Africa in 1991.

A Shadow flies against a Durban backdrop.

David with friends at Cato Ridge, Natal.

Checking a new-build Shadow D Series at Wellington, Cape Province, South Africa.

Filming during Slipstream in Turkey.

David and Bill Paxton in Turkey

Filming in Turkey in 1988. The replica stunt model in the foreground.

Shadow 02 with MIRLS (Mini Infra Red Line Scan) pod, Courtesy British Aerospace Air Weapons Division.

Sea Shadow – in Paradise – the Philippines.

Filming 'Dragonheart' in Slovakia in 1994.

Aerial filming work on location in Slovakia.

The actor Dennis Quaid tries out the cockpit whilst filming in Slovakia. Note the multi-positional camera mounting.

The experimental tailless model for the CFM Image.

The CFM Image prototype at speed.

The Image shows its plan form.

The Image looking somewhat formidable as it taxies to the take-off point in 1994.

The Image's rate of turn was outstanding.

Image – an outstanding sight in the sky.

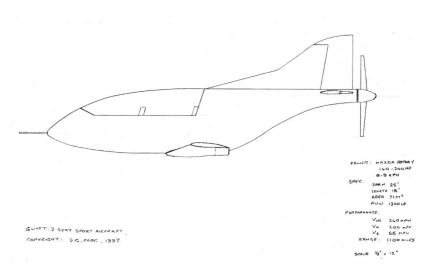

POWER: MAZDA ROTARY
160 - 200 HP
8 - 9 G PH

SPEC:
SPAN 25'
LENGTH 18'
AREA 71 FT²
AUW 1300 LB

PERFORMANCE:
V_{NE} 260 MPH
V_C 200 MPH
V_S 55 MPH
RANGE: 1100 MILES

GLINT: 2 SEAT SPORT AIRCRAFT.
COPYRIGHT: D.G. COOK. 1997.

SCALE ½" = 12"

Glint – a design proposal of 1997.

Glint – a computer generated picture.

A self-portrait of David Cook flying a 60° bank turn in France.

Captain Cook! Engineer, designer and aviator.

Susanne and her daughter Saffron came out to Zimbabwe with me to document the work of the APS for the protection of the black rhino. The Shadow was to be used for aerial spotting surveillance missions and for counting elephants. I was surprised that there only seemed to be eight people on the APS, which was led by Glen Tatum. But it was impressive to see the dedication of these people; they were not paid well and were up against poachers who would willingly kill them for the price of a rhino horn. Armed with military rifles, the poachers were a very dangerous threat to the APS. With the Shadow standing by at Charles Prince Airport, I briefed Glen Tatum, demonstrating to him the plane's capabilities so that he could handle the aircraft when I had gone back to England.

We did some local filming for Susanne's film and I was introduced to my Zimbabwean 'minder'. We Europeans have to be 'minded' in Africa and steered away from hazards.

When we were introduced he said, 'Hello Captain, I am Special.'

'So am I, mate,' I quickly replied.

'No. No. Captain, my name is Mr Special.'

Well, he was a smashing fellow, skin as black as ink and a bit older than me. He was tremendously polite, forever hovering nearby, usually out of earshot, but always being available to help when needed. I liked him very much.

After a few days' of work, Susanne, Saffron and I had a weekend at Victoria Falls, staying in the wonderful Victoria Hotel. I thought the Falls were the greatest thing I had ever seen – one could hide the Niagara Falls in one corner and not even see them. These falls were 3 km long and the depth! No wonder the natives call it 'the Smoke that Thunders'.

Whilst flying at Charles Prince Airport, I experienced a terrifying incident, which demonstrated the completely uncontrollable, unpredictability of nature. I was checking out the Shadow on a local familiarisation flight not too far away from the airfield and keeping my eye on its location, when I received a radio transmission informing me of an international flight due in 15 minutes. 'OK, I'll be overhead in 5 or 6 minutes,' I replied. In any case, there was a huge, ominous cumulonimbus cloud only a few miles away, which was ascending at a frightening rate. It must have been rising to 50,000 feet. The cloud had U-turn warnings written all over it and I responded rapidly. But as I flew back, it suddenly occurred to me that this nimbo cell was very much closer than it had been and I found myself flying with over 100 mph on the clock. The sky was becoming increasingly menacing and the edges of the cloud were enveloping me on both sides. It seemed unbelievable, but this thing seemed to be chasing me. I frantically lined up the aircraft, landed and taxied into position, even omitting to call the tower in my desperation to land as quickly as possible to avoid the inevitable onslaught. As I struggled to tie down the plane, the blackened sky unleashed steel-like shafts of rain that struck the ground with the ferocity of a tidal wave. Thank God, we don't get rain like this in England.

The APS then redeployed to Mana Pools, where the Shadow and Glen's helicopter, a Bell 47, set up near the huge Zambezi River. There were eight of us – two whites and six natives. We had a beer-up on the first camp night, with two fellows banging out a rhythm on tub-sized drums. I started counting the repeat rhythms and got lost after ten. These guys were the equivalent of that fellow on a banjo in the 'Deliverance' film. After two hours of increasing violence on their drums, I felt as though a great deal of my civilisation had departed. I could see how easily this music could prepare one to enter battle without fear. To calm myself, I managed to slip away from Mr Special and wandered the beautiful river-bank in the African twilight. By now I knew enough to know that this period of the day was devoid of day or night animals travelling to or from the river. I returned an hour or so later to much consternation in the camp.

'Where have you been?' questioned Special, distraught at having lost me.

'Oh, just a couple of Ks up the riverbank and back,' I said.

For some reason this reply caused a scene of very uncontrollable laughter and amusement. Eventually Glen told me that I'd just walked through a minefield that was laid during the war by the Smith Regime to prevent their enemy from Zambia crossing the Zambezi! As they say, 'ignorance is bliss'.

The next morning three of us patrolled close to the shore looking for the possible footprints of poachers from Zambia. The bright red flashy Fisher speedboat looked totally incongruous in these surroundings. This was a pleasure riverboat intended for 'yuppies', but had been given by some kind-hearted donor to aid the anti-poaching cause. As we trolled along at 5 knots, the peace was shattered as a huge hippo erupted from the water just aft of the boat. Its head must have been 3 feet in diameter and it was heading straight at us. The Fisher roared to 25 knots for 300 yards or so and resumed its course, whilst we searched for signs of human activity. Within seconds the hippo repeated the same explosive leap from the water as before, only this time it was a mere 20 yards behind us. We abandoned our search with great speed. I was told hippos are the most dangerous animal in Africa and having witnessed this potentially life-threatening scene – I agreed. I was terrified.

That evening, one of the boys came running in, having found a cache of two rhino horns and a pair of elephant tusks hidden 4 km away. Two of the APS immediately left to wait for the return of the poachers. These guys are meant to apprehend them, but usually the poachers are shot 'running away'. After one has seen a mother rhino with her baby killed just for its horn, then one easily understands the treatment of the APS towards those who wish harm to these animals. European values don't apply in Africa, as I quickly learnt. In a village that seemed similar to a Stone Age settlement, I was rebuked by the head of the APS for being too friendly with the native children. The children had seen my interest in a tiny deer, which ran off into the savannah. Within an hour, the children had captured the poor creature and brought it to show me, having snapped all four legs so that it was unable to escape. I was horrified and despaired; this tiny defenceless deer was only about 15 inches long and nearly dead. The APS guy mercifully quickly killed it.

I've never quite figured out why the Chinese need these Rhino horns to be ground up into supposed aphrodisiacs. Next morning at first light, one of the APS who had been sent to the cache came rushing into the camp. The cache was gone. It had been removed very cunningly by the poachers, even though the two anti-poacher lads had the scene staked out. All hell broke loose in our camp as the Bell 47 helicopter and Shadow fired-up, simultaneously an army Puma helicopter arrived. Mug Abe (spells 'E-ba-Gum' backwards) had sent this gunship in to show his concern for the WWF and the DTI film unit, but the DTI film unit with Susanne Campbell Jones had left Zimbabwe before the APS and myself went to Mana Pools. Quickly the Bell 47 and Shadow set about the search for these poachers. We flew very low over savannah-type bush, which was interspersed with patches of jungle. The other chap who was at the stakeout, called us to the area. Suddenly, we saw them – three fellows running across open ground, holding the cache.

'Climb David, climb – they're about to shoot at you!' shouted Glen over the radio.

As I climbed steeply, the Puma gunship swept in and released 20-mm Oerlikon cannon. Suddenly the Shadow and I were in the middle of a gun battle. Even with the engine racket in the Shadow and wearing headphones, I could hear the thump of the guns firing. It wasn't long before two of the poachers were killed, blown to pieces no bigger than a dinner plate. The third poacher escaped. Real life was not like a Hollywood movie.

It was extremely hot that day (near 50°C), stifling in fact, with even the Land Rover struggling in the conditions. My Rotax engine, after all the excitement, slowly lost power and stopped. I remember looking at my altimeter, which read 1800 feet AGL, whilst searching for a landing place. Boulders and rocks were strewn below – best aim for the Zambezi I thought and asked the Bell 47 to follow as I glided down and reached the river. There were sandbanks (quite substantial) here and there on the Zambezi, with bushes and scrub, so I could make a successful landing.

'Don't get out, just sit still,' Glen called over the radio.

It seemed a very long time before he landed beside me; meanwhile I sat there in a high state of anxiety thinking a hippo or some other equally ferocious animal was about to run right through the Shadow at any moment.

The whole camp moved to a sandbank that night. The blackness of the night was all enveloping – an impenetrable world of darkness. I did not like it. We lay in the open on blankets and the thought of sleeping seemed far from my mind that night! What if the river rose up and swept us all away? Special was in a dugout canoe pulled onto the sandbank 50 yards away, when I heard him shouting. All of a sudden, a lioness appeared and raced past us. The white guy lying next to me calmly observed, 'Look, she's got a wet skin suit in her jaws – I bet that's the worst black man she's ever tasted!' It all seemed a long way from Aldringham at the time and, shortly afterwards, I thankfully left Africa to return home.

Europe

I took the Shadow in its trailer to a week-long Aero Exhibition in Friedrichshafen, Germany. It had four days' of static display amongst all the other aircraft from Europe. Gliders, sporting types and microlights (ULMs) crammed huge halls – it was a splendid affair. The Germans had also invited other British microlights so several of our country's manufacturers were in attendance. The final two days were to be a Rally in which various countries were to take part.

An Australian microlight flyer, Carl Booth, had a dental practice in Germany and he organised many of us, accommodating the British and French teams in his house. The French team grabbed the upper levels of the house, leaving the basement to the British. No one minded.

Being a German event, everything was well organised, each team member having been given a young *fraulein* to sort out any possible problems. These young ladies were volunteers who wished to improve their English. My PR *fraulein*, 'Elvi' procured a pile of deutschmarks for me as I had used all my German currency actually getting to the show and the Germans didn't appear to accept Visa cards.

The British team for the Rally looked strong with Graham Slater and Malcolm McBride, Ian Stokes and me. We transferred to the airfield at Friedrichshafen, where we were briefed on the flying tasks we were to perform. For me, it turned out to be two hazardous days of competition and by the end of the final task I felt I had endured at least five close calls endangering my well-being. The following incident demonstrates the point. After flying various routes and photographing landmarks, I arrived over a marked-out area surrounded by forest to try and spot land in a designated rectangular area. Double points were to be awarded if the engine was stopped overhead at 1000 feet. The problem was that there was no windsock to show which direction one should approach the specified area. As the Shadow completed the tasks quicker than the other ULMs, I was the first to arrive. The Shadow hit the box and McBride, overhead, said it almost disappeared in spray on the wet grass. I only just halted in front of a very large, deep ditch. Immediately, a windsock was erected and all the other pilots came in from the other direction – I had landed downwind.

Someone later told me that the ground crew organisers had said, 'The Shadow has landed – let up the windsock.'

'These people are trying to stuff me,' I thought. And so it went on during that day.

I was on track for the next course with all the British team lined up behind me – I am sure all of them were better at navigating than me, but I was being very cautious, as we were right next to the East German border. The French world champion in microlights, Bernard Othrept, had obviously seen our team formating and thought he would do his best to provoke the British. Suddenly he dived from behind me, I only saw his aircraft as it passed underneath the Shadow going very fast, missing me by a few feet. His actions succeeded and gave me such a fright that I miscalculated my navigation for the remainder of the course. Through this reckless piece of flying, we all arrived late for our stated landing times, causing many points to be lost. Later, still steaming from this poor bit of gamesmanship, I saw Bernard in the crew room and grabbed him by his throat.

'Bernard, air law states that when overtaking in the air, you overtake on the right – not beneath or overhead!'

He could see that possible damage to himself was imminent and backed off completely by saying, 'Yes David, that is quite correct.' I had to let it rest with that apology.

Malcolm McBride and myself flew the final task together as his little aircraft was able to keep pace with my Shadow. We had 50 km to fly and had to land precisely at the time that we had predicted to the organisers prior to take-off. I watched my stop-watch very carefully, as Friedrichshafen came into view. There was a designated route and area for the rally aircraft to land as it was a Saturday and a full-blooded air show for the public was taking place. I approached at my determined time; spot on, flying flat out to ensure precision. I couldn't believe my eyes – a Messerschmitt 109 was flying next to the crowd line over our alloted piece of airfield, very low and straight at me at 400 mph. I flew on course lower and lower – the wheels of the Shadow even skimmed the grass once and he still kept coming. We just missed by inches – I'm convinced he didn't see me. This was the final straw. I'd had enough of flying in Germany and was thankful the Rally had finished. I took the incident up with the German air traffic controllers in the tower, but they were unconcerned about the whole affair. I informed them that in England, the pilot of the Messerschmitt would have been jailed. The final stab in the back came when I was placed fifteenth overall in the rally. Fifteenth! I was aware that my timings were off due to the French idiot, but figured on at least third place. Carl Booth told me to calm down and have another beer!

I drove through Switzerland from the Aero 87 to Italy, to our agent near Alessandrea at Mezzana Bigli, with CFM's faithful Peugeot 305 pulling the Shadow in its trailer over the Alps. I took an overnight stop just before Milan, at a small hotel just off the main *autostrata*. The hotelier enquired as to the contents of my trailer and, on hearing about the plane, warned me that there were people around who whisked away vehicles of interest in the night. I suppose the car trailer and Shadow were worth about £35,000 – a considerable investment in those days to be responsible for, travelling alone through Europe. The hotelier said they'd had a customer with a new Porsche who was concerned about its security outside their hotel, so the hotel management had arranged for the car to be parked overnight surrounded by many other vehicles. The following morning, none of the cars were touched, but in the middle of the area where the Porsche had been, there was just an empty space! I was glad to get to our agent the following day with everything still intact.

After a couple of days' work checking out pilots at the agent's flying centre, the agent and I left for the north-east part of Italy to Bassano and Monte Grappa, high in the foothills of the Alps. An International Competition meet had been arranged here with twenty-two manufacturers from all over Europe taking part. The Italian competition organisers, unlike the German organisers, were totally honest, being precise and accurate in their recordings, decisions and judgements.

We had to do timed runs with photography of landmarks as far away as Venice. During one leg of the flight, I suffered a migraine in the air, with fifteen minutes' of very impaired vision. It was frightening not to be able to see properly, especially over totally foreign unknown territory, but I happened to see a delta-shaped shadow on the ground going in my direction and this I steadfastly followed for several miles without ever actually seeing the microlight! This trike microlight saved me from straying from my track and led me to the landmark that had to be photographed. One had to be back at the point of take-off at the time one had stated prior to departure, or marks would be deducted accordingly, but I managed to land within two seconds of my calculated time, which placed me at the head of the listings.

The last task was the flight back to Bassano, where one had to land as near as possible beyond a positioned tape finish line. If the wheels touched the ground before the line, the whole day's points score would be annulled. After stopping beyond the line, the distance was measured back to the tape line. I approached the line in a powered descent, with full flap, and nose high, with the brakes already on. My distance after stopping was less than 10 metres. That's how to do a controlled crash! The Shadow was fine and I was in first place.

Our agent withdrew me from the second day's flying to enable the plane to be displayed for promotion purposes. I was happy to comply with this decision, for the previous day's flying had been sufficiently stressful. But I had enjoyed the Italian competition. It had been so very different from the one I had just attended in Germany.

Fiona Luckhurst, an experienced pilot, loved the Shadow design. She wanted to open a flying school and was building 027 with Peter Troy Davies, to operate as a trainer. As she spoke fluent French, we criss-crossed Europe together in the late 1980s, setting up agents in Denmark, Holland, Belgium and France. We always drove towing the Shadow in its trailer, which demonstrated to the best advantage the plane's mobility and ten-minute rig-up time and equally its ease and speed for disassembly. For example, once on the Isle of Man, a chap wanted to bet me that it would take longer than ten minutes to de-rig the aircraft and put it in the trailer. I told him I'd give him a pound coin for every second that Pat White and I took over the time. At six minutes we closed the trailer door with the Shadow inside. As he had to pay us a pound for every second under ten minutes, he was not surprisingly nowhere to be seen!

ANTIPODES

Dr Ian Ferguson, a world-rated surgeon from Australia, became the agent for our company in Victoria state. He was having difficulties obtaining certification for his UK-approved microlight with the Australian airworthiness authorities based in Melbourne. Consequently, I planned a trip to the southern hemisphere, which would combine a visit to him and Tim Hardwick-Smith in New Zealand. Tim was building his own Shadow and was acting agent for CFM in New Zealand since his return from England, so it would be good to see how he was progressing prior to going to Australia.

New Zealand was the most lovely place I had ever visited. Tim's parents owned a farm and nearly 12,000 sheep in North Island. I visited them for a few days prior to meeting up with Tim in South Island where he was now working as shepherd, having given up all thoughts of engineering. During my stay with them, I had the joy of horse riding and power boating on the river that bordered their estate, the circumference of which was 32 miles and encompassed a part of the beautiful countryside called Taranaki – King Country: a landscape of rolling hills and valleys.

The Kiwis were very proud of having invented the inboard/outboard motorboat device. The motor drives a pump, which delivers a high-speed water jet. This replaces the need for a propeller, which could be damaged when using the boat in shallow water. Tim's parents, Ralf and Janet, tested me regularly with challenges such as how to open gates of great complexity that secured the stock on their estate and questioning me on how many sheep were in a paddock. '1200,' I would say (always give an answer). '3600 mate!' would come back the reply. The snow-capped Mt Egmont was 10 or so miles from the farm. Tim had told me in letters, how he had taken off in his Shadow from the farm and flown straight at the 10,000-foot peak and without turning had flown right over the top, so different from when he had climbed the mountain as a boy with his father and to reach the peak had taken all day.

During my stay, I visited Napier to see an old friend, Terry Aspinall, who had emigrated two years previously. He appeared just the same and hadn't lost his quirky sense of humour. Fooling around in a pub whilst we were having a drink, he challenged a Maori sitting nearby, that he could still see him even if he (Terry) wasn't facing him. The Maori readily took up the challenge and both of them laid $20 on the table. Terry immediately leapt onto the table (I must admit to some slight apprehension at this point!) and with his back to the Maori, pulled down his trousers, where-upon a huge eye was revealed tattooed on his bottom. Quickly replacing his trousers, he jumped down and triumphantly grabbed the money. 'Next few rounds for nothing,' he laughed, holding up his winnings.

Terry and his wife, Emily, drove me to Wellington, where I was to catch my flight to Christchurch, South Island. It was hard parting with such friends.

Tim met me at Christchurch and we then drove for hours to the sheep and cattle station where he worked as a shepherd. There were only three buildings on the estate, the big owner's house and two small cottages. Tim resided in one and Railene, the girl who attended the horse stud, in the other. 'Is she nice?' I asked. 'Only say hello now and then,' replied Tim, who was so reserved in his nature that I was accused by him of being an 'unconscious flirt' because she and I once passed greetings and the time of day. One lived a very solitary existence out here. During the hours of driving from Christchurch, I had counted only five passing cars. Recounting my geography knowledge, I did remind myself that although New Zealand is about the same size as Britain, it only has the population equivalent of Birmingham, 3.5 million.

Whilst helping Tim with his duties as a shepherd I rode a trials-type motorcycle. Tim rode in front on a similar motorcycle with his dog sitting behind on the pillion! We headed for the 2000-foot mountains, where we were to herd the bullocks back to their paddock. As we approached, we could see the bulls already descending the slopes, bellowing loudly and fiercely protesting against their enforced stay amongst the cows, which they had endured for weeks. Having done their duties servicing the cows, they were fed up and definitely wished to be back with their mates – just like us when we meet at the pub, I thought!

I enjoyed the freedom of the motorbikes and rounding up these bulls. Tim said that people who herded like this were called 'kerosene cowboys'.

Before leaving my good friends in New Zealand, I had to visit the science museum in Christchurch, to see the now extinct, giant, flightless moa bird. These were incredible birds, at least 12 feet in height and with legs the diameter of small tree trunks.

From Christchurch I then flew to Melbourne, Australia, crossing the Southern Alps and Mt Cook on the way.

Dennis Brett, one of the CFM 'Godfathers', had accompanied me on the journey to New Zealand. He had visited his brother north of Auckland and now joined me to meet Dr Ian Ferguson in 'Aussieland'.

We transferred straight from the airliner into Ian's SIAI-Marchetti SF260 personal aircraft and flew to his base at Yabba North, an hour's flight. Ian and his wife, Juliet, had a farm station, which provided him with an airfield and hangar to house his microlights. He told me he had informed the airworthiness people in Melbourne that I was arriving from England to help overcome any problems that they found in approving the Shadow – Victoria state, apparently, had never given approval to a microlight. The authorities declined to see me! However, within two weeks of returning to England, I did learn that the Shadow had finally passed certification in Australia.

Ian took us to a glider airfield in his 1930s Bentley and I accomplished my first air-tow with an instructor. We didn't mention that I'd flown before, which was just as well as to all observers of the flight, I reckon it looked like I hadn't! The rudder on the glider whilst under tow, had to be pushed all the way hard left, immediately followed by the opposite rudder, in order to remain in the correct towing position. All this combined with its adverse yaw (that is, the nose of the aircraft tries to go in the opposite direction), had me thinking what awful things gliders were! I had to work really hard to keep in position behind the tow plane and was very relieved when I was cast off at 2000 feet. Released at last, the glider came into its own, serene and controllable, and a very enjoyable flight was completed with the main wheel touching down precisely on the small tarmac strip, which was set in the grass airfield. 'You've flown before,' came the caustic comment from the instructor.

On one of my days at the farm in Yabba North, Ian arranged an open day fly-in party for all his aviation friends. Australian pilots or 'bush' pilots are good. They need to be, flying is often the only viable form of transport and they quickly became hardened with the experience of having to cope with harsh terrain. I was astonished to see aircraft arriving from all directions, often at very low level and some even inverted!

Ian told the assembled crowd that due to the presence of the Great Captain Cook, I would be giving the air display highlight of the day; a statement that filled me somewhat with apprehension. I felt a little less than adequate in front of all these seasoned bush pilots, especially as a Shadow B Series is not exactly 'heavy-metal'. I had to impress, only with approval from these pilots would I gain acceptance. To my good fortune, a nasty fortuitous wind approached Yabba North, just prior to the arrival of a sandstorm. This was to be my opportunity and because of the velocity of the wind, I flew backwards past the gathered crowd standing in front of the hangar. Upon landing, they all grabbed the Shadow and bundled it into the hangar as the sandstorm increased its velocity. To my relief, the display had fulfilled the necessary requirements for their approval!

Later as the weather calmed, a pilot called 'Bill' took passengers up in his Chipmunk aircraft called *Bill's Beauty*. By the greenish hue of the returning passengers' faces, these were obviously not standard straight and level flights to observe the beauty of the local countryside. I only took on the offer to fly with Bill, with the provision that the rear cockpit control stick was reattached – it had been removed to make more room for previous passengers.

'Scared I might die in the air, are you?' crowed Bill.

'Too true,' I thought to myself, observing that Bill was by no means in the prime of youth.

We cavorted all over the sky and at one point as a vertical dive was taking place, I enquired whether he was flying or was it meant to be me? I assumed that he had been.

His reply came, 'You are. Aren't cha mate?'

There appeared to be just enough room to pull out before impact with the ground and I hauled the stick back.

'Struth – you'll pull the wings off,' Bill grunted as we levelled off just in time, thankfully surviving the ordeal, and received the customary cheer from the party. Looking as green I'm sure as all his other passengers, I climbed out of the Chipmunk.

Ian had two wire and rag microlights called BI-RDs (birds I suppose). It was fun flying Dennis Brett around the farm in the two-seater at 30 mph, chasing kangaroos. The other BI-RD was the single-seat model, which I presumed was the 'fighter' version.

Dr Ian Ferguson often received emergency calls for help. To respond to these emergencies, he would fly his SIAI-Marchetti aircraft to wherever he was required. I accompanied him on several of these visits – the Macchi was a superb sport aircraft and we used to bowl along doing aileron rolls when returning from Ian's duties.

On one such call-out at Point Cook, I waited in a rough-looking pub whilst the Ian performed his surgery. Only one Australian was at the far end of the bar and he obviously heard me talking to the barman.

'You're a flaming POM (Prisoner of Her Majesty), aren't cha?'

'Yes.'

'Well, what do you think of the beer?'

'Tastes like piss,' I answered.

'Good on yer mate, let me buy you another.'

I imagine a cultured English reply might not have had such a friendly response! I liked Australians – they are right that most English are 'whingeing bloody poms' and I found that returning their banter, like for like, was the key to acceptance everywhere. An amusing revelation at a 'posh' party in Melbourne, was that I was considered a 'cultured Australian' (is there such an animal?) due to my East Anglian accent. Many of the first immigrants to the Antipodes were from East Anglia, my home, hence the confusion. This was far from the first time when I had been mistaken for being of Australian origin. Customers contacting CFM regularly made the same point.

YEMEN

In this period of the late 1980s, the United Nations was backing a project concerning Yemen's water resources. The work was being undertaken by a team of Dutch scientists and these people took one of the first Shadows to Yemen in their own designed trailer. The aircraft was fitted with a large Hasselblad camera, which was situated in the floor of the rear cockpit, the camera being vertically positioned to fit downwards. This type of camera enhanced areas previously scanned by satellite to show images of underground water sources. The aircraft/trailer had arrived in Hodeidah on the coast of the Red Sea in 1984, but was immediately impounded by the Yemen authorities for over four years and it wasn't until 1988 therefore, that I visited to check out the aircraft and brief pilots on how to handle a Shadow. It takes some believing to understand why a project that is funded with no cost to that country is treated in this manner. After all, it is an assistance programme to help the people in general.

By the time I arrived, the Dutch had almost completed their involvement in the project. What with flight delays in France, a hijacking attempt at Lanaka, Cyprus, and arriving for a transit flight from Sana in the very early hours of the morning, I arrived at the compound outside Hodeidah several days later than planned.

The aircraft was in a sorry state. It had 'cooked' in its trailer over the four-year period of waiting, whilst standing out on an airfield in blistering heat, and drastic servicing was needed to bring the Shadow to an airworthy state. The braking system on this early production aircraft 04 used hydraulics for the disc brakes and all the fluid had turned into grease. The system had to be purged and replenished. I attached a pneumatic line to the pipelines from the airfield fire engine, which forced the grease out of the system. It emerged resembling a huge 10-foot worm, as the lines cleared from the air pressure!

There were acute language difficulties as no one spoke English and I not a word of Yemi. Wherever I went, I was accompanied by a crowd of uniformed Palestinians – armed to the teeth – who, on the whole, seemed very unhelpful to the local people. This airfield was basically a military site that allowed small civilian commuter airliners to land once a week. Security was very tight and the occasional full alert would cause all the airfield defences to be made active. I was warned that an Israeli raid was possible at any time. To my great relief, the air traffic controller spoke fluent English. He briefed me for the test flight and subsequent check-outs of Yemen pilots. I was on no account to look at any military aircraft at the base, nor was I to count them whilst flying. One assumes that when spoken to in English, that the person also possesses a sense of English – not so.

Somewhat amused, I answered 'You mean those eight Tupolov Tu28 bombers and all the MiG21s over there?'

'Yes – you are not to look at them!'

These people certainly took a lot of understanding.

The flight checked out after the controller insisted I backtracked almost 2 miles to the far end of the runway. I wondered if there would be any of the tyres left on the main wheels after travelling that distance in 45°C temperature. The take-off was 60 yards and showed the controller the foolishness of his control. 04 had flight controls only in the front cockpit, so I was damned if I was going to check out someone who had control. If he got into flight difficulties, I would be unable to do anything about the situation. So I sent the first guy off on his flight solo. He had flown DASH7 aircraft, so he was able to sort it all out and train himself.

After a couple of days' work with these people, the driver returned me to the UN compound, only for me to find that it was totally deserted. All the personnel had departed. My enquiries discovered that after three years, the project was either abandoned or finished. My local driver kindly took me to his home for a meal, where I was confronted with what looked like a goat's eye on a tin plate, garnished with a bit of fur on the side. I can recommend it as a good deterrent to hunger!

After returning to the deserted bachelors' quarters at the compound, the driver confirmed that I was now the only person there and the only flight out from Hodeidah was scheduled in three day's time. He parked our Toyota Land Cruiser, contract completed, and bade me farewell. And there I was, abandoned! There was no one to communicate with and no food.

Over the next three days, I survived on bottled water left in the fridge. It didn't bother me unduly; I've never been interested in food that much anyway. But the big worry was that the site had been broken into and was systematically being stripped by bandits (my interpretation of the intruders). The twenty UN Land Cruisers disappeared during the first night – then the apartments and chalets were emptied of contents; even the air conditioning units on the roofs were removed. I made as much noise as possible in my chalet with a radio on at full blast and the air conditioner droning away, but the thieving was working its way ever nearer. Mercifully, the third day appeared before they did and at 03:30 that morning, in total darkness, I trudged out into the desert for the 8-mile walk to the airfield, its welcoming lights on the horizon being my only guide.

The desert was nearly knee deep in discarded plastic water bottles for the first half mile (an image that doesn't immediately spring to mind when envisaging a desert), then numerous tracks led me on towards Hodeidah; a track was used until wrecked, then a new one formed alongside. I reached the airfield after two hours' hard walking. I was determined to get there before the sun became too hot, which would have made the walk unbearable. After having to pay at the airport before I was allowed to leave, I finally departed Yemen praying that I would never ever have to return.

SHADOW MEETS

A Shadow 'meet' would occasionally be arranged by the Shadow Owners' Club and we would have a mass fly-in. Jacob and I would fly in 02 and 108 to a centrally placed location in Essex or Hertfordshire. There was always great excitement amongst the first arrivals to see how many Shadows would attend and sometimes the numbers amounted to forty aircraft. We were a mixed collection of people but we all possessed at least one thing in common, which was of course our Shadow aircraft.

Our European dealer was the Belgian company Euro Shadow, which was operated by Mr Proost and his son Raymond and Pierre Rogiste, the flying instructor. Every summer they used to invite the Shadow Owners' Club to visit them at Moorsele and always received us with a wonderful display of hospitality.

We would all assemble at Headcorn airfield in Kent in order to book out a flight plan to Europe. A mass formation would then fly over the English Channel via France to Belgium. Proper aviators like David Gore, in his Streak, would head the formation using his GPS and radio. I was only too happy following in the rear. Listening to the French ground controllers express surprise (or was it shock?) with their 'Say again?' as the communication told of over thirty Shadows entering foreign airspace, always raised a smile. Once over rural France, people would be waving and jumping up and down at the sight of so many of us. Our formation sometimes streamed out for 2 miles.

One year, the designated day of the meet dawned blanketed with fog accompanied by a heavy drizzle. Consequently, we were late starting from Headcorn, as we waited until the conditions improved slightly. Our formation was much tighter, so that the aircraft ahead could be seen. Mr Proost told me later how he and

Pierre Rogiste had stood dejectedly on the Moorsele airfield, sadly surveying the impossible weather conditions with everything arranged for our arrival, when suddenly, somewhere in the distant gloom they could hear the Shadow formation approaching. Within minutes, he said, it seemed that hundreds of Shadows appeared out of the very low cloud above the airfield. In line, one after the other, they touched down and were warmly welcomed by Mr Proost and Pierre said they cried like children at the unexpected sight of so many Shadows.

One of our formation misjudging his spacing, wildly careered alongside a landing Shadow, fortunately just missing the other aircraft. When he finally pulled to a halt, he sheepishly opened his canopy, expecting to receive a severe reprimand for his actions, but instead found Pierre thrusting a bottle of beer into his hand and shouting, 'Welcome to Belgium!' We were a really happy crowd, all Shadow enthusiasts and enjoying every minute of our meets together.

Another year, when I was unable to attend the Moorsele meet, Jacob flew 02 with the formation. On his return he told me that exactly halfway over the English Channel, during the outbound flight, there had been a huge thump from the engine. To his disbelief, the engine-related instruments still appeared to be reading normally, so with his heart in his mouth he proceeded, praying all would be well and eventually landed safely in Belgium. When he inspected the engine though on Shadow 02, Jacob could see that all the bolts securing the large casting at the front of his Rotax 503 had sheered. The casting that shrouded the cooling fan and positioned the recoil starter, had fallen forward against the firewall, but it mercifully hadn't affected the performance of the engine. Parked in the hangar in Moorsele was a Quicksilver fitted with the same type of engine. It was an ideal source for a temporary emergency repair but no one could find the owner, so a couple of guys helped Jacob 'borrow' the front casting from the Quicksilver and assemble it on 02. A note was left on the Quicksilver saying, 'Many thanks for the engine part – it will be returned to you from England'! This fault or unserviceability was the only trouble that any of the Shadows gave on these trips (except for a Shadow with a main wheel puncture). This was what I found pleasing – the fact that my aircraft could fly away, in mass, to a foreign land for a weekend without incurring a list of failing parts.

In the early 1990s, the Shadow Owners' Club was invited to an Open Day at Duxford Imperial War Museum, for their air show. Twenty-eight Shadows attended and flew a loose trail formation for the crowd. It was an exciting experience for me to fly at the back of the stream, take-off and see all those undercarriage wheels hanging below the climbing aircraft. This sort of flying was quite normal for me, but I did admire those Shadow pilots who flew only for pleasure, coping with flying amongst other aircraft and in front of the public. Being the last to land, I overheard the Second World War Hurricane pilot radio to the tower that if he didn't take off imminently, his engine would blow up due to overheating whilst waiting for the twenty-eight Shadows to land! I hurriedly completed my descent, as I had no wish to be the cause of such damage to one of the actual aircraft that had helped save civilisation and freedom during the Battle of Britain.

DENMARK AND PARIS AIR SHOW

During the summer of 1991, Pat White and I were attending an air show with our agent at Stauning in Denmark when the call came for me to undertake the flying display for the Paris Air Show at Le Bourget. Apparently, Peter Troy Davies, who was to have flown, had turned the Belgian Euro Shadow onto its back whilst taxiing in a strong wind, so the Shadow that was to have been on static display only was to take over the aerial duties for the rest of the week.

Catherine had received the phone call from Mr Proost of Euro Shadow requesting me to replace Peter Troy Davies at the Paris Air Show. She told him I was in Denmark, but that she would try and contact me to pass on the message. She then found the telephone number of Stauning airfield on a presentation ashtray that I had been given on a previous visit and actually succeeded in reaching me at the airfield!

Fortunately, it was our last day in Denmark, which was

probably just as well. The 'Hangar Party' the night before was the rowdiest I'd ever witnessed. There were many visiting pilots who had flown in from all over Northern Europe and there had been vast amounts of drink consumed, accompanied by raucous singing and music. CFM Manager Pat White, with his customary Irish charm, had virtually taken over the party.

I had attempted to curtail my alcohol consumption as I was displaying the next day, but as Pat White and I stumbled back to our caravan later that night, I realised in my dazed state, that the noise I could hear was the dawn chorus. I remember Pat, who was swaying like a tree in the wind in front of me, suddenly dropped backwards like the proverbial log, asleep before he hit the ground. Here he remained, snoring loudly until woken later that morning. Our agent also failed to reach the caravan, for I later discovered him draped head down over a small bush, sound asleep, with one leg pointing skywards! Neither could recall anything of the previous night's celebrations and the agent was extremely nervous and worried when Pat White and I quite successfully convinced him that he had been married during the evening's festivities to a horrendous-looking Yorkshire lady. He consequently spent the remainder of the day skulking in the shadows, obviously trying to avoid any chance meeting with his new bride!

My flight was at midday. I felt far from fit to fly, so I walked to the flight line with a guide on either side so that any unsteadiness in my manner would not be so noticeable to the casual onlooker. Gratefully, I realised I could fly better than I could walk, but I certainly suffered whilst pulling 'g' in manoeuvres. All in all, it was not a wise thing to do after such an evening and definitely not to be recommended as pilot practice.

During our visit I had to take several Danish females for flights, all of whom seemed to be of a different breed from the normal rather reticent ladies I've been accustomed to deal with over the years. One lovely Danish lady definitely appeared not quite so lovely when during a circuit of Padborg airfield, a low sultry voice purred over the intercom, 'Would you like a little violence?' Totally shocked at the suggestion, I could only feebly retort, 'I'll tell your mother.' She then proceeded to spend the next few minutes attempting to climb from her back seat into the front of the cockpit. Anyone who is at all familiar with the layout of the Shadow will know that this would entail a feat of considerable gymnastic ability, but she was undeterred by the enormity of her task. I was more than worried by the safety aspect of the situation and could envisage our lives being put in danger by the stupidity of her behaviour. It was with great relief, therefore, that I managed to land the Shadow without incurring an accident. On another occasion, I was taxiing out to the runway with a very pretty innocent young lady as passenger in the rear seat.

'Will you frighten me?' came her voice over the intercom.

'Of course not,' I said reassuringly. 'I won't frighten you.'

'No, no,' she urgently reiterated. 'Will you frighten me!'

Appearances as they say, are very deceptive!

And so Pat and I departed on the long drive to Le Bourget, Paris, but as we left Denmark we had a distinct feeling that a flight of Viking axes was following our path. What a good lot they all were.

I was lined up to display a Euro Shadow for four days at Le Bourget. (Euro Shadow was the agent for CFM in Europe and based in Belgium.) Shows such as these were really on too big a scale for my aircraft to be displayed to its best advantage. A tenth of the area of Le Bourget would have been more than sufficient for the Shadow's requirements. It was difficult to excite a vast crowd when one was displaying alongside the impressive, awe-inspiring heavy-metal military aircraft with all their accompanying noise, power and capabilities. A Shadow had no raging reheat on take-off and could not shoot vertically into infinity, pouring white vortices from its wings. The purpose of these types of air show is to provide a huge shopping arena for the world's aviation manufacturers to display their latest civil and military hardware. Decisions on a country's defence force can be based on the demonstrations of these aircraft and multi-million dollar deals can take place during the week's show.

This year, 1991, there was an interesting undertone regarding the military might of the air show. Not only was the American Air Force present, but the Russians had also brought their latest aircraft. Most exciting to me was the MiG31 Foxhound – an updated version of the MiG25 Foxbat, which had never been seen in the West before. This huge fighter/interceptor had taken world records in Absolute Speed, Altitude and Closed Circuit, previously held by the US. The secretive USAF SR-71 Blackbird spy plane had to be withdrawn from service because it could be intercepted by the MiG31 Foxhound, which besides possessing greater speed and altitude capabilities, had massive state of the art radar and carried missiles, which were larger than any Shadow aircraft!

My first day at the early morning pilots' briefing was actually the third day of the show. It was presented by a wonderful man, the show organiser, *Monsieur* Dupont. Extremely smart and good-looking, he could easily have stepped straight from a film set. He rapidly got down to the business of the day and embarked on the bollocking of various pilots for discrepancies in their previous day's display, two of whom were subsequently banned from participating in the day's show. *Monsieur* Dupont's reprimands were delivered with civility and cordiality. He merely remarked to the offending pilots, 'You will not fly today, Sirs.' The programme for the day was set out in the notes we had been given, but a Russian representative stood up to declare that the MiG31 would decline to fly. Technical reasons, no doubt, but others informed me that it had not flown at all during the previous days. Today, we were told, the French President, *Monsieur* Mitterand, would be present, so performances were to be of the highest standard.

Later, I watched the President as he and his high-ranking military officers keenly studied the F117 stealth fighter, which was on static display. The plane was heavily guarded by USAF Special Forces and was surrounded by two sets of protective barriers. Security was intense; no one was allowed to touch the special radar-absorbing surfaces of this ultra secret aircraft. I was amused to see a high-ranking French officer's arm pushed violently away by a security soldier, as he was about to lean casually on the plane.

The Shadow was positioned with the French Dassault aircraft and the Russian acrobatic Sukhoi team on the opposite side of the airfield from the crowd line at an area designated 'Bravo'.

Any chauvinistic male would have been silenced on seeing the Russian blonde girl leap from her Sukhoi after giving one of the most mind-numbing displays of acrobatics I had ever seen.

The Dassault Mirage 2000 displayed but, unfortunately, not the wonderful Dassault Rafael, as it had insufficient test hours to take part. Mitterand had been given a display by the Rafael the previous week at which the aircraft had wrecked the runway surface with its afterburners whilst rotating for take-off.

My appointed time of display drew nearer and I slowly taxied the lengthy perimeter track to the runway threshold where I would await the Control Tower's confirmation to proceed. Pausing at the threshold, I surveyed the vast expanse of runway, which stretched endlessly before me and to either side. It was an intimidating sight. '5, 4, 3, 2, 1, Shadow go!' commanded the Control Tower over my headphones and the Shadow and I suddenly became the focal point of the thousands of spectators that lined the far horizon. I had been allotted six minutes performing time. There were only a limited number of manoeuvres I could demonstrate (speed range, climb rate, turning circle); all of which could easily be shown within three minutes. The Shadow was capable of loops but this category aircraft is not allowed by the CAA to undertake acrobatic movements. Six minutes was a dauntingly long time to try and excite the watching crowds.

At air shows I would slow the Streak right down to minimum speed with full flap and solo; it showed about 31 mph but, if I increased the power as well as the angle of attack progressively, I could get the aircraft to stand on its tail with almost zero forward speed. At full power it would somehow even worm its way upwards. The balance, for display purposes, was to match a Harrier jump jet display using not quite full throttle. The lateral axis control took a bit of working at, but it seemed like the turned down wing tips were gripping the air like claws – a fascinating movement to show a crowd. A display at Old Warden, Bedfordshire, which has a short grass runway, ended with my approach, and full stop landing, immediately followed by full acceleration, climb to 200 feet, dive to runway, level out, land and stop all inside half the length of the runway. 'Get out of that,' I used to think, looking at the other aircraft manufacturers! No other aircraft could match a Streak Shadow. It was so much better in lots of ways, to fly at places like Old Warden where the Shadow was in close contact with the onlookers.

The next day's briefing showed, I noted, that the Shadow had been programmed to fly after the MIG31 and before the F117 stealth fighter (real designation Nighthawk). This sequencing was not going to allow me a good viewing of either of these two special interest aircraft. At least the MiG was to fly and the F117, not the example on static display, would make its sole appearance of the week by flying in and out from a base in Germany. It was with rising excitement, therefore, that I watched the formidable MiG31 Foxhound taxi past Bravo. I was waiting in my diminutive Shadow as this mighty weapon of war powered past, the pilot Valeriy Menitskiy raising his hand in acknowledgement.

I was to follow his display, so I trundled behind the MiG, keeping a respectful distance. Suddenly, I realised he had come to a halt and I was far too close to the jet's exhausts. I stopped immediately, but I knew that I was placed in a potentially hazardous position, for if he opened his engines up even slightly when he recommenced taxiing to the runway hold, those two huge 6-foot diameter exhausts would probably turn me into a cinder. Without hesitation, I radioed the Control Tower to warn them of my predicament but even before the controller could tell Menitskiy, I heard the reassuring words over our discreet radio frequency. 'I am aware of the Shadow.' I was so grateful that he had been perceptive of my potential problem.

As the show progressed, I could see something was not quite right as the Foxhound took off with a deep shattering volume of noise and totally disappeared. There was no display routine – nothing. I waited, watching my clock until his five-minute slot had ended. There was still no sign of the Foxhound. It was with some hesitation, therefore, that I moved apprehensively onto the threshold thinking that maybe any moment I could be in the way of a 40-ton jet fighter landing at 180 mph. Le Bourget Control Tower hastened me to 'line up' and I had no option but to go ahead with my six-minute display.

As my routine thankfully drew to a close with no interruptions from the errant Foxhound, I thought that instead of landing and using the exit at the end of the runway as I should, I would land on the first third of the runway and head off to Bravo at the intersect from which I had emerged. If I did this, I reckoned I could save 2 miles of taxiing and be back in time to see the first sighting in public of the F117 stealth fighter display. This proved to be a major error of judgement because on the narrow one-way taxiway I met head on the next display aircraft, the RAF Tucano. The RAF pilot, far from being furious at my mistake, merely smiled and I manoeuvred the Shadow into a smaller area as was possible and we slipped past each other with only millimetres of clearance. The hazard negotiated, I successfully reached Bravo and jumped out of my cockpit just in time to see the F117 stealth fighter make his first fly-past. This technological wonder was the highlight of the 1991 Paris Air Show. However, the gasps from the crowd were not for the Stealth but the MiG31 Foxhound, which suddenly appeared, trailing right behind the Stealth. It was obvious what was happening. The Russians were 'painting' the signature of the F117 with the very powerful and diverse radar sensors – the signature and all its secrets would then be known to the Russians. The Americans freaked – both in the air and on the ground!

Whilst the American in the air performed drastic manoeuvres in his attempt to shake off the tailing MiG, the knee-jerk reaction on the ground was to push onlookers even further back from the static Stealth by the use of their special forces. The two aircraft then disappeared from view, with the MiG31 still in close proximity to the tail of the F117. Fifteen minutes later the MiG31 finally returned to Le Bourget and landed without even giving his display. We had all just witnessed a pure piece of Cold War tactics: Russia 10 points, America 0 points! I am sure there was uproar in the USAF for failing to anticipate the possible occurrence of such an event.

At the debrief the next morning, not a word was mentioned about the previous day's happenings. I think that the French had the diplomacy to 'keep out' of a provocative issue! However, it appeared I was likely to be banned from taking part that day.

'Why was the Shadow taxiing back to Bravo on the incorrect track?' enquired the controller politely.

'I was trying to return quickly, so that I could watch the F117 display,' I answered meekly.

A broad smile spread across the face of *Monsieur* Dupont. 'For you that is good enough excuse. You are forgiven!'

GUERNSEY AND THE STARSTREAK

In October 1991, David Gore, Nigel Ramsey and I decided it would be a challenge to make the flight to the annual Guernsey Fly In, in our respective Shadow aircraft. David Gore, with his homebuilt Streak, was the personification of self-discipline, so he would be the planner and navigator of the expedition, besides which, he possessed a GPS navigational system. Nigel Ramsey, the archetypal 'Ginger' of the Spitfire era, also had a homebuilt Streak and I would fly CFM's 'StarStreak'.

The StarStreak was the latest and ultimate model of the Shadow series. Although all the versions used 70–80 per cent of the same production parts, the StarStreak possessed a shorter boom tube and much less chord (front to trailing edge of a wing) than a Streak. It also had a much greater roll rate and was really agile and effortlessly rocketed around the skies. Initially, I had used the same engine – the Rotax 582 – but an R618 was later fitted. Flying this aircraft, I used to sustain climb rates of 2200 feet per minute and zoom rates of up to 3500 feet for short periods but the delicate handling characteristics of the original Shadows had gone. I was once asked what was the precise colour of the grey spray paint on this first StarStreak. Not knowing and pursuing my normal philosophy of 'always give an answer', I retorted that it was 'Air Superiority Grey'. It seemed I had unwittingly hit on the perfect sales name, as from then on many owners requested this as their colour choice!

The day of our proposed trip dawned grey and overcast. Not exactly the ideal weather for all that flying over water, I gloomily thought. I was more than glad to be met by David Gore and shepherded into Headcorn airfield, Kent, where we were to join up with Nigel Ramsey. These GPS systems do prove invaluable in unpropitious weather conditions for we were forced to fly at under

200 feet across Kent. Using just my map and compass, I would have returned to Suffolk long before now! Our route was to cross the Channel, fly down the French coast to Cherbourg, then out over the sea once more to the Channel Islands and Guernsey. I noted with wry amusement, that our crossing of the English Channel took a mere sixteen minutes from shore to shore, rather less than the time of my 1978 crossing in the VJ-23, which lasted an hour and fifteen minutes!

We refuelled at Abbeville, where the French aviators received us politely. 'Are you *Monsieur* Cook?' enquired one pilot to my amazement. Of course, it was our aircraft that were immediately recognisable, not '*Le Concepteur!*'

As we followed the coast at a height of 4000 feet, we flew over the Normandy bay and beaches, where the remains of the 'D' day Mulberry Harbour were still clearly visible lying in the water below.

The steady monotonous drone of my engine combined with the length of the journey and the very still conditions began to produce a hypnotic effect on my mind and I suddenly realised that I was in danger of losing consciousness. 'I'm too relaxed – that's my problem,' I told myself. 'My breathing is too shallow and I must be fainting because I have an oxygen deficiency,' I deduced. So after ensuring that my radio was turned off, I began yelling in an effort to break my overwhelming state of lethargy. I sang raucously. I jolted and jiggled my body in all feasible directions within the confines of the cockpit – anything to regain alertness and a feeling of normality. My explosions of noise and movement seemed to resolve the problem and I was not, as I was half fearing, suffering from the first stages of some severe medical condition, but this traumatic interlude just reconfirmed my long held opinion that I did not enjoy cross-country flights! Guernsey airport was reached at last, without any further interruptions, and we stream-landed in front of the gathered aircraft. There was a good welcoming party that night for all the visiting pilots but even though our Streaks and StarStreak were the first ever homebuilts to attend Guernsey, we did feel that we were somewhat ostracised by the other private aircraft owners.

The weather the following day was diabolical. The wind blew ferociously and displaying the aircraft was out of the question, only Richard Goode flew a routine in the Sukhoi aircraft and fought with the hazardous conditions. And so the Guernsey Fly In proved to be rather a non-event but we had at least successfully negotiated the journey there and back, a lot of which was over large stretches of water; the return flight from Cherbourg to Southampton was a distance of some 80–90 miles. How infinitely preferable was flying from Thorpeness cricket field – fly one circuit and return!

BOTSWANA

In February 1994, the container that transported the first Streak Shadow to Botswana arrived at Gaberone airport with its seal broken. This aircraft was to be used for surveillance on the Namibian border by the BDF (Botswana Defence Force). The Government was concerned that the plane may have been damaged or sabotaged, so they requested my presence to undertake an airworthiness check.

As the twin-engine commuter aircraft from Johannesburg approached the runway into Gaberone, we were hit by a torrential, tropical downpour. In these conditions it was almost impossible for the pilot to see ahead but as we continued with the approach I assumed that avionics were assisting the pilot to bring us safely to the threshold.

I assumed wrongly, for as I tried to peer through the streaming sheets of water that poured down the passenger window I caught a fleeting glimpse of the runway below to our port and realised we had missed the touchdown point. The pilot opened up once more and we went around to attempt another landing. We were circuiting low over an inhospitable terrain of dense, forbidding jungle, with practically no visibility. The situation was hazardous in the extreme. Rigid with tension and anxiety, I sat there, powerless, and tried to keep calm. I desperately issued instructions to the pilot in my mind. 'Left! Left!' I silently shouted, as the runway slipped by yet again for another aborted touchdown. Finally, to everyone's relief, the pilot succeeded in bringing the plane safely to land, though the rain was undiminished in its ferocity. He had done well under such stressful conditions.

With relief, we exited the aircraft and were greeted by smart airport officials, bearing umbrellas for us, the eight passengers, to use as we paddled our way through the rain to the little airport buildings for arrival checks.

The whole scene was very relaxed and low key, though I was soon prohibited from smoking my pipe when I lit up for a much needed puff after that memorable flight! It was soon apparent that my luggage was missing and that no one had arrived to meet me, so I set off, alone, on a shuttle bus for a motel on the outskirts of Gaberone, where I had a room booked for me by the Botswanan Defence Minister. Clutching my briefcase, which now contained my only possessions, I stared from the bus windows at the passing countryside, as we sped along the road. Huge billboards decorated the sun-baked scrubland, informing the discerning traveller of the tragic statistics concerning sexually active men and women in Botswana – of which, 84 per cent of the male population was HIV positive and 73 per cent of females. It was all rather dispiriting.

Early the next day, a Major Tsitzi arrived at the motel and took me straight to the BDF airfield to inspect the tampered container with its broken seals. Major Tsitzi told me the interference had probably been the work of the South African customs as all container traffic had to dock at Durban, South Africa, and travel overland to Botswana. He elaborated his thoughts by telling me of the frequent sabotage by the South African customs on Botswanan goods and equipment. On one occasion, trucks had been delivered with sand in their fuel tanks and acid had been put in the sump of an engine, which consequently caused severe injuries to a mechanic. The major had no explanations as to why these deeds were perpetrated. Later, when I travelled on to South Africa to visit the Shadowlite factory, I questioned friends who were in the South African police force about this matter of Botswanan sabotage. Although they agreed the acts were indefensible, they did not appear shocked or surprised in any way. 'The South African customs are a power answerable to no one,' was their comment.

I closely inspected the Streak aircraft. The Major's tales of possible sabotage worryingly dominated my thoughts, as I carefully looked at the most vulnerable structural areas, which could have been damaged by someone with aeronautical knowledge. My fears, though, proved groundless and I successfully check-flew the Streak in very hot conditions.

During the following week of operations, I approved three pilots to fly solo after a very limited period of training. One person I cleared to fly solo after having flown only two circuits with touch and gos. These BDF flyers were already proven pilots – instructors, in fact, for students who were being trained on a variety of aircraft and helicopters. They were quite accomplished airmen.

Mr Kumar, the Botswanan Minister of Defence, had arranged to meet me at my motel during my visit. This was now causing me concern, as due to my lost luggage, I had been wearing the same clothes for days and with the lack of any toiletries, my face had taken on a rather grizzled aspect. In fact, my general appearance was deteriorating rapidly and I was in no fit condition to receive a Botswanan Minister but all I could do to rectify this situation was to attempt to 'shave' with the aid of a Stanley blade, which I kept in my sunglasses case as an emergency tool. I needn't have worried. Mr Kumar was very sympathetic to my plight and immediately dismissed his assistant on a mission to purchase me clothes, whilst we talked.

Our meeting went well and we discussed a wide variety of aviation issues. I was already aware of the Botswanan Government's search for the Hunting Strikemaster, a version of the UK's Jet Provost, and offered my assistance if it could be used in any way. The Minister was most interested to hear information concerning the Fairchild A10. The USAF was about to relegate the A10 to second-line use in 1994. This would be an excellent, cheap jet aircraft for the country, though the ammunition used in the seven-barrel 30-mm gun would have to be 'regular' type as the US Government prohibited the export of their standard depleted uranium shells. I then told him of my personal experience flying an A10 simulator at RAF Bentwaters. The USAF simulator computer operators specially presented me with a complex series of fire and engine-out situations and eventually succeeded in forcing me to eject, whereas my son Jacob completed a perfect flight, much to the pleasure and applause of the onlookers!

After I had completed my training of the Botswanan pilots, Major Tsitzi rewarded me with a flight in the Pilitus PC7 tandem cockpit aircraft. This PC7 is a similar aircraft to the RAF Tucano but was probably not as capable. He strapped me into the rear cockpit. The view forwards from the back was surprisingly good. As we took off and approached the end of the runway, I noted we were already flying at 210 knots and were then skimming over the surface of a large lake at a height of 4 feet! 'OK Captain?' enquired the voice of the Major over the intercom. I replied in the affirmative but added that I hoped he wouldn't feel the need to sneeze and, as a precaution, placed my hand next to the control stick so I could pull back instantly if an emergency arose.

It was obvious I was to be given the full treatment! For over 50 miles, we travelled at a height of no more than a 100 feet over an extensive military range area; quite a thrill at a speed of over 200 knots! This low-level flying culminated with a zoom upwards to 10,000 feet with a climb rate of 4000 feet per minute. In my dreams, the Image should have had this type of performance. The plane then entered several very hard acrobatic manoeuvres and I found myself grunting with the pressure of the 'g' forces. Judicially, I switched off the intercom in order that the Major could not hear how my body was reacting to this treatment and only switched it back on again after the pain of 4 to 5 g had subsided! The aircraft was now inverted and side-slipping at the top of a loop.

'You have control Captain,' the Major announced but I had been anticipating his call.

I immediately pulled the control stick hard back, gave full throttle and clicked off the intercom.

'Here's what the ex-RAF can do, pal,' I mumbled as I pulled the plane through a sequence of hard 'g' manoeuvres and was rewarded by the sight of the Major struggling to regain his headset, which had been removed by the force.

I flicked a couple of snap rolls, crossed the controls, clicked on the intercom once more and nonchalantly remarked 'What a lovely little aircraft, Major – you have control?' In no way would I have admitted that in reality, my fifty-three-year-old body was suffering the consequences of such a flight!

ARLINGTON AIR SHOW – BACK TO TEXAS

Shortly after my return home from Botswana, I received a call from Harlow Wise, Laron Aviation, requesting me to assist him at the Arlington Air Show in Washington State. This show was solely for the display of vintage and homebuilt aircraft and I had wanted to attend this event for many years. So it was with great pleasure that I accepted Harlow's request.

Arlington is set in beautiful, forested countryside amongst the mountains just north of Seattle. I finally arrived after two long-haul flights from England, via Fort Worth, Texas, where I was temporarily detained by the US customs. It was a simple problem. I could supply no forwarding address but resolving the matter to the satisfaction of the US Customs officials was not so straightforward. I explained at length that I was an air display pilot on my way to the Arlington Air Show but obviously the air show venue could not provide the required permanent address. All this took a considerable amount of time to prove and it was only after the officials had closely studied my pilot's licence, which showed my Display Rating, that I was allowed to proceed to Seattle.

When I arrived at Arlington, Harlow Wise had already set up with the Korean Twin Shadow and a Streak Shadow on static display. He had retrieved this Streak from a Texas prairie where it had stood unattended for the last three years, which meant I had to spend three of the seven days of the show making the aircraft serviceable for me to fly. Fortunately, the aircraft needed no more than two cans of WD-40 to do the job!

An interesting aspect of attending these sorts of shows was that one never knew who would unexpectedly appear at the company display stand. One day that week, two gentlemen arrived and announced that they were engineers working for the Grumman Aerospace Company. One of them, it transpired, had in the past carried out most of the work on the Hound Dog Missile. They considered the Streak to be the most interesting aeroplane at the show and they were really appreciative to hear and have pointed out, all my design thoughts in creating the Shadow. It was through them that Lockheed later requested Harlow and the Streak to do work with them, though Harlow was restricted from informing me what they had actually had to do, so I cannot comment further.

Another unexpected meeting was with an elderly lady who was on the verge of collapse from the 90-degree heat that day. I asked her to take a seat in the shade of the Laron stand. As she was recovering with a cold drink, she told me about a book she'd just purchased at a neighbouring stand, which was all about Russian women fighter pilots in the Second World War. Her name was Lydia and, as she turned the pages of the book, she indicated to a group of pilots in a photograph and said, 'That's me!' How wonderful, I thought, for this dear lady, who apparently lived just over the Canadian border, to come across such a find. It was fascinating listening to her tales of flying experiences.

The Arlington Air Show was a great event. The weather was ideal with beautiful, hot, clear days and thousands of people attended. Besides the amazing flying to be seen, there were hundreds of stalls, walk-in open-air cinemas and one night, a spectacular flight of hot air balloons magically lit up the dark sky to the accompaniment of music from the Tannoy system

Some of the display flying that week was incredible. The most dynamic flying I have ever seen, was between two unlikely aircraft doing unlikely performances. A Russian Yakovlev, powered by a huge low-throbbing engine, was flown by a Canadian who described his flying as 'with attitude'! He flew a slow, inverted pass alongside the owner of the Robinson Helicopter factory, who was flying one of his machines backwards! As a pilot, I tried to come to terms with this formation. The helicopter pilot couldn't see his flight path because he was flying backwards at 50 mph and the Yak pilot was upside down, flying at a large angle of attack, alongside. Unbelievable! They held this close pairing for the whole length of the airfield to tremendous applause from the crowd.

Another display, the like of which I had never seen before, was by a wire-launched hang glider, which ascended to a height of 1500 feet, trailing a very long streamer. As the hang glider gradually descended, a Pitts Special made repeated attacking passes, cutting the streamer with his propeller. Incited by the manic shrieks from the commentator, the crowd was driven to a state of frenzy as the ribbon became so short that it appeared the next pass by the Pitts Special would surely slice through the hang glider itself!

After the show had ended, Harlow and I set off on the 2800-mile journey back to Texas. We towed the aircraft trailer with his big ol' Dodge Diesel truck, the 5-inch diameter exhaust bellowing out a continuous throaty roar.

It was a traveller's trip crossing the Rockies and the salt flats of Utah. I've always been interested in geography and I was fascinated to see the ribbon-like Snake River as it threaded its way between a range of hills. Nowadays, this river is a placid length of water but, thousands of years ago, it had been very different. The Snake River had been created when the massive lakes of Utah had burst a 2-mile width of the hill range from the torrent of water, which tore across the land towards the sea.

The huge salt flats, where land speed records are attempted, are the previous beds of these huge lakes. A little knowledge does lead to a greater fulfilment of life. I was inwardly satisfied to have been able to 'read' such a catastrophic event that took place millions of years ago.

On our journey, we passed the USAF Colorado Springs Academy, which Harlow had attended for his Air Force pilot training. He bitterly explained that due to political correctness as regards female entrants, he had been dumped on the grounds that he 'was not sufficiently aggressive'. None of the assessors could have possibly known Harlow! His evaluation of the situation was that he did not wear a bra. He had consequently taken up a ground option and had attained the rank of Captain. As we discussed the merits of the Academy, I asked him why the primary USAF training centre had been based at Colorado Springs, which lies at an altitude of 5000 feet. Surely this cannot be helpful for pilots learning to fly, as it means having to cope with high landing speeds and low climb rates. 'It was put there for political reasons?' Harlow drawled. Say no more.

In both the USA and South Africa, the attitudes of political correctness and affirmative action seem to have been carried out to the extreme. They seem to have a situation now where people are employed not for their ability to do the job, but for their colour. I remember a conversation I had with a white lady in South Africa. She told me that because of affirmative action, she had been fired from her top job in a Durban bank and replaced by a black employee who could not do the job, with the result that she had to be re-employed at vast expense, as a consultant, to visit the bank every other night to correct the mistakes made by the new employee. I heard a similar story from the USA from a friend of mine who was head of a department at NASA, Houston. He was to be removed because his department did not employ 'the required number of specified ethnic minorities'. Situations like these surely cannot be right. Of course, there should be equal opportunities for all but to have to employ so many of a certain race regardless of their ability, is an absurd state of affairs.

Ability to do the job should always be the prime consideration when people are employed. This brings to mind another very worrying trend in today's business world and that is the short-sighted policy of companies employing people with knowledge on paper rather than people with knowledge from experience. In manufacturing companies, theoretical knowledge is meaningless without experience in its practical application. The situation now exists in many companies, where many men with years of experience in their work but no paper qualification are being replaced by graduates who possess the necessary piece of paper but no practical knowledge. Without a hardcore of men with practical knowledge, manufacturing companies are bound to decline. The excellent apprenticeship schemes of the past sustained this necessary core of experienced men and it is a tragedy that, in the majority of cases, they no longer exist.

Over the years, the Institute of Mechanical Engineers has, repeatedly, through the Grandfather Clause, offered me the qualification of AMI Mech.E for my achievements in the field of aviation design but I cannot justify its acceptance. I feel that my knowledge has been gained purely through experience and I don't wish to be falsely accredited with theoretical knowledge that I have not learnt. To me, original thinking can only flourish in a mind un-contaminated by the preconceived concepts of others.

Harlow and I had now reached Idaho, on our long journey back to Texas, and we decided to visit Bill Reynolds. Bill made the wooden propellers for our aircraft, so we had had plenty of verbal contact but never met. He lived in Vernal, a tiny, dusty town in the middle of nowhere – ringed with distant scrub-covered hills and tumbleweed, sun-baked earth. We arrived exhausted after a long, hot day's driving and were greeted by Bill thrusting a pint of English brown ale into our hands. He had made the beer from a kit and was anxious to know if it tasted like the real thing. It was powerful stuff and soon provided the desired relaxing effect, so it probably wasn't a wise decision to enquire if I might be allowed to ride his vintage Harley Davidson motorbike, which I had seen standing in the yard.

'Sure,' said Bill, who closely resembled a member of the band ZZ Top, with his long, straight beard and wild, abandoned hair, and he promptly clipped on the seat. I blazed off like in a scene from a film, down the dry, deserted road towards the hills, the all-enveloping silence of the parched landscape torn apart by the loud, staccato roar of the Harley Davidson engine. My sense of unreality was no doubt enhanced by my consumption of the intoxicating home-made brew. However, I was soon frightened back to reality, for when I applied the brakes the handlebars suddenly shot forward and I had the awful fear that perhaps the handlebars were also clipped on like the seat and that they were about to part company with me and the bike. Brought back to my senses, I slowly returned to Bill, who then informed me this movement was normal and part of the design. Apparently, Harley Davidsons have a rubber shock absorber in the handlebars to reduce engine vibra-tion discomfort to the rider.

Bill continued to feed us with a constant supply of his home-made brew and then, in our drunken state, suggested we have a shooting contest. He produced a Chinese SKS rifle that was used extensively by the Viet Cong in the Vietnam conflict and told us how GIs (Government Issue) abandoned their US arms in favour of this gun as, whatever the conditions, it always worked.

'Heard you are a shot, David,' Bill drawled as he showed us the 'piece'.

'Some say,' I muttered, thinking that as my vision was now almost double, the myth regarding my shooting was soon about to end.

To give myself the maximum chance and a justifiable reason for failing to hit the five-gallon water-filled can, I stumbled out into the scrub, clutching the wretched rifle, my one aim to put as much distance as possible between me and the offending can. I heard Bill and Harlow shouting for me to stop and continued purposefully onwards, turning a deaf ear to their call. Reluctantly, I came to a halt and returned to face my challenge. I had achieved my aim, as the target was now a merciful blur in the distance and there was no way in my present condition that I was going to be able to hit the can. I raised the rifle and peered down the sight. Two wavering cans filled my vision. Without any more ado, I fired and the SKS rifle cracked with a sharp recoil. To my utter disbelief, I then saw the can explode, shooting a cascade of water into the sky.

'What a shot!' exclaimed Bill and Harlow in total amazement. No one was more amazed than myself. The luck of the Gods had been with me and my honour and reputation as a shooter remained intact, for now!

Bill owned a friendly Labrador dog and it was whilst I was playing with him later that a really upsetting incident occurred. I had been throwing an old shoe way out into the tumbleweeds across the single-track minor road for this good dog to retrieve. On this occasion though, as he bounded back, I could see a car approaching and knew instinctively that they would collide. I frantically yelled for him to stop but, being in an excitable state, he took no notice and the inevitable happened. The car screeched to a halt but the collision was unavoidable. The Labrador lay very still on the road and we all stood in stunned silence, looking at the scene before us. I felt overwhelmed with remorse and guilt, for it was all my fault. Several minutes must have passed when, suddenly to our joy and amazement, he began to move. He stretched his limbs, slowly raised himself and walked away, none the worse for his near-death encounter, save for a few cuts and bruises!

Before we left the next day, Bill showed us his workshop. His business, Precision Propellers, consisted of only him and his father and they carried out their work in a compact area of sheds. I couldn't help noticing that his stock of 8-foot x 4-foot sheets, of laminated plywood layered by $\frac{1}{32}$-inch plys, were an off-the-shelf purchase. The time-consuming and lengthy process of laying up sheet by sheet wasn't necessary, it seemed, in America.

Ostensibly, propellers are laminated to prevent warping and, therefore, retain their pitch and profile. The propellers (airscrews in America) that I made though, were all from one piece of wood.

The first one was the small 28-inch diameter propeller, which powered the VJ-23E and it was carved from a single section of maple. The second was the 57-inch diameter propeller from the VJ-24W, which Volmer Jensen confirmed could also be made in this way. According to Volmer, the technique of laminating a propeller was evolved by the Germans in the First World War, to prevent the propeller from shattering if it was struck by a stray bullet from the interrupter mechanism whilst firing through the blades.

I took note of Volmer's thoughts on the subject but it did seem to me that the laminated style possessed more rigidity. However, my two types of hand-carved propellers proved perfectly satisfactory.

Regarding the Shadow, it has always been an issue of contention that the 52-inch diameter propeller used was too 'small' but what is a small propeller?

With a big push to cover distance, Harlow and I then drove continuously for some fifteen hours. Eventually, completely exhausted, we pulled in by the side of the highway. It was long after dark and we were miles from anywhere, surrounded only by the silence of the prairie, which stretched around us into the night. The deep sleep of sheer fatigue soon enveloped us as we lay cocooned in our sleeping bags inside our makeshift living quarters in the aircraft trailer. Suddenly, in the midst of sleep, I sensed I could hear a sound – a sound that was persistently growing, filling my head and demanding my attention with its ever-increasing presence. Now fully awake, I lay there, eyes staring, ears straining into the darkness, listening as it grew louder and louder until the sound had become an all engulfing roar. By now, Harlow and I were both sitting bolt upright in our sleeping bags, rigid with fright and frozen with terror as this mind-numbing noise seemed to tear through the trailer. So convinced was I that we were about to die, that I was already visualising Harlow transformed into a skeletal form in this forthcoming scene from Armageddon. We were lucky we didn't die, though we so nearly did. Somehow, in the middle of this vast prairie, we had managed to park for the night within 6 feet of the Santa Fe railroad and the noise was that of a 2-mile long freight train!

The town of Borger is set in the northern panhandle of Texas. This area consisted of some of the flattest ground on earth. There was nothing but snake grass for hundreds of miles and no features to relieve the monotony of the landscape. In fact, when I studied an air chart, I noted a rock of 2-foot diameter was marked!

After we had rested from our transcontinental trip, Harlow flew me to Kansas where I was to pick up an owner's Shadow and fly it back to Borger for various servicing requirements. Our journey took us north-east through Oklahoma into Kansas. As we flew I became more and more concerned about how I would find my way back over this featureless landscape, knowing the limitations of my navigational skills. But I needn't have worried. After attaining a height of 4000 feet AGL – 'Density altitude 8000 feet' – the clarity was unlimited. During the flight of several hours, I could see for at least 60 miles in any direction. It was certainly different from flying in Northern Europe, where visibility was sometimes less than one mile on what might appear, from the ground, a very good day. The flight proceeded without problems except that the aircraft was horribly out of trim. It was trying to roll to port and pitching upwards the whole of the flight and by the time I had landed back at Borger, my arms were really aching.

Over the next few days, we worked on the aircraft's systems and cured all its problems and I then flew the plane back to Guymon, Oklahoma. This area of Northern Texas and Oklahoma was

initially Comanche Indian country. I had always wanted to meet a
Comanche. Where were they? Harlow told me that I would know
when I saw one. This proved correct for, after arriving at Guymon
and parking the Streak on the flight line, as I walked into the
airfield buildings, there he was – the modern day Comanche man;
an imposing, memorable figure of a man, very upright in stature
with chiselled, sculptural features, bronze skin and long raven
black hair tied back from his face. I knew immediately that this race
of mankind was special. I remembered all the comic books I'd read
as a boy, when Kit Carson, as an Indian scout, used to combat this
race. It was a surprise to me that Kit Carson actually existed and
was indeed the local Panhandle, Texan scout. I had thought that,
like Desperate Dan in the *Beano* comic, he was a mythical character
– shame on me in my ignorance.

On reading the local history, I discovered that Kit Carson had
been trapped with some of his men in an area close to Borger
during the 1800s. They had been surrounded by Comanches intent
on taking their scalps, who were clever enough to keep out of range
of the white men's rifles, only charging occasionally to let the men
waste ammunition. It was a stalemate situation that lasted several
days without water. The story read that one of Carson's men
possessed a Sharpe's .50-calibre rifle. He was asked to try to hit the
Comanche Chief who was sitting on his horse a mile away.
Loading the single ½-inch diameter ball in this legendary rifle, he
fired an incredible shot, which knocked the Chief from his horse.
The Chief was unhurt, but following this shot the Comanches
withdrew.

Harlow collected me from Guymon in a hired Bonanza and we
flew to Liberal Air Museum, which contained some wonderful
displayed aircraft. I saw an F14 Tomcat whose pilot had been 'Gus'
Grissom – one of the very first astronauts. I remember him from
the film called 'The Right Stuff'.

As Harlow and I flew back to Texas, we passed right over
the area where Kit Carson had been surrounded. We marked the
occasion by ceremoniously stamping our feet in true Indian
fashion, accompanied by what we hoped were Comanche-like
'whoops', as we circled above the historic sight. We hoped our

actions would meet with the approval of the spirits, though they certainly posed a question mark over the sanity of the perpetrators!

THAILAND

In August 1993, Jacob and I had to visit Thailand to rebuild a crashed Streak, which belonged to Mr Nit; he was a very wealthy businessman with high-up connections in the government. We had to take such an array of aircraft pieces with us that we had to pay excess baggage, though it was nothing compared with the Nigerians who were ahead of us in the queue at Heathrow Airport. Their excess baggage charges amounted to thousands of pounds, according to the official in charge. 'Nigerians always pay in dosh mate, always in dosh,' he confidentially remarked to us as he dealt with our odd assortment of aircraft spares. The delicate fibreglass nose cone was particularly awkward to transport, so as we negotiated Bangkok International, I decided to resolve the problem by wearing it. My rear view must have resembled that of the 'Egg Man'!

Unfortunately, during our flight I had developed a crippling toothache, which was rapidly requiring immediate attention, so Jacob had to explain my predicament to the leader of the military delegation who were awaiting our arrival at the airport. The leader, a robust-looking Para General, immediately steered us through the diplomatic channel, which required no passport clearance, and bustled us into a waiting limousine. Following a hasty communication with the chauffeur, we were whisked to the nearest hospital, escorted by a cavalcade of motorcyclists clearing a way through the heavy traffic of Bangkok city centre. It did occur to me that avoiding all the usual entry procedures at the airport might not necessarily be to our advantage if it came to proving how we'd entered the country. If we didn't enter, how could we depart? However, it was no use pursuing this line of thought; my tooth was the main concern of the moment.

On reaching the hospital, we were marched straight to the dentist department, several floors up in the building, where a poor fellow in the midst of his treatment was literally turned out of the dentist's chair so that the dentist could examine my troublesome mouth. Within minutes, the offending tooth had been removed, to the accompaniment of profuse apologies from the dentist, who appeared to be concerned for his future if he failed to fulfil this treatment successfully!

Mr Nit owned a palatial home in the centre of Bangkok. Its drive-in basement underneath the premises, provided an ideal area for us to rebuild his Streak and the huge fan blowing at 20 mph made it possible for us to work in the very high humidity. Jacob was amused at how fast the epoxy Araldite set. What would normally take a day in England, was hardened in minutes in this climate; consequently the aircraft came together very quickly. I had already consulted with Mr Nit as to the nature of the accident, as he had bought the aircraft from CFM for static display purposes only. Apparently the crash had been caused by his relation with in-sufficient aviation experience, attempting to fly.

Once the aircraft had been repaired and test flown, it was to be put on display in a huge showroom, which he had in his house, alongside an autogyro and a varied selection of exotic cars.

The reconstruction now completed, the army arrived to trans-port us and the plane to a suitable test site. This turned out to be a road built high upon an embankment surrounded by paddy fields. Army vehicles then proceeded to block off the road to all traffic for half a mile or so, in order that the Streak could have a clear runway and be flown.

The test flight was successfully accomplished, though I was slightly apprehensive about the reception I would receive on my return, low pass down the road, which scattered all the observing 'brass'. But I needn't have worried for as I landed the officials' faces were, thankfully, wreathed in smiles.

Our job completed, the in-house mechanic was given a large roll of money (Baht), with the instructions to take Jacob and me out on a 'night for the boys' and to buy us whatever we wanted! An Australian aviator once said to me, 'Bugger the lottery, you can't beat being lost for a week in Bangkok!' But we really didn't know what to expect of this forthcoming outing.

The ostentatious show of wealth from Mr Nit was there for all to see but how he made his money remained a mystery. I did ask him what was the nature of his business but his reply of 'tarmac' certainly didn't account for the baffling presence of the military and this extraordinary display of wealth.

Our designated host escorted us through the thronging streets of Bangkok, trying his utmost to make us spend his entrusted roll of money. We could have had anything we wished but, somehow, it didn't seem quite right to be the receivers of such unlimited material gifts. Jacob instantly regretted enthusing over a costly aquarium at a mere £1500 because we then had the greatest difficulty in politely persuading our host that, actually, he didn't want or need the tank! Eventually, I did succumb to the constant pressure and agreed to accept a superb leather business briefcase with shoulder strap to replace my much used and decidedly cheaper model.

As day progressed to night, we moved from shops to bars and ended up in one of those clubs of dubious repute where, it seemed to me, any form of behaviour was permissible. Naked Thai girls pranced and danced suggestively on a stage behind a long bar, whilst in an enclosure, more naked girls cavorted in a shower of bubbles. It was not the scene for a nineteen-year-old boy to be attending with his father! We sat self-consciously at the bar, drinking beer, being pressed on either side by beautiful, scantily clad girls plying for trade.

I jokingly shouted to Jacob above the music that I'd got mine down to 400 Baht. He replied that he was getting his to pay him! But propriety ruled the day. With the all too real threat of AIDS and letting England down on my part, we kept the faith and managed to leave the bar intact.

This 'fun night for the boys' though, had obviously cost more than envisaged, for at the end of the evening it appeared there wasn't enough cash left to pay the bill. A rather nasty scene then ensued with the 'house heavies' moving in on our group. However, we were rescued by Jacob producing some money, which Mr Nit had given him on arrival to cover everyday expenses. This, without doubt, saved us from certain bodily mutilation; the 'knife men' retreated and we were allowed to leave the bar and Thailand, for as our work was now finished we could return to England. Mr Nit, it seemed, conducted all his financial transactions in cash and so it was that we left Thailand carrying the payment for our work. This meant I had hidden on my person some £5000 in pound notes – a potential mugger's dream victim!

ISLE OF MAN

Not so far from home was the Isle of Man, which I visited with Pat White. We took the trailer and Streak on the famous Steam Packet ferry, as I was to perform at the Jurby Air Show, give demonstrations to potential customers and check out an aircraft we'd sold to Lou Barham and Margaret Dodd.

The crossing was in glorious sunshine but there was quite a swell and strong wind. I sat and relaxed in the lounge but Pat decided to soak up the sun on the foredeck. Suddenly a dejected figure appeared, dripping in front of me. 'Pat!' I exclaimed. 'Whatever have you done? Fallen overboard?' Poor Pat, he'd been on the receiving end of a huge wave that had washed over the deck whilst he had been peacefully sunbathing in his deckchair!

The wind blew steadily during our visit. It was a relentless 35 mph on one day, so extreme care had to be taken on the ground whilst handling the aircraft. That day, the Yamaha Motor Cycle Team just so happened to be testing their machines on the runway at Jurby. The coincidence was too much to ignore, the temptation too great – the thought of out-flying the speedy motorbikes below, irresistible. A young lad was inadvertently the unwitting passenger in the rear seat, when after holding off at 200 feet – his presence temporarily forgotten – I swooped from the sky, diving at the racing motorbike as it blazed down the runway beneath the plane. I then continued the flight heading straight for the Yamaha works crew and pulled the aircraft up into an exhilarating 3-g vertical climb over their heads. I estimated our ground speed must have been a breathtaking 160 mph down wind. The sudden appearance of the plane must have caused shock and concern to those below, so having succumbed to temp- tation, I concluded the flight in a responsible manner and then proceeded to apologise profusely to all those concerned.

Poor Lou Barham had flown that day too and had unknowingly overflown the Remembrance Day Memorial Parade taking place in Douglas town. His fairly low and noisy fly-past had coincided exactly with the two-minute silence. The outraged Mayor traced him and rang to say that the Town Council were taking action. Lou was elderly, mild and kind-hearted and his error had been a genuine mistake. I felt very sorry for him in his distress, so I contacted the Mayor of Douglas and informed him that far from being 'out of order', Mr Lou Barham, an ex-Hurricaine pilot, was giving his own personal tribute to our war dead and all was forgiven.

CHAPTER 5

Production Overseas

UNITED STATES OF AMERICA

In August 1990, the first CFM aircraft to enter the USA arrived in its trailer at Brooklyn, NYC. This was to be an example aircraft on which to base production at Laron Aircraft, CFM's agents in the States who had bought the rights to manufacture. After collecting the aircraft and trailer, Byron Goddard met me at JFK airport as I had agreed that it would be a worthwhile venture to display and so promote the Shadow at various air shows in the NE and Mid Western States on its journey down to New Mexico. We headed south passing through West Virginia, Pennsylvania, and Indiana to Ohio. The ex-secretary of CFM was Sue Norton, previously from Leiston, who had married an American. She and her family kindly put Byron and me up for a few days whilst we sorted out the airworthiness acceptance for the aircraft in Vandalia, Ohio.

I talked to the 'heat' as the FAA (Federal Aviation Administration) is known over there, for about an hour. I showed the aeronautical engineers our UK compliance. They expressed surprise that we had actually load-tested the airframe and total amazement that Shadow 02 and Streak 108 had both survived the ultimate load tests and were still flying more than twelve years for 02 and seven years for 108 later at that time. A visual appraisal was then made with the Streak assembled in the car park outside the FAA offices. I confidently recounted that all the welding, for example, was done by a CAA-approved welder. 'I don't care who did it – I'm not going to fly it,' was the typical reply. Their opinion of our CAA was that 'Those people are mean'. The Streak was approved by the FAA in hours.

On reflection, it did seem unbelievable that the Shadow's elevator electric trim system had taken eleven months for the CAA to approve even though an identical system passed by the PFA had been in use for a long time on the Streak. There is much to say for the method of approval in the US. It is marvellous for manufacturers, but is it good for owners? Nothing would persuade me to fly a US homebuilt or kitplane under that sort of approval. Due to the emphasis on freedom for the individual, there are many things in the US that to us in Europe, seem very lax in the area of safety. To me, it appears that, overall, life is regarded as cheap in the US. I consider many of the regulations in the UK to be too bureaucratic but surely rules on car safety belts and motorcycle helmets are a good thing? Americans don't like being 'made' to comply. For instance, it is absurd to me that cars are allowed to travel on sandy beaches in California because of 'freedom' for the individual, with no consideration of the possible dangers to children playing. Yet you cannot have an alcoholic drink in public and road speed limits seem to be from an earlier age of motoring. Householders can be fined for failure to have their front lawn cut and edge trimmed or for leaving out a garbage bin for too long after collection. Freedom USA? To me it often had the appearance of a police state. In general, I found the US population hostile to the police force, whereas in the UK I consider most citizens find the police acceptable.

The Experimental Aircraft Association (EAA) put on an annual North East Meet at Marion, Ohio. The Streak was to make its debut at this event. When we arrived at Marion, two problems were immediately apparent. The FAA officials at the show had not received official clearance for the Streak to fly in the US. The organisers of the show had denied authorisations for the display, which had been booked earlier by Byron Goddard for the Laron company. Laron had been set up by David Owen, Harlow Wise and Byron to produce and build Streaks and Shadows for the US market, when CFM had found that the exporting costs added to the UK prices had eliminated competitive sales from this potential market.

I confronted the Marion EAA authorities and it began to emerge that the real reason the Streak could not be flown in the display was because of a type of 'closed shop' for performing air show pilots. Being foreign or 'alien' as they call anyone visiting who is not from the US, I was not going to be allowed to join the select few. I argued that I had travelled some 4000 miles to display my aircraft, which I was sure would be appreciated by the US public. Eventually, the EAA organisers relented but stated that I would have to put my case to the 'select few' (the pilots taking part that weekend) and that I would also have to accept their verdict.

In the pilots' briefing room, I was presented and invited to stand in front of them and present my case. I was interrogated by a bunch of seemingly very hardened mature aviators, some of whom obviously bore battle scars from previous flying experiences. They all resembled aerobatic championship pilots.

'OK David, convince us why you should fly in our display,' demanded one of the audience. I proceeded to give what I considered to be a passable delivery of my forty years' flying experience: the 1500 hours on this type, displays in twenty-two countries, and opening slots at the world's major air shows such as SBAC Farnborough and Le Bourget Paris Air Show. I also recounted the Streak's eight years in production with zero structural problems, zero modifications, no bulletins, no air directives (ADs), its World Class records under FAI rules. All in all, I was 'the Man'.

My five-minute speech was met with complete silence. Eventually, the organiser of the show dryly said, 'OK Mr England, you can display your airplane here but you are first display routine.' The stipulation was meant to put maximum pressure on me but unknown to them, it didn't work that way for Mr England!

There was a large attendance at the show, with the aircraft lined up on display until thirty minutes before the start – at which point participants moved their respective machines via a taxiway to the airfield side of the barrier. I started my engine and was about to taxi through the barrier, when the local FAA officials (the 'heat'), suddenly turned up and asked me to shut down. Apparently there was still confusion concerning the paperwork and clearance of the aircraft. In the USA, the FAA have the power to bus an entire town population out and away from a air show if they are not satisfied with the safety of a situation. Thus, one can well imagine the tightness of control at these events. I very patiently waited whilst the forms and clearances were studied. The time for the beginning of the show was drawing near and I was meant to be first on. However, the deliberations still continued until finally, Byron protested to these FAA officers and they reluctantly allowed me to start up my engine with a mere three minutes remaining before the commencement of the display.

Thankful to be moving, at last, I taxied through the well organised marshals to the 'live' side and was then confronted by a late-arriving private visitor taxiing in the opposite direction to the public side of the barrier. We met head on with insufficient room to pass and stopped – neither having a reverse gear! An aggressive official in an agitated state roared up to me on a four-wheel motorbike.

'Where the hell do you think you are going?' he screamed.

'I'm first on,' I yelled back, trying to be heard above the roar of engines.

'First on what?'

'First on in the display,' I retorted, trying to contain my feelings, now having reached the limit of my endurance.

The official then reversed his rage onto the facing Cessna crew and almost threw his aircraft from the taxiway. The taxiway was built up at least 12 inches above the level of the surrounding grass and with the roughness of the ground must have nearly broken the Cessna's undercarriage.

At last I was free to do my display except that the 'heat' had made the proviso that I was to remove any extreme manoeuvres from my routine until they had made an assessment of my flying abilities. My instructions for the following day's display would depend on this judgement. If I had not possessed many years of flying experience, the necessary confidence to perform would long since have evaporated under all this pressure. I thought that it was disgraceful.

A Taylorcraft type aircraft was to depart before me in order that it might gain altitude during my display to then be ready to commence its routine once I had landed. I waited at the intersection 'hold' with no sign of any aircraft movement. On my radio I heard a frustrated air traffic controller comment, 'We got an air show here?' The silence continued, then suddenly to my relief a 1940s Taylorcraft appeared and lined up on the runway. I watched as its engine wound up. Smoke canisters began to pour out streams of swirling white cloud, which quickly obscured the whole stationary aircraft.

'This is Zulu, five fower, niner, we have us an air show. Yippee. . . . . ' shouted the pilot of the Taylorcraft.

I recognised the raw southern accent from the previous day's meeting. The owner of the voice had made a striking impression with his shock of white hair, burn-scarred face, dressed in black and walking with the aid of a black and silver-handled cane. I had never heard anything like him on a radio frequency, but this was a discreet number.

His aircraft burst out of an all-enveloping cloud of smoke and I was finally cleared for take-off. Adhering to the enforced restrictions, my first display in the USA was a restrained and consequently boring routine. As I came in to land, I saw the Taylorcraft pilot start his routine by throwing his aircraft through at least five show-stopping inverted spins. These were no ordinary pilots.

Prior to the show the following day, a time-to-climb competition took place. To my regret, the Streak was unable to take part as applications had to be made on the previous day. I think my entry had been barred after some of the competitors had seen the capabilities of the Streak. Anyhow, a Sonerai won the 0 to 3000 feet event with a time that I knew my Streak could have halved.

That second day, the FAA cleared me to perform 80 per cent of my normal display. A facility at the airfield enabled pilots to talk to the crowd, so I explained how by facing the aircraft into wind I could 'park' in the air. This manoeuvre was received with a lot of applause and appreciation. I also mentioned the refusal of the organisers to allow me to enter the time-to-climb competition, to which the crowd responded with gratifying signs of their displeasure. After the show had finished at the end of the day, I was deeply touched when every single display pilot called by and congratulated me on my effort. It was unexpected, quite genuine and personally rewarding after having endured one of the most pressured situations I had ever known.

One thing now was certain; I was definitely 'in' on the air show circuit USA. I remember Byron's despaired face and his statement that he could only ever dream of being in my position of acceptance. I'm not sure how one achieves this status but when one is a 'known' entity in aviation, things seem to happen with much more ease. This applied, I'm sure, when I proposed to get the Streak categorised as semi-aerobatic with the UK authorities. They enquired why I had put in the request. I replied that with the Streak's ability to be semi-aerobatic, my air show routines could be construed as 'out of category' regarding its present categorisation. The authorities then asked if that was the sole reason. When I confirmed, I was told to please not apply for semi-aerobatic clearance for the Streak because people would probably kill themselves using the aircraft this way, but that a cautious blind eye would be given at any of my routines!

The CAA department dealing with displays showed common sense – but I'm sure this only happens if one is a 'known' pilot. It must be so very difficult for those who have not yet attained this level.

With the conclusion of the show at Marion, Ohio, I returned to England and left Byron to carry on to New Mexico State where the new factory was to be opened.

It wasn't long before Steve Emmerson went out to see how production was progressing. There seemed to be a problem with the process of bonding aluminium to aluminium. After a week of investigation, he discovered that the problem was being caused by some sort of solution in the water supply, which prevented the bonding process. A factor that gave rise to much greater concern, was that the parts that were being made in-house at the factory, were not of an acceptable standard. Due to the remoteness of this area, there was a complete lack of an engineering infrastructure and this was creating difficulties for Laron. The local people were not engineers. They raised cows for beef or drilled for oil. There were many parts on the aircraft that were easily available in the UK but were not so in the USA. For example, the brakes used on the aircraft originated from mopeds, but mopeds were not an accepted mode of transport in America and this applied to many other items. Laron would have to overcome these manufacturing problems.

A year or so later, I met up with them again in Florida where up to 10,000 aircraft attended a meet called 'Sun 'n' Fun'. The Laron Streak was flown by me in-between the 'display showcase'. It was fascinating to witness three different circuits at differing heights all operating at the same time. I flew around the ultralight circuit, passing twenty-three ultralight aircraft on my way. The engine temperature seemed very high. The Laron crew later revealed that no oil had been added to the fuel and the two-stroke Rotax had therefore flown on straight gas. There was no one to blame but the pilot. I had accepted the fuel and assumed these guys knew and operated this aircraft. It was my fault for not checking. For the next circuit I applied full flap and a lot of power and flew so slowly that I was overtaken by the majority of the US ultralights, much to their pleasure. But to those watching, it showed the great speed range of the Streak. Not only was it the fastest but pretty much the slowest aircraft in view. My solo flight must clearly have upset the showcase organisers, for I was nearly grounded and was told if I gave a routine like that again they would halt all flying. To me, it had been the normal Streak display. I was instructed that I was not to climb at more than 60 degrees and was accused of flying upside down at one point. I tried to explain that it was probably due to the angle at which they were viewing the display but all to no avail and from thereafter I had to curtail my routine by 50 per cent.

Whilst parked at the Laron stand during the meet, I happened to notice two fellows studying the Streak. After overhearing one of them remark, 'How in the hell does this thing go so fast?' I introduced myself and discovered that one of the gentlemen was Homer Kolb – a manufacturer of ultralights in the USA.

'This airplane gets its speed from over a hundred different secrets,' I said. 'The turbulators on these struts are one of them, but

I'm not going to tell you about any others.' To my amusement these two very established aviators then spent considerable time studying the design for 'other secrets'!

Unlike the UK where the categorised definitions were set by the FAI, there was no specific microlight category for aircraft in the US. All these types of machines were listed as 'Ultralights' and were restricted to being single-seaters and flying at a maximum 63 mph. The Streak, therefore, was put at a disadvantage having to conform to these ultralight regulations.

So often, it seems, in so many aspects of life, the US adopts an isolationist policy regardless of other systems worldwide. It is a pity that being so dominant in their own right, the Americans appear to know little, or are even aware of the rest of the world. Ronnie Regan even thought Scotland was in England! One flying type in Texas even asked me if we pilots had air navigation charts and pop rivets over in the UK! I assured him that we did and we also had British supersonic airliners and fighter jets that took off vertically!

PRODUCTION: SOUTH AFRICA

In the early 1990s, Africa became the next continent to manufacture the Shadow aircraft. Len and Lesley Alford set up a factory in South Africa at Pinewood near Durban. My father had been born in Johannesburg and I felt this would be a great asset when the time came to visit their premises and check the aircraft production. This proved to be correct and I got on well with all the South Africans I met.

The day I arrived in Durban was 5 November and the people were celebrating with a huge firework display in acknowledgement of Guy Fawkes! The glorious weather though, convinced me that this wasn't England.

The facilities for Shadow/Streak production were vastly more suited here than in New Mexico or the Texas Panhandle where Laron later moved. Even fibrelam was available from an industrial area next to the factory at Pinewood.

I stayed with the Alfords in Natal, near Kloof. It was a beautiful area with flowering trees and very lush countryside. In 1991, my first visit showed me that there were superb roads, telephone systems and all other infrastructures – very different from the rest of Africa. One could even drink water from the tap and all this after forty years of sanctions. Keeping my nose out of politics was not possible in these surroundings; I just hoped that with the coming necessary changes, South Africa would not become like the rest of Africa.

The first Shadow and first Streak in Len's factory were reaching completion. I helped to finish these two aircraft and check them out, which meant their firm's 'Shadowlite' would then be underway. After preliminary flight checks during the week, the two aircraft were ready for their weekend presentation flights to the Cato Ridge Microlight Club, some 15 miles from Kloof.

It was an enthusiastic club and many people turned up to witness these microlights from England. Len and Lesley had taken considerable financial risk and investment to reach this stage. Joos Skeepers, an elderly, financially secure, backer had put his faith in Len, even though many others present thought the aircraft were 'paper tigers'. Len Alford had previously visited CFM and informed the club members that these types of aircraft were outstanding. All the members of the microlight club were now waiting at Cato Ridge to see if Len's appraisal of the Shadow had been justified.

This scepticism was soon put to rest. I gave a 100 per cent display routine of rate climbs and vertical dives, both at high speed and passes performed at an near impossible slow speed. Turns were tight with 4-g flat 360s and minimum radius slow-speed 360s at low altitude and a final full loop from straight and level was enough to convince everyone present that they had not witnessed a performance of this standard before in their flying careers. I received a rapturous applause upon landing and could only point to the Streak and say that's what it can do . . . I don't think I had to buy a beer at the club for a week!

Joos was overjoyed, slapping his Afrikaner thigh and roaring approval. These people are usually quite self-contained and don't have too much appreciation for the English but Joos was overwhelming with his kindness to me. He even offered me accommodation in South Africa and was willing to put me up in one of his new houses, which were being built near the factory – a housing estate that was one of his investments. He was also determined to track my heritage and discovered to my surprise that my grandmother was indeed an Afrikaner – not Fancourt as I'd understood, but Fernkirk. The aircraft were a hit with the other pilots. Len had previously only flown flexwing types but it wasn't long before I checked him out in the Shadow. He learnt very quickly as the Shadow possesses such docile and forgiving characteristics. It's another step up again to fly a Streak with its accompanying leap in sharpness and performance.

During my visit I stayed with Len's parents, Ralph and Eunice, who showed me great courtesy and kindness. Ralph ran a company producing modified trucks for commercial and UN uses. Everyone I encountered was so interested and enthusiastic about the Shadow. In those weeks I made many close friends at Cato Ridge.

Late one afternoon as my work was now almost completed, a few of the Cato club members, noticing my interest in their firearms, took me to visit a quarry nearby, which was used as a shooting target practice area for the AWB (Afrikaner WeerBond). Some of these guys were there with their weapons – a vast selection of armoury that in England would be under tight control and restricted to a few shooting clubs. I was allowed to fire a wide range of shotguns, pistols and rifles at targets and was coached in their handling and use. During RAF training I had gained marksman status and at home I possess an air rifle but I was not experienced with weapons such as these. Firing the Winchester rifle with its superb accuracy was particularly satisfying. The AWB fellows seemed very serious and were different characters from the people I met at Cato Ridge whilst we were there.

A competition arose amongst the gathering, whereby two persons stood back to back with a .22 pistol, safety on, ran 10 metres and shot at a bean can 25 feet away. The first to hit the can went on through to the next round – an elimination process. I progressed to great shouts of encouragement from my flying friends and reached the final shoot-out stage. A huge AWB man stood back to back with me. His name was Pietre. These guys were not amused that this 'little white form' as I was named, had proven such a shot and had got through to the final of their eliminations contest. The huge Pietre proceeded to run to the shooting point but I decided to walk – I could hear him shooting before I was even in my place. I carefully released the safety, took one shot and my can ricocheted into the air. Unbelievably, I had won the contest, which gave rise to much cheering from the Cato Ridge guys. Apparently, this was very embarrassing for the AWB. Len said, 'You don't seem to realise what you have done. These fellows fire 1000 rounds a year with personal weapons and they've just been humiliated.' The AWB did, however, present me with a special white cap with suitable neo-Nazi badge of which only fifty had ever been made. I asked Len whether I should wear it to which he quickly advised, 'I wouldn't if I were you!' We laughed it off and I told him that I had envisaged the bean can as though it were a MiG aircraft in my sights.

The year from 1991 until the time of the 'vote for all' in South Africa was an exceptionally tense period. Natal encompasses Kwa Zulu. The tribe of Zulus preferred independence and the ANC (African National Congress), with Nelson Mandela leading, wanted South Africa as one country. The dealings with my aircraft placed me in the Kwa Zulu territory and a state of war existed as they vied for power. This was vividly brought home to me when I saw that the pub we had visited the previous day had been blown to smithereens on the next! The minority white population was not involved in this struggle at all – it was a 'black' affair.

I found it amazing how the white people were so self-sufficient. They virtually ignored black people as though they were not even there. I rated their capabilities as twice that of an average English male and four times that of the average English female. These people could handle themselves. Having grown up in the isolation of East Suffolk where only white people populated the area, I was well out of my depth and did not comment on the situation between black and white in South Africa. I was only interested in my flying business. Five or six visits to South Africa over the years have left me, politically, in no man's land. In England my comments would be seen as Right Wing – in South Africa they were that of typical 'do-gooder' European. To spend time amongst the people in South Africa is the only way to form opinions.

It was strange indeed to learn that white people's dogs only bit black people and that black people's dogs bit only whites! This fact was demonstrated at the Alfords. They had never asked or trained their bulldogs to bite anybody and yet whilst walking in the beautiful grounds of their Kloof house, I was often charged at by 'Precious', one of the guard bulldogs. However, at a distance of 15 feet it would see I was white and break away. Usually I stood rigid – petrified I was going to be attacked. But I never was. Poor Anna, the Zulu housekeeper, lived in permanent fear of these dogs. She had been attacked several times and the dogs duly beaten. She was always compensated by the Alfords.

One weekend we took two aircraft, a Shadow and a Streak, on a cross-country flight to Hawick airfield near Pietermarisburg. Len and John Young flew the Shadow and I flew their Streak with Len's wife Lesley as passenger in the back. At Hawick we noted that during the journey the main battery on the Streak had boiled and spat acid all over the engine and rear fuselage. The reason for this wasn't obvious, so we washed the area with clean water and proceeded to fly back in formation. However, twenty minutes into the flight, with the Shadow leading and the Streak tucked slightly aft to starboard, the engine suddenly stopped. I quickly radioed the Shadow but John Young appeared unaware of any call and continued flying ahead. Then to my relief the Shadow turned. Later I learnt that Len, seated in the back, had heard my message and had then quickly taken over the controls and followed us down. We were above the tribal lands of Zulu country. Below was a landscape of rounded hills covered in sugarcane crops. At least our altitude was good, so there was some time in hand before a decision had to be made, but I failed to see any suitable area where I could successfully land. In the silence of our glide, I asked Lesley if she'd noticed anywhere. 'I don't really know,' was all she said. She seemed calmly unaffected by the seriousness of the situation and unaware that we might be dead within the next few minutes.

Matters were becoming urgent; we had now descended below the level of some of the hills and were skimming between them. If I do find somewhere to land and manage to survive, I'll probably be boiled up in a pot with a few vegetables – I gloomily thought as I pessimistically surveyed the countryside, which was rapidly rushing up to meet us. Suddenly a large farmhouse appeared with a track leading to the property. The landing would have to be on that track . . . I lined up the aircraft, approached at speed and we zoomed towards it. To my horror, I then saw power lines strung across our descent path. We shot over one set, under the next and came into land. It seemed an eternity before the wheels touched down and I realised we were flying downhill, with banks dangerously close encompassing either side. We eventually came to a halt without a scratch, but it had been a very tight landing. As I contemplated the aircraft straddling the track, I calculated there was less than a foot clearance from each wing tip to the banks.

Len's Shadow roared overhead, having witnessed our safe landing, and flew off to get help. I always hated flying other than solo. The responsibility for the safety of others weighed heavily on my mind. I imagined the rescue team arriving and having to say to Len, 'I've wrecked your aircraft, killed your wife – but I'm OK!' They were unbearable thoughts. Swarms of little black children suddenly appeared as if from nowhere. A diminutive five-year-old white boy and his equally small black friend raced up to us. 'The coon boy and I watched you coming down,' the white boy shouted. This comment ought to remind all where we are . . . As the crowd of children was all very excited by the unexpected arrival of the aircraft, I put the largest twelve-year-old in charge to keep the others in check. He was delighted with his new rank and immediately took control.

Lesley and I wandered up to a large house, which I could now see through the high sugar cane. It resembled a stately home in England. We were invited in by a maid who showed us into an elegant, cool living room where an obviously rich family sat drinking tea from the thinnest porcelain cups I had ever seen. Lesley introduced herself as an 'Alford' and the name was immediately recognised. These people farmed sugar cane and trained dressage horses to an international standard. I felt like a hooligan standing before them in my tee shirt and jeans, drenched with perspiration and slightly traumatised by the recent happenings. But we were made most welcome. In this remote place I don't suppose they get that many people 'dropping in' on them.

It took Len Alford and his friends several hours before they reached us, as they had difficulties in locating the house. Ken, an electrical wizard, soon declared that there was nothing wrong with the aircraft systems and the Streak responded by starting immediately. So I nominated myself to fly back even though the take-off run would be almost as difficult to negotiate as the landing, with the close banks and overhead wires. It should be mentioned that the ground level here was 2500 feet or more above sea level and the temperature usually 30°C or more, which meant that the take-off run was longer than in 'English' conditions. Cato Ridge was only 8 miles distant and could be seen high on a bluff from the ground where we were standing. Take-off achieved, I climbed overhead to gain a good altitude in the event of the engine stopping again and headed towards Cato Ridge to the accompanying gestures of all on the ground below, faithfully pointing to the direction I had to take. Landing back at Cato Ridge, Bill Gore, an Irish chap with whom I had made friends, handed me a beer saying that the story was already out that I'd put down in an impossible place without putting as much as a scratch on the Streak. I think that, as weekend flyers, they overrated my flying skills and didn't realise just how much flying I did as my work.

Over a beer and whilst awaiting the return of the rescue crew, Bill related a horrendous tale involving his flying.

Returning one day from a mild cross-country flight in his Flightstar microlight – a basic second-generation copy of the original American design – he overflew a huge bowl-like formation of rock that lay just between him and Cato Ridge. Unfortunately, it was the time of day when cloud formed exactly over this area. As Bill knew where he was, he chose to fly straight into the cloud, expecting to emerge from the other side in less than five minutes. This was a potentially very dangerous thing to do for unless one's aircraft possesses instruments for flying 'blind', it usually only takes thirty seconds or less before one's sense of balance is lost. Without an apparent horizon, there is no awareness of straight and level without. He survived the 'white out' purely through quick thinking. He hung his stopwatch by its lanyard above him, so that it acted like a plumber's bobweight. After twenty-two interminable minutes, he finally saw the ground a mere 10 feet below and landed, heart thumping. He said that he'd never ever been so pleased as that moment, to see the native people surrounding his aircraft. 'Only someone Irish could have done this!' I added. It was a remarkable piece of flying from someone who didn't even contemplate how or why the aircraft flew at all.

Eventually, my rescue crew returned and we celebrated survival of the day late into that night.

Len Alford and I flew by airliner from Durban to Cape Town to check out a Shadow built by a couple who lived near Wellington. This was a most beautiful area of vineyards, citrus fruit-producing farmlands, mountains and pasture – a lovely place. Mike farmed a citrus estate and these people had made an immaculate 'C' Series Shadow powered by a Rotax 582 engine – the one used for the Streak.

The aircraft checked out perfectly when I flew it from his prepared airstrip, which was cut out between the lemon trees. Unfortunately, it was not sufficiently large enough for checking the owner out to fly solo, so I flew his plane to a private tarmac airstrip, which belonged to 'Mr Olive Trees' – a dear, elderly man who had started out with a small patch of land that had now expanded to such an extent that he was known as Mr Olive of SA. He owned a twin-engined aircraft and had given us permission to use his facilities for training.

The strip was set in the most exquisite surroundings. The rolling countryside was covered in olive trees, backed by majestic 7000-foot high mountains, which rose from one end of his runway. Mr Olive enthusiastically watched the flying instruction and during a rest between flights, he told me that he'd never seen any aircraft climb so well as this Shadow. Boasting about my design, as usual, I said that flying solo, I reckoned I could climb right over the 7000 -foot peaks starting from the end of his runway. 'Go on, then,' was his reply! Loving a challenge and maybe the possibility of another sale, I duly complied. The Shadow certainly responded well but naturally as I climbed higher and higher the mountain face loomed nearer and nearer, so in the end I had to steer through a gap between the peaks rather than fly over the absolute summit. The plane just made it, leaving me thinking that sometimes perhaps I ought not to be so hasty with my big mouth!

A similar occurrence happened at Cato Ridge when John Joubert announced that his Beaver microlight could out-climb the Streak. I confronted him and received a succession of excuses ranging from unserviceability and other reasons as to why a challenge of the first to 1000 feet could not be done.

Following this, the wives of the Cato Ridge flyers printed a challenge in the *Durban Times* personal column. It was a dreadful piece of twisted words and phrases concerning Beavers and Streaking that even the most hardened fellow would have denied writing. It left no doubt for the reader though, that the challenge to John Joubert was for Saturday morning at 6.30 am, Cato Ridge; 0 to 1000 feet with an observer flying in an orbit at that height with two witnesses.

I was actually quite friendly with John and his wife – there certainly wasn't any animosity between us but this involved a lot of pride on both sides. I was fiercely proud of my design and would challenge anyone who disputed its capabilities.

The Beaver looked good with the latest equipment and sported the best propeller from Arplast. Both aircraft had similar engines, but I weighed less than John, which was to my advantage. A large crowd had assembled at the designated date and time – through having read the intriguing entry in the *Durban Times*.

The aircraft were flagged off the start line by the Cato Ridge Club safety officer and observed by a Shadow that was circling at 1000 feet in order to confirm which plane was the first to pass this altitude. The Streak and I shot through the orbit into an overcast sky and disappeared from viewers on the ground at around 1050 feet. It had climbed, in the American phrase, 'like a homesick angel'.

On landing, John Joubert congratulated me. I would have bought him a beer, but celebrations even at that time of day – breakfast time

– were the expected deal; nearly a pint of brandy had to be drunk by the winner, to the taunts and cheers of the onlookers. Needless to say my flying was definitely finished for that day!

One day, the Alford family kindly arranged a visit to a real Zulu village – something that I was interested in witnessing as the white and black races lived separately. There were about 1500 people living within a compound in thatched circular huts, which were surrounded by an anti-lion thorn fence. It certainly gave the appearance of being genuine and not set up for tourists – I couldn't see a BMW parked around the corner.

We were greeted with a village parade, sat down and given a display stick fight. These knobbed sticks were used with great speed and dexterity and must have been a deadly weapon. I could see easily how I could have been overcome in seconds. The interior of the circular main communal hut must have been 50 feet across, and half-naked girls then performed dances for us to the rhythm of a tremendous drum beat and traditional Zulu foot stamping.

As honoured guests, we were offered their tribal beer to drink. We sat in a ceremonial circle next to the chief. The drink was first tasted by the chief's wife, only then did the chief drink from the bowl and pass it to the visitors. I did notice that all the Alfords only pretended to drink but when my turn came I decided to be more adventurous, caution not being one of my attributes. Besides which, it was a very hot day and I was thirsty. The grey-looking liquid resembled very thin porridge and definitely didn't look very appetising but I drank enthusiastically with beer spilling from each side of the bowl.

The Zulus who were watching my every move cheered wildly – likewise the Alford females, for as a reward for showing such enthusiasm I was offered the prize of four young Zulu girls. I was escorted to where a group of near naked, nubile twelve to fourteen-year-old girls stood and was told to make my choice, to the accompaniment of shrieks of laughter and screams of delight from the Alford women. Lesley and Eunice could see my acute embarrassment at the predicament. I didn't know what to do. Surely it would be a cultural insult to reject their generosity. I imagined the outcome of this incident would be the conclusion of my life in the boiling pot. I frantically sought a solution to my ghastly predicament from my now beer-befuddled brain. 'I've been ill . . .' I murmured weakly. To my utter relief, this remark seemed to have been understood by the Zulus. Even so, it still did not deter them from proffering certain bits of female flesh for me to feel and fondle! The whole visit had been a more than memorable experience but I have to admit to being most thankful when the ordeal was over! Any one of those girls would have eaten my 'little white form' for breakfast!

On another occasion, I accompanied Joos Skeepers to Durban. We travelled in style, for like Ralph Alford he possessed a top of the range Mercedes.

At the Mercedes service centre I asked the manager (tongue in cheek), 'Where are all the Jaguars?'

His response was to point to an oil patch in one of the bays and say, 'That's where the last Jaguar stood! Do you know why the English cannot build computers? . . . Because they can't make them leak oil!'

Ralph Alford previously had even mused that he was going to send me an oil drip tray for my Jaguar – as a Christmas present! There is some truth in all this, as English engines do tend to leak oil.

Several times I found it hard to believe I was in Natal. Once, I was in an ex-railway building in Kloof village, which had been converted into a pub. On the wall were the nameplate castings from steam engines and other equipment from Richard Garrett, Leiston – the very place of my work for fifteen years back in Suffolk, England! Beer mats, too, were evocative of home as they showed all the types of Adnam's beers from Southwold – a few miles up the coast from where I lived. It seemed totally incredible to see all this so far from home!

I returned to England with many fine memories of all the kindness and generosity that I had received from the people of South Africa.

CHAPTER 6

Military

TURKISH AIR FORCE, IRAQI AIR FORCE AND RAF

In 1988 we received an order from the Turkish Air Force. The two
Streak Shadows were to be built to specific requirements: three
separate fuel tanks with individual means of selection; blackened
rear polycarbonate canopies to prevent unwanted viewing of the
sophisticated thermal imagery that was to be fitted in the floor of
the rear cockpit of which we possessed only the drawings for the
aperture and its fixing hard points, the sensitive equipment being
for restricted 'eyes' only; and thick Kevlar anti-bullet protection
throughout the front cockpit. The effectiveness of the Kevlar
armour was demonstrated to us at the British Armoury, Enfield,
when a .45 calibre handgun was held against it and fired. Although
there was no penetration of the armour, the resounding impact of
the bullet on the pilot's body would not be a very pleasant
experience.

The Turkish Air Force, unbeknown to us at the time, were trying
to secure their border with Iraq – particularly the Kurdish area.
Their F16 fighters had been using sensors in an attempt to intercept intruders crossing over their mountain range. However, the
endurance of the aircraft was too short; they were therefore limited
in their effectiveness. The Turkish forces then used helicopters and
lost three of these within a month from hostile ground fire. The
Streaks had the advantage of being able to fly very quietly at a high
altitude, whilst scanning for heat sources from 14,000 feet. In the
West, we seem to have sympathy for the much-maligned Kurdish

180

people. I personally did not feel at ease producing aircraft to undertake such a task, but Turkey was a legitimate member of NATO and I had a company to run with employees who had families, which relied on the income generated.

Various other military people also visited CFM, amongst which was a delegation of Iraqi Air Force officers. Their two-day visit culminated in an order for two Streaks for assessment. I clearly remember relating to them the story of my recent confrontation with a RAF Group Captain and his entourage. I had put to him the perfectly reasonable suggestion that 1000 of my aircraft could be purchased for the equivalent price of one fast jet fighter-bomber and that each one of these aircraft armed with a Sidewinder missile could wipe out any country's air defence system in a day. This was 1990. When the Gulf War started within two years, we at CFM pondered the significance of my theory. If Saddam procured hundreds of Sidewinder-equipped Streaks, then the coalition forces could have been under great threat. For sure, the West's fighters would have been able to knock these Streaks down like flies, but if there had been hundreds of Streaks, each capable of taking out a multi-million dollar jet with a Sidewinder, who would have been able to predict the outcome? I jokingly told my employees that if there was any likelihood of this occurring – through Iraqi copying of the two supplied – that we'd better lock the factory, chuck the keys and run! However, thankfully the embodiment of my theorising did not come to pass, maybe because the Air Force officers we met were amongst the sixty high-ranking officers in the Iraqi Air Force who had then been executed by the Saddam regime during the intervening years.

SURVEILLANCE, LINE SCAN, SAS, INDIAN AIR FORCE, DEA AND RAF

The Flight Dynamics Department of British Aerospace requested CFM and Shadow 02 to attend a meeting at the BA Centre at Hatfield, Hertfordshire. The purpose of this meeting was to brief us on the possible use of a device called a Mini Infra-Red Line Scan (MIRLS). John Wibberley and David Clarke displayed the aircraft's capabilities to the assembled gathering of boffins who were sufficiently impressed to ask if the Shadow could be used for trials with their line scan.

The MIRLS was incredible; it could detect, passively, heat losses from buildings and factories and could 'see' runway damage. It would be of great advantage to the Military in that it could be used day or night above cloud, to analyse the movements and positions of enemy troops, as it was able to pick out people, armies, tanks, vehicles, snipers and anything that possessed a temperature different from the ambient surroundings . . . All this information was on a rolling drum of paper, which could also be simultaneously tractor-beamed back to a base. The MIRLS was only a receptor of signals, emitting none except when using the tractor beam.

Whilst at Hatfield, we were kept well away from a part of the airfield where Flight Dynamics operated. I made the error of casually enquiring how many people worked there. This brought a sharp response as to why did I want to know?

Following this meeting, several of these boffins then came to Suffolk and I worked with them, doing several sorties in the plane using the MIRLS situated in the rear cockpit. It received information via a slot in the floor, working with a scan of more than 180 degrees to compensate any rolling movement made by the aircraft. When the information was decoded, these high-powered technicians showed me that the information on the scan was so detailed that I could have recognised people I knew on the ground. These trials would have been just as successful had I been flying at night or above cloud. With all this high-tech stuff about, I was very amused to hear one of the boffins comment whilst I was tying down the Shadow into its trailer, 'It always comes down in the end David, to a piece of string!'

In the mysterious world of surveillance, I was sometimes requested to perform tasks by unknown people who originated from I knew not where. During the SBAC show at Farnborough in 1986, the Shadow with its fitted British Aerospace MIRLS line scan was asked to do a run over the aircraft that were positioned in front of the crowd and, in particular, the Russian aircraft. The run involved a violation of the flying limits for displaying aircraft. I was not prepared to lose my flying licence undertaking this flight. CFM depended upon me to promote the aircraft and I was responsible for twenty to thirty employees and their families, so Peter Troy Davies volunteered to do the SBAC display in Shadow 02. Thankfully, he only received a mild rebuke from the SBAC committee as he claimed he was forced to fly beyond the targeted area by a gust, which blew the aircraft off course. No one ever knew that information was being received and recorded by this flight. I did not know the value of the information, but I did know that the MIRLS could see the location of fuel tanks, fly-by-wire systems and many other items that the eye could not perceive.

At the request of British Aerospace, we attended several military hardware shows with the BAe Shadow. To indicate the presence of the MIRLS, a promotional pod was attached beneath the fuse-lage bearing suitable logos and inscriptions, but in reality of course, it was empty!

The SAS special forces, in particular, showed interest in the Shadow. My cousin, David Gibley, had been a Major in the regiment for four years and I asked him if he would kindly inform various contacts of his in the army about the aircraft's military potential.

My cousin and I had grown up together and we both remember, with amusement, the time in 1944 when we were four years old, huddled together with fright in an Anderson shelter when a doodlebug (V-1) exploded less than 200 yards away. We recall clutching each other, grizzling in terror as the whole world seemed to crash around us in the darkness. There wasn't much counselling given in those days!

The SAS's main interest in the Shadow was its ability to take off from water and transform itself to land-use by the mere re-connection of the nose leg with its one bolt.

Brian Harrison planned and designed most of the equipment needed for the Sea Shadow model. Besides the SAS, a floats con-figuration was being requested by other interested customers and the finished version looked superb, making the Shadow appear born for use on water.

I obtained permission for trials on Thorpeness lake, but was restricted to taxi trials only. Peter Troy Davies did one taxi run, then lined up and took off flying over the village out to sea. The whole trial was very successful and we managed to exceed the limitations of our permission. Float version Shadows were consequently sold to several foreign countries.

In April 1988, the Indian Ambassador for this country with a Wing Commander from the Indian Air Force came to visit me with two special requests. The Indian Air Force wished to investigate the possibilities of arming a Shadow, which could then patrol the remote boarder areas of India, with a view to discouraging unwanted intruders. The Shadow's role was not to be openly aggressive; the mere knowledge of the aircraft armaments was to be a sufficient deterrent in itself. Armament specialists came to the factory with various proposals, which culminated in the choice of a Minigun 7.62-mm multi-barrel weapon to be situated in the rear cockpit, which would function by projecting out of the starboard side of the plane pointing forwards. The only major problem would be the discarded cases and links. The Minigun could fire 2000 rounds per minute and carry sufficient ammunition for two minutes' firing. These specialists took a fibrelam monocoque to Enfield for firing trials and reported superb anti-vibration absorption by this material. The armament package was completed with a passive gun sight, a red-dot marker for the pilot that was taken from a US Marine AV-8 (Harrier).

The other Indian request was really unusual. The very valuable Russian fighter interceptors, MiG25 Foxbats, operated from the airfield at Poona, near Bombay and they were having problems with bird strikes during take-off and landing phases. Apparently, these were huge birds and already catastrophic collisions had occurred leading to the loss of a MiG25. The only means of frightening the birds was, it seemed, the howl of a hunting dog. It was proposed that clearance of birds from the airfield could be done by a Shadow flying in a confined and restricted area, issuing a recorded hunting dog howl!

I showed the Wing Commander how, with practice, a Shadow could be flown circulating in an area only the size of our cricket pitch. Such a small area would allow the approach or take-off by the jets to continue without interruption. I carried out a study with the help of a local hi-fi business. We devised a system that could issue 500 watts of hunting-dog howl from the Shadow – an extraordinary sight and sound!

Another unusual request was from an anonymous American, who asked me to perform an unconventional flight demonstration. He wished me to fly the plane until out of his earshot and to return as quietly as possible, descending from the approach to end up directly behind him. I suspected this guy was from the Drugs Enforcement Agency (DEA), as he was also proposing the attachment of Stinger missiles to a Shadow. Anyhow, I flew out of earshot as requested, at a good altitude, and, with the engine out, I glided into Thorpeness cricket field. Silently, I landed on the grass and stopped 20 yards behind this man who was still facing the other way. Opening the canopy, I shouted, 'Was that quiet enough?' By his startled reaction, the plane must have fulfilled his requirements. He hadn't heard a thing! And sales later followed.

Mike Plewman, who was running CFM jointly with myself at the time, informed me one day that the RAF Training Command was interested in having a test session with a view to using the aircraft for training purposes.

He mentioned that the Group Captain of RAF Valley was the very same fellow that I had caused to be grounded when I was at Cranwell. He had been a Flight Lieutenant instructor during training and this fellow was now to assess the Shadow! What a strange coincidence. The incident had happened when an Empire Test Pilot's two-seat Hawker Hunter T7 had made an approach at Cranwell and had been 'bounced' by the Flight Lieutenant who was flying a Jet Provost. I had been watching from the flight line, as these two jets got into a turning combat at very low altitude. Suddenly the Hunter stalled and plunged into the ground. Both pilots were killed. The subsequent inquiry had me as one of the witnesses, so I was one of those responsible for grounding the Flight Lieutenant.

I decided to let Mike Plewman handle this one and kept a very low profile, doing only the display! Mike was an ex-Lieutenant-Colonel from the army anyway and well suited to handling people whom I thought were not quite real! Some time after this session, I heard that the head of the RAF Training Command had left the RAF and become a Director of Grob – a German company that specialised in gliders. The MOD consequently purchased sixty Grob-powered gliders for the RAF, which were later retired as unsuitable . . .

Meanwhile, I was confronted with a facetious Air Commodore who was determined, it seemed, to downplay any attributes the Shadow might possess for military use. One question he put to me was, 'What battle damage can it take?' 'None,' I replied, answering him in the same vein. 'But,' I added, 'a thousand Shadows would cost about the same as the price of one Tornado fighter-bomber and could each drop a 200-lb bomb on a target. And if fitted with a Sidewinder missile, these same number of Shadows could wipe out all RAF Defence fighters in a day – added to which, the aircraft would not need airfields as school playing fields, football grounds or any clear 100-yard strip would allow operation.' He then enquired 'where I would get a 1000 pilots?' I replied that it would not be a problem as very little training was required to fly a Shadow. CFM got nowhere with the RAF. It seemed to me that the Shadow would not provide the right image and prestige to an Air Defence Command. A row of Shadows on the flight line would hardly present the same deterrent to a supposed enemy as an equivalent row of powerful multi-million pound jet fighters.

LIEUTENANT-COLONEL THOMPSON

In the late 1970s, the number one 'hotshot' pilot in the USAF was Lieutenant-Colonel Tommy Thompson. He tested the Fairchild A10 tankbuster and formed the first wing at our neighbouring airfield, RAF Bentwaters. Lieutenant-Colonel Thompson had completed 200 missions in Vietnam and the development of the A10 was the result of aircraft design failure in that conflict.

I knew Thompson well, as he lodged in my village of Aldringham. We had over time consumed many beers in the local pub, talking aviation. He had the coldest eyes I'd ever seen – just like a hawk – he was the definitive killer when in the air. I used to goad Thompson about having to have 'top cover' with fighters like F15s, whilst the A10s were in-the-mud killing tanks. He'd reply, 'I'd trade head-on passes with anyone.' The A10 had a huge gun weighing nearly 2 tons with seven rotating 30-mm barrels. It spat huge depleted uranium cannon shells out at 70 per second.

At some air displays we often crossed paths, both of us showing what our particular aircraft could do – as opposed to our own capabilities as pilots. I admired Thompson for this, for he would lift off and temporarily disappear, flying below tree lines, ground hugging – only to suddenly reappear in a pop-up manoeuvre to feign shooting at an imaginary target on the airfield and then to simply 'disappear' again. This was displaying the role of his flying mount to the full.

He collected 'display of the day' at Biggin Air Pageant. When I congratulated him in the Officers' Mess afterwards, he kindly told me that the sight of my legs hanging below the VJ-23 foot-launched hang glider, 'cracked him up' and I should have earned the award . . . not that I agreed.

Later in the year, my wife and boys, Gary and Jacob, watched with me as Thompson gave an incredible flying performance at our local USAF Bentwaters open day. He then flew on to RAF Chicksands in Bedfordshire for a further air show. Only half an hour later, we all heard the public announcement that he had been killed whilst giving that display.

Apart from the initial sadness of losing a friend and for his family's loss, there was also the huge undermining of personal confidence concerning flying. If the best of the best get caught out, what about one's self?

It had been a reoccurring horrid scene throughout the whole of my flying career. It also lays heavily on the personal responsibility every pilot has to his family and friends. If you want to do hotshot flying, such as air shows and demonstrations – the aerial description that fits my job – then one's precision and concentration on the task in hand had better never be anything but perfect. I used to know my limits and the aircraft's limits and never exceeded them. Usually, a 90 per cent display would suffice in front of big public crowds at air shows, whereas locally I flew the 'envelope'.

A few times when overseas, I did have to fly the envelope of the Streak Shadow, and by the end of the display emerged soaked in perspiration through the expended effort. One such display was at Kjula airfield, Stockholm. After my display, the pilots of the Saab Viggens of the Swedish Air Defence Squadron called me over, saying 'Are you the pilot of the red Streak Shadow? For you this tee shirt is free.' Quite an honour, as this tee shirt with their unique Squadron badge was for them only to wear.

In France, after another maximum effort, I was announced as the 'heroic ancient RAF pilot'! I hoped that it translated as 'ex-RAF'. Many elderly French people wanted to shake my hand – they all had the 'Free French' badge, which was shown to be behind their coat or jacket lapels. The French were very enthusiastic about flying, but these people wanted to remind themselves of the close connection with England during the Second World War. That, too, was an honour.

The USAF authorities later came to England to investigate the cause of Lieutenant-Colonel Thompson's crash. I was having a quiet beer in the Dolphin Inn in Thorpeness with a friend. When we overheard these Americans mention Thompson, I introduced myself as his former colleague. They were very interested in what I had to say. They couldn't accept that the crash of the A10 and consequent death of Thompson had been an accident. The most bizarre theory was that whilst flying so low, he had been shot through the aircraft canopy by a sniper from behind the Iron Curtain!

Every part of that A10 was subsequently shipped back to the United States for investigation.

WORKING WITH THE LAW

In 1987, the local police asked me to help them find a missing man suffering from senile dementia, who had wandered out from his home in Aldeburgh.

Scanning the ground from my aircraft, I found him within half an hour, lying in an area surrounded by gorse about 1½ miles from Aldeburgh on the Thorpeness road. He had been lying there for three days but thankfully recovered, none the worse for his experience.

This success was widely covered by the press and two TV companies; Anglia and BBC Norwich.

On a regular basis, the police forces over Norfolk and Suffolk then used me and my Shadow to find people or clear certain areas for them. I searched for suicide cases, people missing through illness or, as in one case, who were trapped. But the most extensive search was for a murderer who had stabbed his mother thirty times and was on the run deep in the Norfolk Broads.

I was briefed that he had the habit of having to wash his hands at least every twenty minutes, which implied that he would be in the vicinity of water. The police gave me permission to use school playing fields for refuelling. We searched for most of a day using SWAT teams and dogs. I flew at 300 feet above the terrain, which was heavily wooded, or marshland with reed beds and lakes.

I eventually saw him looking up from a wood. With radio contact, I brought in the SWAT team. He then escaped in a van, which I followed for some miles, cutting corners so that I was always in touch. It was quite a challenge to hold back at least 1–1½ miles, whilst keeping the van in sight, flying the aircraft and reading relevant road numbers to enable the police to intercept, but we succeeded and he was finally caught in the wilds of Norfolk.

The Shadow didn't need an observer, as it could fly very slowly to undertake a search. Also, of course, brief inattention to the controls would not result in a stall or spin due to the forgiving characteristics of the Shadow.

I had several meetings with chief constables to discuss these aircraft being used in their forces. Further investigations due to Britain's over regulated system showed that such operations would involve 'aerial work'. The CAA required any aircraft performing aerial work to be fully certified and the pilot qualified to commercial licence level. As microlights were only 'approved' with non-certified engines and could only fly with a 'D' licence especially set up for this type, the use of them by the police was not possible. So here we had a vehicle that could do a job saving thousands of police search hours, but which they were not allowed to use.

One chief constable with a certain amount of aircraft knowledge rejected the Shadow's use for the police force because it wasn't fully instrument rated, which would have allowed it to fly at night or in poor weather conditions. I told him that as far as I was aware, search duties couldn't take place at night or in poor weather, as it was a physical impossibility.

Another chief constable's area encompassed coastal waters and rivers and he was obviously a 'yacht man'. He said 'officially' that the Shadow was no good for the police because at £20,000 it didn't cost enough! That same force bought a £250,000 launch that could reach 15 knots to trawl the rivers and inland coastal waters for smuggling purposes. Police forces mainly use helicopters, which are very versatile and capable, but cost a fortune to run.

Common sense in this country is sometimes absent. The relaxing of aerial rules by the CAA would allow all sorts of aerial surveillance to help organisations like local authorities to oversee crowd assemblies, riot control, missing persons and various other law enforcement procedures, all at minimal cost to the tax payers.

CHAPTER 7

Films

SLIPSTREAM

One day, in 1987, an impressive black AMG Mercedes drew up outside the factory. It was owned by the film special effects director, Brian Johnson, who had come for the purpose of buying a Shadow aircraft. We immediately became friends and have had a lasting association ever since.

Early in his career, Brian had created most of those fantastic effects for the film '2001: A Space Odyssey'. He broke new ground with George Lucas and Gary Kurz in the making of this film. I remember '2001: A Space Odyssey' for being the first totally believable film about space. Since then, Brian has worked on 'The Everlasting Story', 'Star Wars', 'Aliens' and other major film releases for which he has won many awards.

It was in 1987, whilst formulating a film at Pinewood Studios called 'Slipstream' – a film set in the future after the earth has suffered a disaster of apocalyptic proportions – that Brian Johnson and Gary Kurz proposed the two unusual aircraft required in this £7 million production to be the Optica and the Shadow. I think Brian was the Shadow's main advocate. The Optica was a private venture. It possessed a peculiar airframe layout and was an aircraft to be used for surveillance purposes. It had three side-by-side seats in what looked like a bug's head – in short, its appearance presented an unusual sight, as did the Shadow. It is a feature of films to use unusual objects and places to entertain the public. The Bond films are a prime example.

The 'Slipstream' film used two Shadows painted in the most extraordinary colour schemes. One was for studio work and one for the flying, which I was to undertake. The Optica was to be flown by the gifted pilot, Derrick Piggott. Derrick had flown for various and numerous films in the past and was very experienced in this type of work. I was shocked to hear the very small fee that he had received for these past flying films. This type of work can be very demanding – even dangerous – so without much idea myself of fees, Brian helped both Derrick and I to receive a fitting fee. To be paid for flying in the UK is termed 'aerial work' by our authorities, thus all my fees went straight to CFM and I personally received no money.

When he was younger, Derrick Piggott had been the stunt flyer stand-in for the actor George Peppard and made the memorable pass under that bridge in the film 'Blue Max'. Each flight missed the bridge support uprights by only a couple of feet. It is a tribute to his skill that he made that pass over twenty times.

In the film 'Slipstream' I had to represent the American actor Billy Paxton ('Apollo 13', 'Twister', etc.) with a wig and identical clothing. The passenger in my aircraft was Bob Peck (best known for 'Edge of Darkness'), but for the flying sequences a very realistic dummy took his place.

In my first take I had to use the Pinewood grounds as an airfield – the first time apparently in the studio's history. I took off from alongside the huge Bond 007 studio, my altitude limited to 200 feet by the proximity of Heathrow International Airport. Over the next few days, the flights went well and then the whole crew moved to Settle, in the Yorkshire Dales.

I soon realised that every person involved with the film was the best at their specific job and I felt honoured to be in such company. I was completely fooled on one occasion, due to the brilliance of the make-up artists. I had just endured my own makeover session, when I was approached by an African who obviously knew me well, talking to me on intimate terms. I was becoming progressively uneasy and unnerved, when the African revealed he was Brian! Even with the knowledge of this fact, I took a lot of convincing!

In my experience, only the military had been capable of efficient organisation and management, but the organisation and management in the film industry that I witnessed was superb.

Helicopters and their pilots were used for filming the aerial shots. These people usually came from the Flying Pictures company and were also experts in their field. Marc Wolf and David Paris were probably two of the most experienced flying film operators anywhere in the world. They always did the flying shots for the James Bond films.

Derrick Piggott and I worked with David Paris throughout the making of 'Slipstream'. The helicopter used was a Bell 206 Jet Ranger with a gyro-stabilised pod housing the camera, which was attached to its side. The Shadow and Jet Ranger had a similar speed envelope, so we often filmed together rather than with Derrick and the Optica.

One of the film sequences in Yorkshire was at the formidable Gordale Scar. This is an awe-inspiring 200-foot deep canyon that broadens to approximately 150 yards across from wall to wall and travels for a distance of ¾ mile before petering out into the open country. Additional microlights were needed for this shoot and I had to lead a long line of these microlights over the brim of the canyon at its widest point and plunge into its depths and then fly its length. None of this somewhat hazardous flying actually featured in the finished film, which I felt was a shame as these microlight pilots made great efforts to please, whilst combating with far from easy flying circumstances. I had to negotiate the canyon without much clearance on either side of my wing tips. It was a dangerous thing to do with unpredictable air currents and massive broken rocks lying just below. This was not the time to make an error. If any fault had occurred during my runs, there would have been no reserves for flight safety. Several repeat runs were usually required during a film shoot, as different film speeds or light settings were covered, each of which would produce a varying effect of the same scene – the best then being used for the final version. Then there were the unforeseen errors made through faulty equipment or failures for other unknown reasons, even if the flight run itself was perfect. Altogether, I made over sixty passes down Gordale Scar and didn't enjoy one of them!

The other danger in that part of Yorkshire was the low-flying military jet aircraft. On one filming session, I radioed to Derrick that two fast jets were coming across the open end of Gordale Scar just as he was about to exit. He didn't reply. Quite how they all missed, I'm not too sure, but he didn't see them at all. I began to wonder if he should change his glasses – or maybe stop flying!

On another session, whilst flying near the town of Skipton, I was tucked up behind a Quicksilver microlight. The Shadow was at minimum speed with full flap; I was trying hard not to overshoot this slow aircraft and right on my tail was the Jet Ranger. I could 'feel' it through my elevator, which sporadically jerked, indicating the closeness of the helicopter. Suddenly, looking to my left, I saw three RAF Buccaneer fighter bombers in formation, heading straight in our direction at the same height. 'Traffic at 9 o'clock,' I yelled. The Quicksilver hit his spoilers and dropped away like a stone, leaving the two of us still hanging there. Just as they missed us by a few feet, another three Buccaneers from the same direction flew past us, but 300 feet ahead. One of them appeared slightly to jink his wings in acknowledgement, yet they remained in tight formation. This second near miss was incidental in comparison with the first, which had seemed a positive strike situation. A few months after this incident, a CAA statement was published in aviation magazines, requesting the multi-coloured microlight that was flying in Yorkshire on a specific date to confirm to their authorities a 'near miss' report by an RAF Buccaneer. Obviously the second trio of Buccaneers had reported the meeting with the Shadow but didn't mention the helicopter. This was from the formation that had passed some 300 feet distance – not the lot that missed us by feet!

Aircraft near misses in the UK airspace have to be reported to the relevant authorities. The film people had obtained proper clearance for our flying activities in this particular area of Yorkshire. They had issued a NOTAM (notice to airmen) so in theory, no other aircraft were supposed to be flying in that area. I duly reported to the Air Miss Group Captain that I had been the 'near missed multi-coloured microlight', but that the three Buccaneers who had made the notification to the authorities were not in actual fact the three aircraft that had so very nearly hit us that day. I also wrote vociferously to this Board, covering the complete failure of the RAF to abide by NOTAMs. This was not the first happening of its kind. We had already reported near miss incidents on several occasions, which occurred whilst flying in the Malham area of Gordale, Yorkshire, but the RAF denied that any of their aircraft were responsible and said they must have been NATO German planes. Filming at low altitude through forests and canyons was dangerous enough without the constant threat of low-flying fast jets.

One of the interesting shots created was achieved by setting up a camera and crew on top of a large rounded hill. The Shadow was instructed to fly in the valley below, and then whilst climbing, hug the contours and finally skim over the surface at top speed, narrowly missing the camera and crew. I always tried to carry out what was required as precisely as possible, so if they wanted a low pass I assured them it would be low! The first pass seemed to be acceptable, then through my radio I was requested to do a second run. As I flew up and over the curved summit, I noticed the camera was in place on its tripod, but there was no sign of the crew. I completed the run and on landing, asked what had happened to the crew. The crew apparently had hidden, because no one would stand there to face another pass at such a low altitude! They had set the camera running and then dived for any available cover. We filmed in fascinating and wonderful hills and dales, flying over miles of deserted countryside, some of which looked like lunar landscapes of limestone scree. There were no major roads in this part of the world, but I used to land on minor single-track byways whenever possible, when I needed refuelling.

During the production of a film, there are two film units. The first unit usually works on the set with the actors and the second unit creates all the action scenes. Sometimes the Shadow was used for some filming purposes, operating an Eymo camera fixed to various places such as a wing strut or undercarriage leg.

After completing our filming in Yorkshire, we spent two days in a large chalk quarry just north of Dunstable, Bedfordshire. The Shadow and Optica both took off from the floor of the quarry, which was half a mile across and surrounded by steep, high white walls of chalk. A strange coincidence was that only a mile from this quarry was the tiny village of Tilsworth and, when I flew, I could look down on the house and place where I was born in July 1940 – the start of the Battle of Britain. My mother, being pregnant, had been evacuated from Thorpeness on the east coast of Suffolk because of the imminent threat of an invasion from Germany, but I have no memories of this area as we returned to Suffolk when I was just two months old.

Sometimes film requirements can become worryingly hazardous. Whilst working at this location, I had an accident with the Shadow. The storyline necessitated the Shadow, already two up, to have a third person (in reality a dummy) lying on top of the centre wing. I endeavoured to ensure the security of all this but on take-off the aircraft became completely uncontrollable. I hurriedly cut the engine power and hit the ground causing a ground loop. Thankfully, we were unhurt and no damage had occurred but it left me shaken. It seemed that objects could be hung anywhere on the plane except the top of the centre of its wing. The dummy in this position must have upset the airflow over the tailplane, which made any pitch control impossible. The idea of three in a Shadow was obviously not going to work, so the storyline had to be changed.

The next move for the crew was to Turkey, where we were to film in the area of Cappadocia, south of Ankara. This strange landscape has desert-like features with hundreds of rock columns, each topped with a large boulder. The Shadow was transported to Turkey in its trailer, inside a juggernaut lorry, and driven to the site by one of the film crew. The Optica had to fly there. It pleased me no end to hear that Derrick Piggott needed to have an airline pilot with him to work all the avionics and GPS for navigation. Here was one of the finest 'flyers' around, but he was as hopeless as myself at piloting. I think he and I should be termed 'aeroplaners'.

As we disembarked at Istanbul, I asked Billy Paxton if he'd ever seen the film 'Midnight Express'. He clamped his hand over my mouth, saying that we were the first film unit in eight years that had been allowed into Turkey. The Turkish Government had been very embarrassed by that film, the result of which had been the virtual end of the tourist industry in that part of the world. At Istanbul, we all transferred on another flight to Ankara followed by a four- or five-hour bus ride south.

I didn't really know where I was, but the following morning saw me unloading my Shadow from the trailer with its incredible paint scheme. As I checked everything out, it became obvious that the truck had been in some sort of accident whilst travelling from England to Turkey. The Shadow had broken free from its tie-down, due to the trailer having crashed around inside the truck.

A huge row ensued between the film organisers and the driver of the truck because the main teleflex control cable for operating the Shadow's elevator had been snapped and the aircraft could not fly. A new teleflex was needed. I have previously mentioned that film crews comprise amazing people and this incident proves the point. During that first night at 04:00 hours, there was a knock on my bedroom door and there stood a fellow waiting to hand me the replacement part from CFM! The hotshot production assistant girls and secretaries had sent a courier on a motorcycle to CFM. The motorcyclist had then handed the teleflex replacement part to a Turkish airline captain, who off-loaded it onto a taxi driver at Ankara and he had driven for four hours to deliver the new control cable to me. Incredible!

Derrick Piggott had to use a Turkish military airbase somewhere not too far away, but because of the Shadow's short take-off, I could use roads wherever the main crew were in position. Amusingly different from the UK, were the police assigned to our film unit. They halted the traffic, even on a main route – once at either end of a quarter-mile stretch – so that I could use the road as a runway.

The flying conditions were difficult. We were about 4000 feet AMSL and it was very hot and thermic. Derrick, with his under-powered Optica, had problems whilst flying in closed valleys, finding it difficult on occasions to climb sufficiently to rise above the sides.

One morning, my brief for filming was to fly to an area named an 'open museum'. 'Just follow this road for about 50 km when you will see a box canyon. That's where the crew will be.' Off I went, following the said road. Whilst trolling along, I realised that I didn't know where I'd come from (not even the name), let alone where I was heading. If I crashed, I couldn't speak Turkish and hadn't even any local money. The road below was the only re-assuring factor.

The radio crackled in my ears, 'Hello, where am I?' It was Derrick Piggott.

Responding, I replied, 'Where do you think you are, "Lester"?' (I'd decided to call him 'Lester' after Lester Piggott, the jockey).

'Stick to radio procedure, David,' came the clipped English reply from Derrick.

He reported he was near a large lake, which, fortunately, I could see on my map. Assuming we were both destined for the same area, I told him to fly 210 degrees at 1000 feet and look for me at 2000 feet. For nearly ten minutes, I circled in vain above in-hospitable terrain. To my relief, at last, 'I can see you!' came over the radio and we flew on together. I landed on the road at the mouth of a wide canyon whose walls rose an intimidating 1500 feet on either side and whose far end was completely closed, the canyon narrowing to a width of 300 feet – an awesome and worrying sight for a flyer. We had reached our intended destina-tion. I tied the Shadow down, grateful that I had survived the journey and met up with some of Brian Johnson's special effects crew whom I had worked with in England.

One of these special effects guys was called Phil. He was a mad character. When not filming, he ran a pub back in England with his partner who had always been the love of his life. He then proceeded to tell me this incredible tale of how he had in the past, attended his partner's wedding to another. However, when she had seen him, Phil, standing outside the church after the ceremony she had broken away from her new husband and run to Phil to the ensuing disbelief of all present and had then driven away with him!

Phil was also the complete film buff. He seemed to know every film ever made and all the actors in their respective roles. I quizzed him on several films, wanting names or title. He reminded me that a film title was 'High Flight', which I needed to know. 'That actress was Mary Ure,' he replied to another query and then when I remarked Elizabeth Alexander was my favourite-looking actress, he pointed out certain members of our crew that had worked with her.

A strange incident occurred later that day at the canyon. Phil and I were walking along the road and we happened to be passing a telephone box. Suddenly it started to ring. We stared at each other in disbelief.

'Shall I answer it?' asked Phil.

'Whatever for?' I said. 'You can't speak Turkish.'

But Phil just had to respond – the compelling force of the ringing telephone was too much to resist. He disappeared into the box, then seemed to be involved in an animated conversation with the unknown caller. He then leaned out of the door and said, 'It's for you, David!'

'Don't be daft,' I retorted dismissively.

'No, really,' he said, insisting I speak to the mystery caller.

Feeling like a fool, I picked up the telephone. It was Brian Johnson speaking from England! Although not on location with us, he had previously reconnoitred the area as a filming location and had taken the telephone box number for reference. He had deduced that we would be filming at this site on this particular day! One couldn't really improve on that for timing!

David Paris, the Jet Ranger helicopter pilot, was responsible for flying the camera crew. He told me that the first run involved him hovering at the entrance of the canyon to film Derrick in the Optica, who was scheduled to fly head-on towards them and below the Jet Ranger. Paris said that his accompanying Turkish observer (a military requirement) started to 'nip sixpences' as the Optica approached so closely that it seemed inevitable the two planes would hit. The helicopter held station but almost as soon as the Optica had passed underneath, the radio crackled, 'Optica to helicopter – where are you?' After this, David Paris declared that there was no way he was going to fly with the Optica again until the pilot was issued with new glasses. He was obviously shaken but was still able to laugh, as he recalled the Turk's white face as he related this episode to me afterwards.

The action didn't stop here because Derrick then flew into the narrowing box-canyon in an aircraft that possessed no performance ability to climb and clear its sheer rock walls. Realising that as he progressed, the width was drastically diminishing, Derrick flew near to the canyon wall and executed a 180-degree turn with his wings at a 90-degree bank angle – a fantastic manoeuvre. Not only did he do this once but several times that day! What a flyer.

I also had to fly several times in the canyon that day. Thankfully, my power-to-weight ratio in the Shadow was sufficient to allow me to climb the necessary 1500 feet to clear the canyon's closed end. On one flight, I thought I would attempt a similar flat 180-degree turn at the point where Derrick had manoeuvred. I achieved the turn but was never confident that sufficient width existed. I concluded that Derrick, even though his eyesight was far from perfect, was doing a wonderful job.

Later, skimming across the summit of 1000-foot rock mesas and swooping down close to their sides was great fun. The Jet Ranger, flying only a few feet off the wing tip, filming at 100 mph, made the background surface of the rock a complete blur, which was the whole object of the 'take'. Cameraman Terry Cole told me the resulting footage contained some of the best aerial shots he had ever taken. Even David Paris got excited with the flying we were doing.

The film wasn't a success, but it was sad that due to editorial cutting, cinema viewers were deprived of these dramatic aerial sequences. The crew, who had all worked on dozens of films, knew before filming was completed that it would not be a box-office hit. With Gary Kurz producing and such well-known actors as Mark Hammel (Luke Skywalker), Ben Kingsley, Bob Peck and Billy Paxton, the film should have been a success. I waited to see the finished result before I could believe them, but I later found their assessment to be correct.

On my return to England, there were further scenes to film for our Second Unit, which entailed flying amongst some of the world's largest hot air balloons. These balloons created a wondrous sight, a fantasy world in a multitude of shapes and colours floating silently in the sky above Surrey and Hampshire. My flying instructions were to pass as close as possible to one specified red balloon. I found this extremely difficult. It was very hard to calculate accurately the distances involved with an enormous balloon at 4000 feet. I finally resolved the problem by passing over it rather than alongside. I seemed more able to judge this distance.

I worried needlessly in the end, as virtually none of these flying shots were shown in the finished film.

'Slipstream' was given a Royal Premiere in Leicester Square, London, in the presence of the Duke and Duchess of York. I gained permission for the whole factory personnel to attend and hired a coach to take us all to London. One of the wives told me she had often watched on television, film stars arriving for film premieres and walking into the cinema on the red carpet with all the crowds shouting and clapping. She could not believe that it was now happening to her as she and her husband walked that same route. Inside the cinema, the stars and people involved in the making of the film were introduced to their Royal Highnesses. The Duchess of York took particular interest in the flyers, Derrick Piggott and myself, as she was undertaking flight training herself at the time. She was wearing a full-skirted taffeta dress, which was shaped much shorter at the front than the back. As she laughed at something I'd said, she leaned back and I thought we were all going to see the 'crown jewels'. 'Steady,' I shouted. To which she roared with laughter, fully aware of my concern for her possible predicament!

SHELL ADVERTISEMENT

Whilst completing the filming for 'Slipstream' in the autumn of 1988, another filming request occurred when I was recommended by Flying Pictures to fly a Streak Shadow in an advertisement for Shell Oil. This was to take place near the coastal village of Portreath in Cornwall. As Brian Johnson was between films at the time and was always so enthusiastic about the aircraft, he accompanied me to assist in the handling of the plane. Our arrival in Cornwall coincided with the rapid deterioration of the weather and the wind blew wildly for days, accompanied by banks of horizontal sleeting rain. Eventually, with the weather showing no immediate signs of improvement and boredom getting the better of us, we rigged up the Streak and flew in what Brian measured as a 55 mph wind! It proved to be an exciting flight!

The action of the shoot was performed by Marc Wolf, who was probably the best flying film shooter in the world. It entailed flying his Jet Ranger helicopter close to the ground, towards the edge of the 300-foot cliffs following a set route, which was to be crossed intermittently by a succession of various animals and people, creating a 'near miss' effect. This would culminate in the near miss of myself as I flew in over the sea towards the cliffs, at which point our paths would meet. Execution and timing of the action was crucial and several runs were completed with masterful expertise by Marc Wolf. The rumoured cost of this and other action sequences was £1 million.

Money certainly appeared to be no problem. One evening, the film crew and participants were taken out for dinner in Falmouth. During the evening, Brian, knowing my inability to resist a challenge, made it known that I had no interest in food and preferred desserts and cream. At the point in the evening when my judgement was severely impaired by the consumption of red wine, the challenge was issued for me to demonstrate my love of cream by eating the whole contents of a large jug of clotted cream, which stood on the table. I can vividly recall the sight of the spoon standing vertically in the jug; such was the solidity of the cream. However, honour was at stake, so putting aside any qualms or misgivings about possible side effects, I duly dug in and completed the task! The unbelievable conclusion to this magnificent meal provided by the generosity of Shell Oil was that I was the only person who was not ill the following day!

After all this, the completed TV advertisement apparently showed no Streak Shadow. It took my son Jacob to spot it. He recorded the advertisement and on slowing the speed right down, noticed the flash of the red Streak fly past on two frames.

It seems incredible that so much money, time and effort had to be used to create such a minimal effect.

'Superwings'

In 1995, a film crew from Holland arrived at CFM. They were producing a film called 'Superwings' about microlights for the Discovery TV Channel and wanted to film the Streak Shadow.

Having already filmed other microlights, the crew had very defined opinions about the capabilities of such machines.

'You are in for a shock,' I told them, 'the CFM Streak is another order of performance altogether.'

I positioned the crew on Thorpeness cricket field so that they could film the angle of climb immediately after take-off and warned them that it would be dramatic in comparison with other microlights. They duly set up the camera at a distance of 150 yards. 'Come closer,' I shouted and beckoned them nearer. '50 yards or even less.' I told them I could be higher than 300 feet altitude by the time I flew over their original position. As I've previously mentioned, the Streak demonstrator was nothing less than violent in its manoeuvrability in the air when set up with very little fuel, and an overall empty weight limit of less than 380 lb. The rotation angle filmed was 70 degrees up, the acceleration 0–60 mph in under four seconds. I had told them that they were in for a shock! The climbing Streak could sustain a 70-degree angle of climb and this wasn't a zoom manoeuvre. This was not the best angle of climb for 'rate of climb' but it did look spectacular. The 'Superwings' crew quickly realised the plane's capabilities and decided to film from the 30-foot cliff tops at Thorpeness, whilst I displayed over the beach and sea. I demonstrated a landing on the sandy beach and noticed that the sandbank, just off shore, was being revealed as the tide went out, so whilst waiting during a pause from filming, I decided to fly off the beach and do a 'touch and go' on the newly exposed sandbank. I thought that if the sand proved hard enough for a landing, this would make excellent film footage for the camera crew, who were positioned directly opposite the sandbank on the cliff top.

I duly carried out a 'touch and go' on the 50-yard strip of enticing sand and looked back to check my tyre tracks. There were none, which confirmed my opinion that it would be firm enough to land. Lining the plane up, I touched down and stopped. To my horror, the wheels immediately began to sink. This was no firm landing surface; it was quicksand. My supposed wheel tracks that I had previously looked for must have instantly puddled away. Cursing myself for such a gross error of judgement and with no distance now to lift off, I had to somehow turn the plane about and taxi to the far end of the sandbank in order to attempt a take-off. I was filled with the chilling knowledge that lift-off was by no means a certainty in these conditions. Using as much power as I could muster, I roared the Streak forward, down its improvised runway, dragging the reluctant wheels through the sucking sand and willed the plane to become airborne before we were engulfed by the icy waters of the North Sea.

I was aware that Pat White had already perceived the potential dangers of the situation and had bolted down the cliff face to the beach in anticipation of initiating my rescue 150 yards from shore. My mouth was biscuit dry, as the plane finally lurched into the air just above the breaking waves and I thought what a shot this could have been for 'Superwings'; my final moments captured on film for all to see, the scene of the rapidly disappearing Shadow being pulled downwards beneath the sea, with maybe the final dramatic touch of my hand desperately clawing upwards for help!

Joking apart, it had been a near thing. The film crew had been totally unaware of my predicament, but I should have known better. I had known all my life of the sand's unpredictability. My father's younger brother had been lost in the 1930s at this very place and his body never found.

'DRAGONHEART'

In 1994, CFM was contacted by a film company who wished to use a Shadow and me in the making of their film 'Dragonheart'.

Dragonheart was a legendary tale from medieval times and contained all the right ingredients to appeal to an audience of all ages. This $92 million film was to be shot in Slovakia and would star Dennis Quaid as the dragon slayer and would feature the voice of Sean Connery as the dragon.

Apparently, Flying Pictures, based at Fairoaks, had recommended the Shadow and me when Bob Cohen, the director, had told them that he needed an aircraft with a really smooth, aerial platform to carry out the filming of the dragon's point of view (POV).

Flying for film work is very different from flying purely for one's own pleasure. One has to be totally competent and capable of instantly performing any manoeuvre that is required. Often flying in hazardous conditions and circumstances, one has to be able to accurately repeat that flight many times before all the varying filming angles are completed. Besides the actual flying, one must be totally reliable, disciplined and committed in every way. With up to $100,000 a day expenditure when on location, the director does not want to hear that the aircraft engine will not start or that the aircraft has failed to arrive at the appointed time on the set. Pay in the film industry is high but this is because everyone in the crew is of the highest standard and possesses all the above qualities.

Before the Shadow could undertake this film work, I had to design a mount that would safely secure the $90,000 camera on the front of the aircraft. I was beginning to realise that this film work was too big a venture for me to organise on my own, so I contacted my friend Brian Johnson, who was in the film world and, asked him if he would consider being my manager. Through his enthusiasm and love of the Shadow, he agreed to my proposal and immediately took over all the financial dealings with the film company. He was the ideal manager, as he was familiar with the scene and knew how to sort out any problem or transaction. He purchased a vehicle, trailer and the aircraft on behalf of 'Dragonheart'. The vehicle, an LHD Range Rover, had belonged to an Arab Sheik and would be perfect for towing the aircraft and trailer across Europe to Slovakia.

He also advised me knowledgeably on how to charge the film

company for the camera mount that I had designed. In actual materials, the cost was nominal – a mere £4.50! But his suggested figure of £5000 was for the engineering skill necessary to devise such a fixture, without which, filming would be impossible. This mount was adjustable in pitch and could be fitted 45 degrees port or starboard and proved vibration free, exactly what Bob Cohen required. I personally felt that £5000 was an excessive figure to charge the film company but, in this industry, all finances are high and as my camera mount worked perfectly and did the job, no one cared as to its cost.

I thought it would be a good idea to take Jacob with Brian and me to Slovakia. He would be an invaluable asset with his practical engineering abilities, knowledge of the plane and flying skills. I also considered it would be good experience for him to witness what was demanded when flying for films. One day I was going to have to give up the continuous pressure of flying and perhaps he would be able to replace me in this work. There was a general feeling amongst my friends that my flying was becoming a little too good and this is a clear danger point for a pilot. If one becomes too confident, safety tends to take second place. A signal, therefore, that perhaps I should be standing down in the very near future before fate intervened.

We drove to Slovakia with all the usual problems of transporting an aircraft through different European countries with the frustrations of the carnet and queuing in long lines of trucks at customs but, eventually, we arrived in Bratislava where we joined up with the Special Effects Unit (SPX). They weren't the crew Brian normally worked with but they were all English and knew Brian.

The film was to be shot east of Kosice, almost at the border of the Ukraine. It was a wild and rugged countryside of waterfalls, forests and ancient castles, which straddled the rough-hewn hilltops. My first 'take' was to be flying towards one of these castles. Reaching the site entailed yet another long drive. It seemed time had stood still in this faraway part of the world. Life was as it must have been in the Middle Ages. Weather-gnarled old women, entirely clad in black, heads tightly tied with headscarves, sat companionably in the sun, unmoved by Brian's greetings of 'Hello Mum!' as we drove slowly past.

On reaching the location site, we found a disused agricultural spraying airstrip where we could prepare the aircraft. It was obvious that once the Russians had moved out of this land during the break up of the Soviet Union, life had quickly slipped back into the pastoral ways of old. But flying in a country like this without all the necessary permits granted by the authorities, could be a hazardous or even fatal occupation. There was the ever real threat that I could be shot down as a foreign intruder, so to prevent this possibility, I had to carry reams of official paperwork, in case I needed to prove my identity and clearances.

Film shooting involved many hours of static activity. One can be in position, on call, from 06:00 hours and yet it may be 16:00 hours before one is required for action. Whenever that call comes, one has to be instantly focused and ready to perform.

The high-tech nature of the filming provided the director with my POV (point of view). This was achieved through placing a small video camera on the aircraft and he could then direct me for the operation of the main camera, which was mounted directly in front of me. It meant my view forward beyond this large device was not good.

Carrying out the director's orders as to where to fly and what to do, remembering to turn the camera on and off, whilst coping with flying the aircraft with this severely restricted view, plus having to have a constant awareness of where to land and exit in an emergency, demanded the highest levels of concentration and was exhausting work.

I often had to repeat a flying sequence several times in order that the cameraman could use differing film types and speeds of exposure. The director of the SPX unit told me one evening that after my first low-level run at a stockade where I had to scatter the people and horses in my role of the dragon, he had covered his face with his hands, so convinced was he that I was going to collide with the actors and animals! Apparently, the scattering effect hadn't required much acting on the part of those present! This sequence had to be carried out identically another four times, for which I was rewarded with the director's compliment, 'That fellow is the Right Stuff!' This was a compliment indeed, for he was referring to the aviation film of that name, which relates the lives of the top American pilots in the 1960s, who trained to be the first men in space. Dennis Quaid, coincidentally, was one of the stars of this film and there is the memorable quote (that he repeated to me!) from him when he says, 'You wanna know who's the best pilot in the world? Well you're looking at him!' I know I'm far from the best pilot in the world, but I do know that I'm good at undertaking what is demanded of me in the film world.

Slovakia was in the grip of an unrelenting heat wave that summer and the temperature in my cockpit reached 50°C on many occasions. Far more of a problem was that the constant excessively high temperature was causing the Shadow's Rotax 618 engine to overheat. Fortunately we had brought with us, in case of such an emergency, the engine from CFM's Streak demonstrator, the regular Rotax 582, so Jacob was able to change the engine and resolve our predicament.

On one of our designated days at the agricultural strip, the crew decided to take a much-needed lunch break, and Brian suggested we quenched our thirst at the local village bar. As we entered the large room, which acted as the bar, the dozen or so locals seated there fell silent. Brian, smiling broadly, took charge of the situation and gesticulating expansively, ordered beer for ourselves and everyone present. The atmosphere immediately lightened and the suspicious work-worn faces of the villagers were wreathed in smiles.

These were very poor people. Our $50 a day allowance from the film company was probably the equivalent of a month's wages to these people and it was embarrassing to be so rich in comparison.

The beer was wonderful and we soon discovered that all these local people knew exactly who we were and what we were doing. We weren't equipped with gifts like explorers of old, but I did have the coloured promotion leaflets on the Shadow and Streak, which I gave to the village children who treated them as treasure.

A visit we made at another time to another bar turned out to be not such an enjoyable event. My birthday occurred whilst we were on location, so Jacob, Brian and I decided to celebrate the occasion with a few drinks. The choice of venue was limited but we opted for the Russian-built hotel in Kosice, a rather bleak-looking edifice, but appearances aren't everything. Unfortunately, the interior wasn't much better. The bar revealed itself to be a vast, near empty lounge, with what I took to be piped music of the worst kind to provide an atmosphere of conviviality. Undeterred, we ordered our drinks, determined to make the most of the evening, though alcohol consumption would be strictly limited, with flying programmed for the next morning.

However, as the evening wore on, I became increasingly annoyed by this ghastly intrusive music, which was making any form of conversation impossible, so I ventured to ask the waitress if it could possibly be turned down. My request was received with an icy hostility. Unbeknown to me at the time, it was live music being performed by two musicians, hidden from my view, at the far end of the bar, one of whom was the waitress's boyfriend. My innocent remark did nothing to promote harmonious racial relationships, for that night Brian (who had made the mistake of endorsing my request) and I suffered the most dreadful bout of sickness. To me, there was no doubt in my mind that the waitress had 'spiked' our drinks as revenge for insulting the musical talents of her beloved.

The waitress wasn't the only one to be upset. The producer, Raffaella de Laurentiis, was extremely upset the next day, when she learned from the film set doctor that there was no way Brian and I would be fit for work. She was furious that I had obviously indulged myself with an excess of drink whilst celebrating my birthday.

Our next location was in the west of Slovakia, where we rigged up beside a large lake ringed by forests and the distant Tatra mountains. I was to simulate the dragon's POV as it dived into the water and, as the dragon supposedly possessed 80-foot wings, the diving action would have to be closely followed by a splash of appropriate dimensions as it entered the water. This would be created by a Russian helicopter dropping a massive 8-ton rectangular block of concrete. All good fun!

I began my filming run from the centre of the lake and flew towards the assistant director Herb and his crew, who were watching from the shore. As I approached, he radioed me to turn left. I was pretty sure he had meant right, as he was facing me, but I carried out his instruction. This resulted, I later heard, in Herb, who was a hardened New York tough guy, throwing a complete tantrum at my misinterpretation of his order. Later that day, I had a face-to-face confrontation with this intimidating character. I politely explained that for the past few hundred years in seamanship and in eighty or so years of aviation, the words left and right have not been used, purely to avoid this kind of confusion. The terms port and starboard are always used in reference to direction. Port is always to the left when facing forward in a craft and, starboard to the right. If he had issued the instruction to turn to starboard, the error would not have occurred. Apparently, this was the first time that the crew had ever witnessed anyone daring to correct Herb and it was a memorable event!

My next challenge on behalf of the dragon was to fly into a cloud of black smoke to create vortices, which would depict the dragon's departure in one of the scenes; vortices being the curling motions of air, which would supposedly show where the dragon had flown. Accordingly, an area of some 100 square yards was covered with old car tyres and set alight, which produced a satisfyingly impressive eruption of dense, sooty smoke, which blotted out the sky. It didn't seem very sane to be deliberately performing a low-level run into a seemingly solid mass of smoke as black as night, with zero visibility, but that was what I had to do.

I approached it apprehensively at full speed and shot through the swirling darkness, praying for the clear air to appear as soon as possible and emerged with a plane as black as the smoke I'd passed through. The flight did not produce vortices of any significance and I soon realised that this was because the plane did not possess sufficient inertia to move the air. To overcome this problem on the next attempt, I flew to what I estimated to be the centre of the massive smoke stack and executed a hard 'g' turn. I then flew out to where I hoped daylight would exist. This time the vortices were excellent but I had to execute this manoeuvre at least another eight times, such are the demands of flying for special effects.

Whilst waiting at our airstrip for the call to do yet another hazardous flight into the smoke, I was fortunate enough to witness one of the world's wonders. It was late August and the intense drowsy heat enveloped the landscape. We were positioned on a remote hillside, on yet another disused agricultural airstrip. Below us lay the village and meadows, motionless in the hot, shimmering light, and the far forested hills were lost in the distant haze. I was lying stretched out on the warm, dry grass, staring idly at the sky above, when suddenly, slowly drifting into view, came hundreds and hundreds of pure white storks high, high overhead on their migration south. Flying from the direction of Poland, these stately, elegant birds were gliding by in silent formation, with no wing movements, at what I estimated to be a height of about 8000 feet, their wings outstretched across the deep, blue sky.

These storks, from all over Northern Europe, were travelling back to Africa and had been making this journey for thousands of years. It was a very humbling experience to realise that this event would have occurred regardless of my existence or that of mankind and I felt most privileged to have seen such a moving, glorious sight.

The film unit gradually worked its way westwards, towards Bratislava. Whilst passing through Zilina, I attempted to buy some much-needed tobacco for my pipe. Stopping at a convenient street kiosk, I discovered that the only tobacco available was the local brand, which went by the impressive name of 'Taras Bulba'. Apparently, he had been a legendary warlord in olden times who'd done his part in ransacking this part of the world. If the name was anything to go by, this would be powerful stuff! The girl shop assistant though, had other ideas. Far from trying to sell the tobacco to me, she did her utmost to deter me from the purchase and I had the greatest difficulty in persuading her to part with a packet. I couldn't help remarking that she had a lot to learn about salesmanship and capitalism! Powerful it certainly was, much to the amusement of the onlooking film crew, who waited with relish to see how I would fare when I 'lit up'!

Dennis Quaid and I became quite good friends during the time we spent together on set. Being a pilot himself, he appreciated the flying characteristics of the Shadow, especially its extreme slow speed capabilities. I seriously thought he intended to buy one after the completion of the film but our friendship came to an abrupt halt after I refused to give him a lift in the plane. It was a very awkward situation to handle and came about because one day, when neither he nor I were needed by the film director, he asked me if I would take him to Bratislava, some 120 miles, so that he could get a flight to Paris to see his baby son and wife, Meg Ryan, who was making 'French Kiss' at that time with Kevin Kline. I had to explain that the aircraft was not mine. It was owned by the film company and I was under very strict limitations with flight permits and paperwork as to where I could fly and what I could do. To undertake an off-the-record flight, was just not possible. I also had to consider the possibility that if we suffered an accident in the plane and he was injured, I would be held responsible for all that would entail and the production of the film would be in jeopardy.

He obviously didn't understand the implications of what I had tried to explain about the situation, for after that I was avoided and given the cold shoulder.

As our location sites drew nearer to Bratislava, I found myself flying over vast tracts of beautiful deciduous forests and hills. Usually, my filming work was to fly at under 20 feet but this day, whilst waiting for the usual call, I flew to a height of 3000 feet. At this height I could look down on this incredible scene of endless beech and oak trees, interspersed with the occasional pine that covered the land as far as the eye could see.

The film unit was set up in a few clear acres in the forest, where the grass was carpeted with fragile, purple autumn crocus. I found it hard to comprehend how people seemed totally unaware of their beauty and walked on them with no regard for their existence.

The flying was exciting stuff. I would be briefed concerning the 'take' required, then I would carry out the instructions as I saw fit. It entailed low-level flying through the forest fire breaks at only one-third of the tree height, with the camera set to the side filming the flashing trees as the plane sped past. I often thought that if I did go down or crash, I would never be found in this boundless area of trees.

All aviation law and conventional flying restrictions are abandoned in film flying. Inevitably the flying is frequently low level and often requires flying directly at buildings, objects or even people, to within very close limits. This was the case in another of the dragon's POV shots when I had to fly very low down a long tree-covered slope, straight towards an actress who had been tied to a vertical pole mounted in a cart and then pull upwards at the very last moment. It must have been a terrifying experience for the actress and, hardly surprisingly, produced a genuine look of horror on her face at each of my three flights. I had the feeling that the shots were not close enough but a film technician reckoned that I had a third of a second remaining before she would have been hit! It was always helpful when the ground crew or director were in contact with me on flights such as this because they could advise me on the plane's height and distance from the target.

Brian Johnson was an invaluable help to me at all times. Being a Shadow and Streak flyer himself, he could appreciate and anticipate any difficulties that might arise regarding location sites and the flying tasks demanded. As shooting came to an end, he remarked that during the whole of the filming, I hadn't had to do any retakes through any fault of my flying. This fact hadn't even occurred to me but it was a welcome compliment from someone who was so used to working with the film industry.

We finally completed the 104 days of the shoot. Later, back in the USA, the computer experts would digitalize the Shadow to become the Dragon. I had flown a total time of twenty-four hours in the making of 'Dragonheart', out of which there would be maybe only six minutes shown in the actual film. A full day's filming by the crew, working from dawn until near dark, would only produce three to four minutes' a day of film that would be used in the final version.

It is not until one's been involved in the making of a full-length feature film, that one can really appreciate the enormous amount of work that's done to create those two hours the public will see in the finished film.

CHAPTER 8

Shadow 'D' Series and CFM Liquidation

At the beginning of 1996, the Shadow 'D' Series was awaiting certification by the PFA. Their engineering department delayed the certification to such an extent that CFM's finances were completely drained. The Shadow design was now fourteen years old and had been flying for thirteen years with the best known safety record of any aircraft, let alone that of microlights, yet we were still required to execute endless structural tests on the aircraft and to produce endless streams of data. The PFA even requested that the CAA's chief check pilot, Bob Cole, be sent to assess the design. On the conclusion of his flight, he dismissed the plane as 'boringly safe'. Our feelings of helplessness and frustration knew no bounds. So what was the reasoning and logic behind the PFA's obvious reluctance to grant the certification of the 'D' Series? I cannot understand, even today, but the outcome of their behaviour succeeded in the downfall of the company. To be a viable business, we had to make a minimum of two sales a month and we were unable to do this due to the delaying tactics of the PFA in authorising the certification with the result that the company had to go into the hands of the Receiver.

At the liquidation of CFM, the accountant laid intense pressure on the two directors – Pat White and my son Jacob – accusing them of the highly illegal act of knowingly running a company that was not profitable. It all seemed so unjustified to me. What did he know of the reality of all those years of striving? To lay blame on Jacob seemed so wrong. He had only been a director for two years and that was only because after thirteen years of struggling to fulfil so many roles in the company, I was completely exhausted and asked him if he would take over my directorship. This he had agreed to do and Catherine and I had then put in a further major investment to help the company. He should not have been made to bear the brunt of these accusations at the liquidation, when he had no dealings with the finances. If Catherine and I had had any perception of the problems that were to come, we would never have encouraged his involvement in this capacity. As it is, we must be found guilty of naivety in the harsh light of the business world where the only realities are the figures on the balance sheet and the company's production of the finest microlight in the world for fifteen years was worthless.

After protracted negotiations, the company was eventually taken over in November 1996. It was soon made obvious to me by the new owner that my services were not required and I had no option but to leave CFM – the company that I'd formed all those years ago in the early 1980s. I did not even possess design rights on the aircraft, as these had been forfeited to CFM for a royalty on each Shadow sale — royalties that, in reality, I had never received and yet on which I had been made to pay tax. It was not a very happy period.

CFM continued for another six years before finally collapsing. Most of the original employees left the company and with no new designs, or designer, the company now called CFM Aircraft only lasted that length of time because a long awaited order from the Indian Air Force, which we at CFM had been negotiating, came to fruition. This was the largest single order for any microlight ever placed but it came too late for the survival of CFM.

Strangely, my redundancy was a relief. I had been involved since 1973 with homebuilt aircraft and all their associated risk. It was wonderful, in a way, to have the stress of it all removed. Having been flying since I was fourteen years of age, I had been lucky enough to have got away without being killed for forty-two years and it was the right time to stop. Anyway, the permissive uninhibited flying required for making of major feature films had resulted in my boredom with normal flying practices and I no longer had the driving desire to fly. It appeared as though I had 'done my bit' and so was now satisfied. My only remaining interest was that of designing aircraft. I could have built a prototype Glint and, no doubt, if it had fulfilled its potential of 300-mph top speed and 1000-mile range, a market could have been developed and I could have then produced kits for sale. Not bloody likely!

It was time for contemplation in my beautiful area of Suffolk; walks on deserted beaches, heathlands and woods. I now knew what my father had meant when I asked, as a lad, 'Why haven't we got a car?'

'Because I have already arrived where I want to be,' he had replied.

Epilogue

Following the collapse of CFM, Laron in Texas sold out to Airborne Innovations. This was a company run by a group of people who were also NASA employees at the Johnson Space Centre, Houston. I was asked to visit Houston to help them begin production of the Streak and Shadow design. It was of great interest to me to visit the complex where these NASA employees worked, as it was where the astronauts undertook their training. I was fortunate enough to be able to sit in and peruse the interior of the International Space Station (ISS). The many logical techniques used in this satellite were fascinating to observe.

I was interested to see in the ISS that although there is no up or down when weightless in space, the 'floor' areas were coloured green and 'ceilings' blue. This was for the human brain to acquire some sort of orientation. Numerous other helpful considerations were apparent. I learnt that an automatic landing sequence procedure was available on the Shuttle, whereby the landing could be completely handled by the computer. However, this had never been used by any pilot to date, as they much preferred to be in charge of the manual controls and use their own judgement.

The one and only profitable aspect of NASA was their high-altitude research programme. This was conducted from B57 aircraft, which NASA had acquired after their retirement from the US Air Force. This plane was, in reality, the English Electric Canberra, which years before had been made under licence by Martin Co. as the B57. These planes were now nearing completion of their working life and only two were currently operating, which meant that NASA would need to find a replacement aircraft to take over this research programme.

One of the scientists, the Head of Engineering, really liked my design drawings of the modified StarStreak, which were to have been used to build an aircraft to attempt a class altitude record for Airborne Innovations. If the secret 'fuel cell' could be used, he mused, an unmanned StarStreak with a 50-foot wingspan and high aspect ratio might be a viable alternative to the ageing B57. The fuel cell ran on liquid hydrogen, which produced electricity. This, in turn, ran an electric motor, which powered a conventional propeller. My calculations showed that a StarStreak in this form was a genuine possibility. The liquid hydrogen tank would be formed around the fuselage with 2½-inch insulating foam, which would give the aircraft a profile of a rubber dinghy. Without a crew or engine and other normally accepted equipment, the weight when complete would be similar to a normal StarStreak. I did query the weight and size of a 60+ hp electric motor but was assured that modern technology had made these much smaller and lighter than in the past.

I was asked if I would consider working confidentially for NASA for three years, to develop this idea. My reply was emphatically in the negative. I couldn't even contemplate working in that over-hot, steamy climate for that length of time. The US may be geographically awesome but I knew that whatever was said in the interview, I did not want the job on any terms. Anyway, I knew I possessed one trait that would make me totally unacceptable in their eyes and that was my inability and refusal to use a computer. I did all my work with the aid of a slide rule, an unknown device in these days of electronics!

I duly faced the interviewing board of three NASA representatives, who interrogated me at length. Besides the obvious technical questions, there were numerous questions relating to my personality and character, such as 'What would you like most of all in the world, if given the chance?' I replied with reckless abandonment, 'A chicken suit!' I added that it must be yellow and have the beak, comb and big feet. This remark completely confounded the team of experts and gave them plenty of food for thought and proof, I hoped, that I was not suitable for any position in their establishment! Eventually, one of them asked what would I then do with a chicken suit? Revelling in the moment, I said I would race around my garden in England, making the appropriate sound effects! Needless to say, I succeeded in my attempt to fail the interview and returned, thankfully, back home!

Reluctantly, I did have to leave my beloved Suffolk yet again, for in 2001 I was visited by a charming Pakistani, Lieutenant-Colonel Ajab Khan, Deputy Military Secretary to the Chief Executive of the Pakistani Government. He and a friend, Brigadier Zaka Bhangoo, intended to circumnavigate the globe in his StarStreak, to raise funds for a children's charity. I quickly discovered that Ajab was very knowledgeable about aviation and we were soon deep into conversation. I listened to his fascinating accounts of flying his StarStreak high in the mountains of Pakistan. These are mountains of great heights, K2 being the second highest mountain on Earth. During one journey, the plane was flying in a canyon at 14,000 feet AMSL, the sides of which rose up a further 12,000 feet!

These flights were all part of the preliminary testing for their proposed world adventure.

It was during one nine-hour endurance flight, when Zaka was flying solo, the length of Pakistan, that fuel contamination caused the engine to misfire and he was forced to put down on a dry river bed. The damage inflicted on the aircraft required my technical expertise to repair, hence Ajab's visit to Suffolk.

I had no real desire to undertake the work, but felt I could not refuse my help when the world flight was in the aid of sick and needy children.

I decided to ask my friend Mick Newman if he would consider accompanying me on the visit. He was a yacht designer and builder and had also built and flew his own Shadow, so he would make an ideal accomplice to do the job. He enthusiastically agreed and so, in the early summer of 2002, we set off for Pakistan. Mike and I must have made an odd-looking couple, as we stood before the United Arab Emirates' officials at the flight check-in, Heathrow, vainly trying to persuade them that we had been informed that we did not need visas. Mike's appearance in his thirties-style crumpled linen suit, sandals and little round sunglasses obviously didn't help matters. We probably resembled more a pair of spooks rather than acquaintances of the Pakistani Government!

Eventually, with less than ten minutes to spare before the check-in closed, the officials received a fax from the Pakistan Government confirming that our statements were correct and that we could enter the country without the necessary visas.

After this fraught beginning to our travels, the actual journey passed uneventfully and Zaka met us, as planned, at Islamabad Airport. We entered a country on a war footing. Over one million soldiers lined the border with India, which was less than 60 miles away. According to the British press, the area was in a state of great alert, with both Pakistan and India threatening the use of nuclear weapons if the countries came to war and the situation demanded such shows of force. To us, life seemed pretty normal, the only signs of imminent war being the military government's gun posts on most road interceptions.

We were staying in a hotel in Jawlapindi and transported each day to an Army Air Corps base where we were to repair the aircraft, which was awaiting our arrival in one of the hangars. The heat was intolerable within the confines of the hangar and I found the work conditions unbearable until my suffering was noted and a large fan installed, which did improve the situation considerably. We were treated with great courtesy and respect and were very well looked after during our stay. Zaka may well have been retired but all the serving ranks treated him as their superior, even Ajab called him 'Sir'. Apparently, Zaka was and is regarded as one of the finest helicopter pilots in the world, with over 8000 flying hours to his name, and he was a constant source of fascinating stories. One day, the Base Commander arrived at the hangar to inspect our progress. He was a very imposing figure, extremely smart, still with the air of an ex-Sandhurst graduate. He related to me an incident concerning Bin Laden and his escape from Afghanistan, which I found totally incredible. He told me that following the recent upheavals in that country, a Pakistani soldier had apprehended Bin Laden at a border crossing and had later reported the incident to his Captain. The soldier had done his duty and shown him 'animosity' through the act of letting the air out of the tyres of the moped on which he was travelling. 'What happened then?' I commented in total disbelief. 'He was allowed to continue his journey into Pakistan.' I'm ashamed to say that my involuntary response was to laugh outright at this outrageous statement but the unflinching, unmoving face of the Brigadier then made me wish I had not succumbed to such flippant behaviour. 'This must be remembered is Muslim to Muslim, Mr David,' the Brigadier replied.

I will leave everyone to draw their own conclusions concerning that episode!

Zaka, Ajab, Mick and I all became great friends, each admiring each other's capabilities. The repair work was completed but without a test flight, as the Rotax 914 had not been returned from its shock-test before we had to return to England.

Mick and I left with the knowledge that we would all meet again in the near future, when Zaka and Ajab stopped in the UK on their proposed world flight. Sadly, to date, this flight has still not occurred due to the state of present world politics.

Throughout my flying activities from 1984 to 1996, I have had the privilege to have worked and flown in over thirty different countries, undertaking the most varied forms of flying in the most varied of circumstances and have met, I'm sure, some of the friendliest people on Earth. Many people have said to me that I should put down my experiences on paper but I have not felt confident to do so; an engineer/aviator/designer is not necessarily able to write a book. Structure, grammar and spelling are not attributes I am renowned to possess!

Initially, I reckoned that if I started writing and continued writing through that following night, I would be completed by morning! Needless to say, the enormity of this task has proved to take considerably longer than I originally estimated.

The one thing that has given me the most satisfaction in my career, is that the Shadow series has proved beyond any doubt that it is aerodynamically and structurally sound. The responsibility of an aircraft designer is a heavy one and it gives me immense pleasure that my designs have given endless joy to thousands of people without ever inflicting harm.

In the seclusion of my East Suffolk countryside, I still carry on with the design thought, 'Do we need an aeroplane to fly? Why not put on this conceived rig and go?'

Currently I am eyeing up the fantastic strength-to-weight ratio of my giant Hogweed trunks for wing spars. If constructed to the design of a dragonfly that has had millions of years' of development – just maybe . . .

They say there are 'No-Old-Bold-Pilots'.

David Cook – Aviator – Achievements

1944
Initial interest in aviation was inspired by watching the P51 fighters of 357 Sqn Leiston passing at low level over my home in Thorpeness on their way to Germany. I was four years old.

1951
The Bentwaters 81st TFS with F84 and F86 jets maintained my interest, as did the Thorpeness based USAF fighter pilots. During this period many model aeroplanes were built and flown from the cricket pitch.

1959 to 1963
RAF service –Initially in Airframes, later flew with T11 Vampire, Jet Provost T3/T4, Hunter T7 and Victor B1A

1973
Built the VJ-23 rigid wing hang glider in an attempt to win the Selsey Birdman Rally. Won in '74 and '75 however, the organisers did not pay the £3,000 prize even though I covered the distance.

1975-77
Won every hang gliding competition entered, both National and International, with the VJ-23.

1977
Designed and built power unit for VJ-23e. Also made the propeller.

1978
Flew the English Channel to France (first hang glider to do so). Lowest powered flight crossing in the history of aviation. Bleriot had 25hp, I had 9hp in the VJ-23e.

1978
Royal Aero Club. Presentation of "'Medal of Achievement" from HRH Prince Charles.

1978
Invited to Glendale California by designer Volmer Jensen who purchased the engine Installation Rights from me for the VJ. I flew several of his designs and we became close friends. I also met Volmer's friend, Irv Culver who had designed the VJ wing. (Drooped L/E - unique - and in principle used later on my Shadow series)

1979
With Neil Moran we designed and built 'Musfly', a man powered aircraft.
    The VJ-23e over the years was displayed at more than 80 major air shows. I was sponsored by Duckhams Oils. Highest honour was first on opening the show at SBAC Farnborough 1980. This machine was an exhibit at the Shuttleworth Collection, Old Warden, for several years before being transferred to Manchester Air/Space museum, where it currently resides.

1980
Volmer and I modified his VJ24 foot-launched design in 3 weeks to a wheeled/powered version -VJ24w, probably the world's first microlight, again built in my basement. This aircraft was displayed at major air shows in the UK for several years. Currently at Newark air museum.

1981
Working at Blois Aviation at Yoxford building imported microlights and instructing more than 50 pupils to fly.

1982
Design of the Shadow. Even in 2006 it was still considered one of the best micro lights in the world. My son Jacob is still flying the prototype, (02) twenty four years later.

1983
Shadow takes FIA world speed record over 3km - cat. CI-A/O. Pilot D Cook.

Shadow takes FIA distance record. Parham Suffolk to St. Just, (Land's End) More than double the distance of previous records! Pilot, P Troy Davies.

1984
Production started for Shadow Aircraft at Leiston as CFM. (Cook Flying Machines)

1986
Shadow flown from Biggin Hill to Sydney Australia by Eve Jackson.

International competition 'Dawn to Dusk' won by D Cook/D Southwell. 67 airfields (of the 8th air force) visited in a day, with shadow 02.

Precision Navigators Award
Duke of Edinburgh Award

Microlight Award
Outright Winner all categories
Presented by HRH Duke and Duchess of York.

Shadow and Optica used in the film "Slipstream". I was stand-in for Billy Paxton (Apollo 13 film). Filmed in England and Turkey.

1987
Shadow won British Design Award. Presented by HRH Prince Philip

Attended Royal Premier for "Slipstream" at Leicester Square. Duke and Duchess of York attended. I took the whole CFM factory personnel and spouses.

HRH Prince Philip visits CFM in Leiston as President of WWF for presentation of Shadow to Zimbabwe -I told him, "We were so proud to have the 'King' to come to poor Leiston"!

1988
Invited, with wife, to Buckingham Palace garden party, met the Queen and all.

Segrave trophy presented to Eve Jackson - D Cook Segrave medal.

1992
U.K. National category altitude records:
Shadow 23,600 ft UK Microlight category
Streak 27,150 ft FIA Microlight category
Took place from Thorpeness, Suffolk cricket field.

1994
Shadow chosen as aerial unit for filming 'Dragonheart' a $92m production shot in Slovakia. I flew P.O.V. & computerised track.
The stars - Dennis Quaid and Sean Connery.

Time to climb records: 0 – 3000metres Both Shadow and Streak halved existing records -unconfirmed by F.I.A. Pilots D Cook & J Cook.
Crew David Foster

Overseas flying experience with my own designed aircraft:

New Zealand. Eire, Guernsey, Australia, Thailand, India, Turkey
Italy, France, Germany, Belgium, Holland, Denmark, Sweden,
Botswana, South Africa, USA (14 States), Slovakia, Yemen, Greece,
Zimbabwe. 1994 (contd.)
Lectures:
Cambridge University of Engineering
Royal Aeronautical Society
NEC
Universities (Mostly under the auspices of the IMechE)
Rolls Royce Annual Lecture, Paulerspury

INTERNATIONAL AIR SHOWS:

SBAC Farnborough, 1980/86
Le Bourget Paris
Sun'n Fun - Florida
Stauning Lufthan - Denmark
Aero 87 - Friedrichshafen - Germany
Kjula - Sweden
Koksede - Belgium.

MILITARY WORK:

British Aerospace; Trials with Linescan (infra red) used with boffins locally and at Hatfield for trials.

A covert equipped Shadow used at Farnborough SBAC 1986, to Scan all the Russian military aircraft present.

Yemen:

World Health Organisation (Dutch UN) supposedly to be operated for water resource search using Hasselbladd cameras. After training crews I saw the PLO take over

Turkey:

Specialised Streak versions — bullet proof- using thermal imagery Equipment - replaced helicopters - and F16, on border work Against Kurds.

India:

Armed version for border surveillance using 7.6mm chain gun. Installation trials held in Enfield, London.

UK.

RAF demo at High Wycome.

D.E.A. Assignment for silent covert intrusions.

Botswana.

Specialised Streak versions. Border patrol against Namibia. Used By B.D.F.

Iraq:

Study by delegation for sidewinder version (no fixed base required - 1/5000 cost of a fighter)

Zimbabwe:

Sponsored by Goldfields Trust., used by anti poacher squad, protecting Black Rhino also used for Elephant counts.

World Distance Flights: In Shadow & Streak versions

England / Australia	Eve Jackson
England / India	V.P.Singhalia
England/ Australia	B Milton
England / Beijing	James Edmunds
USA, coast to coast	Andy Nightingale

| U.K. Hurn / Kirkwell | 2 Shadows non stop |
| | B Milton and P Troy Davis. |

International Competitions: (microlights)

Germany -	Aero 87 Friedrichshafen
Italy -	Bosano Monti Grappa
France-	Toulouse.

Private Airshows: VJ23e
Mostly with Ken Wallis, e.g. 'It's a Knockout' final. Arundel.

DESIGN WORK:

VJ23 to VJ-23e engine mounting, systems, and propeller.
Musfly - manpowered aircraft.
VJ-24 to VJ-24w (wheels), First Microlight.
Shadow series: A, B, B-D, C-D, D, G, and Float versions.
Streak. Star Streak. Image. Twin Shadow. Glint-(paper study)
DTI 'Smart'award.
British Design award.

TV/FILMS:

Blue Peter visit.
BBC Look East x 20.
ITA. About Anglia x 15.
Discovery channel - Superwings
DTI in Zimbabwe
Shell Advert for TV.

FEATURED IN:

News Papers
Magazines
Readers Digest - The Story.
The Colin Chapman story ,
Gordon Kinsey's "Aviation, Flight Over the Eastern Counties
since 1937"
"To Beijing", by James Edmunds.
"To Australia", by Brian Milton.

Final Note

Since this book was first written, in 2002, the author wishes it to be known that in 2005 the CAA Airworthiness Division grounded the Shadow Series fleet with what it termed a 'non compliant undercarriage'. This had previously been approved in 1985 by the CAA. Also that the elevator was causing it to flutter. These two Directives (ADs) needed major modifications. This was after 21 years of service by 450 of the type worldwide. No other country's airworthiness authorities found it necessary to comply with these modifications.

As a direct result of these actions by the UK CAA, the production of these aircraft under the name of Bella Aircraft went into liquidation. The Shadow Series are now orphan aircraft.

David Cook
2007